HQ76.45.U52 S683 2012
Pray the gay away :
33663005156944
EGN

DATE DUE

BRODART, CO.   Cat. No. 23-221

PRAY THE GAY AWAY

Pray the Gay Away

The Extraordinary Lives of Bible Belt Gays

Bernadette Barton

NEW YORK UNIVERSITY PRESS
New York and London

NEW YORK UNIVERSITY PRESS
New York and London
www.nyupress.org

References to Internet websites (URLs) were accurate at the time of writing.
Neither the author nor New York University Press is responsible for
URLs that may have expired or changed since the manuscript was prepared.

LIBRARY OF CONGRESS CATALOGING-IN-PUBLICATION DATA
Barton, Bernadette.
Pray the gay away : the extraordinary lives of Bible belt gays / Bernadette Barton.
p. cm.
Includes bibliographical references and index.
ISBN 978-0-8147-8637-6 (cl: alk. paper)
ISBN 978-0-8147-6472-5 (ebook)
ISBN 978-0-8147-2442-2 (ebook)
1. Homophobia—Southern States. 2. Gays—Southern States. 3. Christianity and culture—
Southern States. I. Title.
HQ76.45.U52S683 2012
306.76'60975--dc23
2012026535

New York University Press books are printed on acid-free paper,
and their binding materials are chosen for strength and durability.
We strive to use environmentally responsible suppliers and materials
to the greatest extent possible in publishing our books.

Manufactured in the United States of America
10 9 8 7 6 5 4 3 2 1

For all the Bible Belt gays in my life,
especially Anna and Charles.

CONTENTS

ACKNOWLEDGMENTS

I appreciate the opportunity to acknowledge all of the people who supported this work and shaped the book you are reading. I concur with many other authors who say that this simply would not be the book it is without the generous collaboration of dozens of people as well as time and resources from my home institution, Morehead State University. I am very grateful for all the support this study received, and will do my very best to recognize all of those who contributed to it. First, I would like to thank the Bible Belt gays who participated in formal audiotaped interviews with me. Their willingness to share deeply personal information and hunt within themselves to offer creative insights from their life narratives is the substance of this book. I would especially like to thank Misty Dyer and Joshua Taylor for giving so generously in this way.

Second, I am indebted to many scholars, colleagues, and students who contributed intellectual feedback and support during different stages of this project. These include Shondrah Tarrezz Nash, Jeff Jones, Dawne Moon, Clarenda Phillips, Charles Homer Combs, Ric Caric, Constance L. Hardesty, Eric Swank, Patricia K. Jennings, Merri Lisa Haney-Johnson, Sharon Rostosky, Verta Taylor, Leila Rupp, Rebecca Ropers-Huilman, Emily Askew, Ann Andaloro, Ann Ciasullo, Daniel Phelps, Jason Rosenhouse, Glenn Branch, Lynne Gerber, Royal Berglee, Lisa Hinkle, Jennifer Martin, Michelle Fiore, Jessica Roe, Justin Clark, Danielle Story, Toni Hobbs, Kristy Hayes, Leslie Weaver, Erika Shira, and all of the students from my Religion and Inequality class. I further appreciate the editors and anonymous reviewers with the *Journal of Homosexuality*, *Feminist Formations*, and *Qualitative Sociology* for their very helpful feedback. Special thanks to Kathleen M. Blee and Ashley Currier for generously sharing substantive feedback on several chapters of this book. I appreciate Kathy Blee for helping shape the research design of *Pray the Gay Away* when it was just a nugget of an idea, and finally for continuing to act as a scholarly mentor to me through several stages of my professional career.

Third, I am also grateful to the many individuals who invited me to present a public lecture based on this work titled "The Toxic Closet: Being Gay in the Bible Belt." The positive responses of audience members, most of whom were Bible Belt gays, invigorated me and improved the work. Thanks to Merri Lisa Haney-Johnson and the Bodies of Knowledge Symposium at the University of South Carolina–Spartanburg, Jody Cofer and the Murray State University Alliance, Katie Goldey and the University of Kentucky Outsource, Meredith Redlin, Christine Stewart-Nunez, Lawrence Novotny, Tyler Pecker and the South Dakota State University Gay Straight Alliance, Randall Mills and the Big Sandy Gay Straight Alliance, Minh Nguyen and the Chautau-qua Lecture Series at Eastern Kentucky University, Sheena Thompson, Toni Hobbs and the Morehead State University Allyance, Susan Bordo and the Gender and Women's Studies Program at the University of Kentucky, Mat-thew Gabriele and Benjamin Sax at Virginia Tech, Daniel Mahan, Kimberly Boggs, and Kathy Edwards with Ashland Community and Technical College, and Blake Jones with the Social Work Program at the University of Kentucky.

I especially appreciate Ashley Currier, Lowell Kane, the members of the Queer Studies Working Group and the GLBT Center at Texas A&M, College Station for bringing me to campus as a guest researcher in 2008. I collected valuable data during this visit. Special thanks to journalists Jacque E. Day, Stephanie Pappas, Mary Dee Wenniger, and Mary Helen Conroy for featur-ing this work in news stories. Finally, I would like to recognize the following organizations for their support of this work: Kentucky Fairness, Kentucky Equality Federation, Lexington Fairness, JustFund Kentucky, Kentuckians for the Commonwealth, and Women in Higher Education

My colleagues at Morehead State University continue to create a support-ive environment for the discussion and dissemination of research. I thank Clarenda Phillips, Ric Caric, Phillip Krummrich, Scott Davison, Karen Tay-lor, Ann Andaloro, Jennifer Reis, Cynthia Ann Faulkner, Samuel Faulkner, Rebecca Katz, Timothy Hare, Janelle Hare, Paul Steele, Ann Rathbun, Mad-die Decker, Suzanne Tallichet, Bob Bylund, Jennifer Madden, Bruce Mat-tingly, David Rudy, M. Scott McBride, Tom Kmetz, and Janet Cline. Special thanks to Ray Bailey with the Camden-Carroll Library Technology Service Center for patiently supplying technological support for my "Toxic Closet" presentations. I am also indebted to the Office of Research and Creative Productions, the Institute for Regional Analysis and Public Policy, the Cau-dill College of Arts, Humanities, and Social Sciences, the Interdisciplinary Women's Studies Program and the Department of Sociology, Social Work, and Criminology at Morehead State University for providing research and travel funds, and release time, to complete this project. Many units of More-head State University participated in the creation of this work. When I con-sider the potentially controversial nature of the subject matter, I am truly grateful for the unwavering institutional support I have received over the past six years.

I feel fortunate to be a New York University Press author and appreciate the opportunity to publish another book with such an excellent staff. Special thanks to several anonymous reviewers whose feedback greatly improved the overall manuscript. Thanks also to Aiden Amos and Despina Papazoglou Gimbel for helpful and timely assistance, and Mary Sutherland for meticulous copyediting. Finally, I cannot say enough good things about my editor Ilene Kalish, and I know that I am not the only one who feels this way. Ilene substantively shaped the direction of *Pray the Gay Away* from the first proposal I submitted and continued to give essential editorial feedback on many drafts of the manuscript over the past several years. Ilene has acted as compass, captain, and counselor to this project—guiding and encouraging me to make *Pray the Gay Away* the best book it could be. Thank you Ilene! I am your biggest fan.

My friends and family have encouraged me, expressed interest, and engaged in many conversations about *Pray the Gay Away*. The seed of this book was born during a conversation with my oldest friend, Charles Homer Combs. As we discussed what I might research next, Charles suggested, "why don't you study rural queers?" and hence *Pray the Gay Away* was conceived. A big thank you and warm hug to Charles, as well as to Ginger Shank, Donna Hale, Sue Sartin, Jeff Jones, Lisa Tolliver, Teri Wood, Shelley White, Dina Schaper, Neal Linville, Connie Hardesty, Lisa Hinkle, Patricia Estes, Shawn Burns, Patricia K. Jennings, Shondrah Tarrezz Nash, Cynthia Ann Faulkner, Ashley Currier, Patricia Gallaway, Mathew Gallaway, Janet Gallaway, Gunilla Haac, Robert Fyke, and Rebecca Croucher. As always, I am grateful for the loving support of my parents Catherine Ziesmer and T. Colin Barton who encourage me in all my endeavors and believe that I can accomplish anything to which I apply myself. I also appreciate my siblings Joelle Nims and Colin V. Barton for both their thoughtful feedback on the project and, in general, keeping me anchored in the world.

Finally, I acknowledge my partner, Anna Blanton. This project consumed much of my time and energy over the past several years and hence, much of hers. During this time, she participated in and endured many conversations about the work and much probing into her personal experiences. Anna also generously agreed to allow me to share some of her story of life as a Bible Belt gay and of our story as a couple in the following pages. Thank you honey! I appreciate that our relationship continues to be a platform for all kinds of creative expansion and I look forward to growing older with Anna.

"In the Eyes of the Lord"

What are the words you do not yet have? What do you need to say? What are the tyrannies you swallow day by day and attempt to make your own, until you will sicken and die of them, still in silence?
—Audre Lorde, *The Transformation of Silence into Language and Action*

I live in a small town in Kentucky. Although I have lived in Kentucky for 20 years, 17 of these in lesbian relationships, I had not personally experienced, or, to be more precise—noticed—much homophobia until a spring day in 2003 when a lean man wearing a Christian fish belt buckle and a black T-shirt called homosexuality an "abomination" to me in my own backyard.

Anna, my partner, and I had just moved from Lexington to Thomasville, Kentucky,[1] a town closer to my workplace where houses are inexpensive. I was digging in the garden, pulling out a few random weeds before planting tomato, pepper, and cucumber plants when "Jim" walked up to the fence bordering our yard and that of our 90+-year-old neighbor, Ms. Smith. Jim belonged to the same church parish as Ms. Smith and had come over to till her backyard so she could put in her garden that season. He introduced himself to me and, when he saw me digging in a tough patch, offered to till the area I was weeding. He seemed nice, was very persistent, and figured out that I was an easy sell when it came to an extra pair of hands in the backyard. Jim pushed his tiller through our gate and began working while I weeded nearby.

When he finished and I was offering him a glass of water, he immediately inquired, "Are you married?" I knew this was a precursor to asking me on a date. I have a conventional feminine appearance, which makes most people assume that I am heterosexual.

"No," I responded, "I'm involved with someone." Although not legally married, Anna and I traveled to Vermont in 2002 to be officially joined in a civil union. I struggled then with Jim, and still struggle at times, to find the best way to answer questions about my marital status. Heteronormative assumptions and potential homophobia lurk behind this question, depending upon who is doing the asking and why.

Jim inquired, "Do you go to church?"

"No," I said, and then took my own leap of faith. "We're gay, and the churches around here aren't very supportive of it."

He paused, looked confused, and examined me closely. A long moment passed. He announced, "It's an abomination in the eyes of the Lord."[2]

Stunned, I just stood there looking at him. The air grew thick. I felt dazed, afraid, shamed, and weirdly, curious. "Someone just called me an abomination in my own backyard," I thought, "This isn't supposed to happen." I felt like an anthropologist stumbling upon an unexpected and unpleasant finding about my own life.

Jim added, "I'll pray for you," then there was a long pause, "that you grow good vegetables." We chatted briefly about soil quality. Meanwhile, I didn't recognize myself. I am a very outspoken, some might even say opinionated, person and was surprised by my reticence. I found that I was reluctant to confront him about his homophobic comment. What if he decided to burn a cross on our lawn? Looking at myself from far away, I listened to him pontificate about his relationship to the Lord in the righteous tones of the born again.

The act of speaking with nonbelievers or sinners about the Christian God is a form of testimony called "witnessing." Witnessing is premised on the fundamentalist doctrine that the faithful are charged to seize every opportunity to introduce God into an unbeliever's life and let the power of the Lord work on changing his or her heart, and win another soul for God.[3] Although witnessing is commonplace in the Bible Belt, this was the first time I personally experienced it. "The Lord called me," Jim confided, lowering his voice, as I stood frozen beside him, a hostage in my own backyard. "I believe in the Lord. I'm so close to God, I left my wife and children. She went one way and I went the high way. My relationship with the Lord was more important."

"Just like the apostles," I thought but didn't say so. I made an inquiring sound.

"I just don't get into all that sleeping around, going from bed to bed," Jim elaborated.

"But you were married," I inquired, puzzled.

"My wife wanted to sleep around," he clarified.

"So she wanted a non-monogamous relationship?" I responded.

He stopped and peered at me puzzled. After a moment he continued, "I believe in the creator," he added, "not evolution."

"I believe in a creator too, but I also believe in evolution." I responded. He blinked at me. "I mean, it's possible to believe in both, don't you think? They aren't irreconcilable. There's so much scientific evidence to support evolution."

He shook his head slowly, "I don't think so," he said with some doubt.

Our conversation lapsed into a strained silence. I was waiting for him to leave, but he was only halfway through the glass of water.

"I haven't seen my children in two years. It's up to God. God will bring them back to me."

"They must miss you very much," I said carefully, thinking that this was a safe, nonjudgmental, not-going-to-get-me-called-any-more-names comment.

"You know the story of the prodigal son?" he explained, "The son had to leave, and it was the hardest thing for his father to let him go. But when he came back, the father went out to meet him. That's what I will do. My door is always open for them to come back to me. I'm leaving it up to the Lord, I'm not going to bother with lawyers and court and all that. God will bring them home."

While thinking privately that he would be much better off with a good lawyer, I asked, "How old are your children?"

Distracted, he changed his demeanor from preacher to person, Jim answered "12, 14, 17, and 18. But I've spoken with the oldest."

"Gosh, that would be hard for the youngest ones to come to you. The prodigal son was a grown up, wasn't he?" He looked at me blankly, and almost nodded. "Did your oldest child explain why the others hadn't come to see you or talk with you?"

"No. We just spoke on the phone. We are still reconciling."

"Reconciling from what?" I thought to myself.

He continued, "That's what happens when you disobey the Lord, you get spanked."

I wondered, "What on earth is he talking about? Something he did to his wife, to his kids? Is he referring to my abominable behavior again?"

He clarified, "I believe in discipline, corporal punishment. If my kids break a rule, I spank them. I mean, I don't beat them or anything," he backtracked, "but I believe in discipline. The courts didn't see it my way."

"Okay, this guy is really creepy," I thought. "And he's in my backyard." With some follow-up innocuous pleasantries, Jim wheeled his tiller to the gate. He left and I went inside my not-so-safe-feeling home. This encounter with Jim—and his rambling, scary, illogical worldview—was a watershed moment. I suddenly realized that, "Yes, I am in a same-sex relationship while living in the Bible Belt."

Reflecting upon this interaction with Jim, I recognize that my fears that he was violent, that he might "burn a cross on our lawn" were, if not completely unfounded, at least very unlikely. At the same time, while most conservative Christians would not engage in violence against another person, they do ascribe to a religious ideology that constructs the behavior of an entire group of people as an "abomination." This influences social attitudes and behaviors, and is the regional context within which I based the research for this book. I argue that Bible Belt Christian attitudes create and maintain a homophobic status quo. Conventions of small-town life, rules that govern southern manners, and the power wielded by Christian institutions and Christians within secular institutions all serve as a foundation for both passive and active homophobia.

People in the Bible Belt, like Jim, regularly query acquaintances, "What church do you belong to?" The answer to this question conveys a wealth of information, not only about the particular Christian denomination (i.e., Old Regular vs. Free Will Baptist) but also signifies a set of potential political and social attitudes as well as class status. Bible Belt Christians practice what I call "compulsory Christianity," communicative exchanges that involve presenting one's Christian identity to others in routine social interactions.[4] Not only is this an easily observable social norm, but religious leaders explicitly tell parishioners to spread Christ's message. For example, while attending local churches for this study, I heard preachers and other religious authority figures directly instruct parishioners to share the word of God outside the church walls: "Teachers, see your classroom as a vessel of God and your students as an opportunity to spread God's word." Church members were specifically instructed to perceive their workplaces, schools, day-care centers, doctor's offices, and libraries as battleground spaces in which Christians might find opportunities to spread the message of salvation.

Because most Christian churches in the Bible Belt (including Baptist, Methodist, Pentecostal, Roman Catholic, and nondenominational megachurches) construct homosexuality as sinful, lesbians and gay men from the region must choose between staying in what I call the "toxic closet" or risk rejection and ostracism from the people who are supposed to care for them the most—their families, friends, and neighbors.[5] The lesbians and gay men I interviewed also heard from family members, teachers, peers, neighbors, and preachers that these gay feelings—that they could not stop with any force of will—damned them to hell. No matter how hard they tried, and close to 60 percent of the Bible Belt gays I interviewed tried really hard, some weeping at the altar in front of their congregations week after week, they still could not *pray the gay away*. Donald, who is 52, white, from Indiana originally and currently a long-term resident of Louisville, Kentucky, summed it up this way: "In other words, we say to God, 'If I'm going to hell because of this, then take it away from me.' There isn't a gay person that hasn't asked that at one point in time in one way or other."

Many feared their uncontrollable attractions doomed them to hell. For example, Linda, who is white, 29, and from Texas, whose father was a preacher with the Disciples of Christ, prayed many times for her salvation:

I would go outside to smoke, and I remember that I would often stand outside while I was smoking and just weep silently, I'd just weep and weep, and I'd ask God, "I don't understand, how can you say that you love me, that you love me so much that you sent your son, your perfect son to suffer and die for me so that I wouldn't have to go to hell just because of being a sinner, how can you say you love me and yet for one thing that I cannot control, that I cannot stop, God knows I've tried, but you would send me to burn in hell forever separated from you, forever."

Central to this book are interviews with Bible Belt gays like Donald and Linda, a group of people simultaneously on the front line of our national culture war over "family values" and ones rarely cast as leading characters in stories about American culture.

Some of the Bible Belt gays in *Pray the Gay Away* include people rejected by their families, like Joshua, for coming out, and some who do not come out to their families for fear of rejection, like Ron. Joshua,[6] who is 29, white, and from a suburb outside of Atlanta, grew up in a Southern Baptist home and attended private Christian schools for most of his childhood and adolescence. His parents disowned him when he refused to get treatment for his same-sex attractions. Joshua explained that sharing stories like his was especially important because "this isn't just some sort of abstract political talking point or political agenda on either side of the debate. At the end of the day this impacts individuals: your son, your daughter, your neighbor, your teacher, your friend." He continued:

> As juniors in high school we would go to abortion rallies as field trips with our class and we would march around with *Stop Abortion Now* posters. The dots were connected for us—political action and Christianity. We understood why these needed to be partners. I think that's why it's important here in the United States, particularly here in the South, because we live in the Bible Belt, Flannery O'Connor called it the Christ-haunted South. We live in a part of the country where these ideologies, fundamentalist ideology, have so much currency.

Ron, a 36-year-old white man from Eastern Kentucky, generously shared his story with me in my university office one cold February afternoon. Ron never told his parents that he is gay. When Ron began to feel same-sex attractions at age eleven, he did not have anyone to discuss these feelings with; he related, "I feared that if it would be discovered, I almost felt like I may be in danger, physical danger, if I told it." Ron explained that he worried that if his parents learned he was homosexual they might "harm me, get rough with me, kick me out, withhold their love."

As I interviewed and discussed my research with dozens of Bible Belt gays, I learned that Josh's story and Ron's fears were relatively commonplace. Home is not a haven for many Bible Belt gays; in fact, home may be more dangerous than the streets. A 2006 National Gay and Lesbian Task Force study found that of homeless teens, 20–40 percent identify as gay.[7] If one considers that the most generous estimates of the percentage of gay people in the general population is 10 percent, such a statistic illustrates an alarming overrepresentation of gay youth among the homeless. When I pressed Ron further to explore if now, at the age of thirty-six, he thought his parents would really have beaten, killed, or ostracized him, he said, "No, but I do think that I would have been taken to counseling, maybe even prayed over. The terminology is referred to as 'laying hands upon.'" "Laying on of hands"—a touch that cures or enlightens—is a spiritual practice in many religious traditions. Within Christianity, laying on of hands can be either a symbolic or a literal invocation of the Holy Spirit into another. It can also border on violence, as was the case with Chris who is white, forty-two, and from Eastern Kentucky.

When Chris came out to her family at the age of 27, her father (a state trooper) and mother put their arms around her in a suffocating embrace and ordered the devil to leave Chris and enter her father. Chris explained what happened:

They were both there and they came up to me and they hugged me and they put their arms around me, a grip so tight you couldn't get out of it, literally saying that the devil needs to come out of me and into my father. They literally thought that an evil spirit had come into my life and had taken me over and that the only way that they could help me is to take it from me and put it on themselves. You know, here they were fifty, late fifties. And they had lived their lives. They felt like they were making the decision that whatever had come upon me, had taken control of my life, to come into them, so that I would have an okay start.

Frightened, Chris struggled to free herself. With both parents blocking the front door, Chris ran to the basement exit, her father chasing her down the stairs. She managed to escape. Later she learned her parents thought if only they could have kept Chris at home (she speculated that they planned to handcuff her in the basement) until their family preacher came to pray the "devil of homosexuality" out of her, she might have been cured. As psychologically traumatic as this experience was, and as Chris herself called it, "the most harrowing experience I have ever gone through," she still interpreted this event as evidence that her parents loved and cared for her. They had made a calculated decision that Chris's father as head of the household was best equipped to handle the devil, and both acted to spare Chris this suffering.

Most remarkable to me as I digested the implications of her story, Chris's partner, Deanna, who had been listening in, sadly added, "At least Chris's parents fought for her. My parents didn't even care enough to try." Completely rejected by her southern Ohio Roman Catholic family for being a lesbian, Deanna perceived Chris's familial relationships as far superior to her own. Over time Chris's parents grew to accept that Chris and Deanna were "best friends," and the couple is welcome in their home. After 16 years, Deanna's parents still refuse contact with her.

Like Ron, Chris, and Deanna, the Bible Belt gays interviewed for this book divulged many painful stories of rejection and abuse from the people closest to them. Patty, who is white, 40, and from Eastern Kentucky, explained that she was not invited to swim in her aunt's pool as a young "butch" girl, but her cousin and brother were. Imagine a hot summer day, the tantalizing blue gleam of the pool, the sounds of other children, even your own siblings, splashing and laughing, and you aren't allowed to swim because there is something about you the adults think is diseased and polluting. This example conjures up images of the kind of Jim Crow segregation in the South that African Americans endured before the civil rights movement.

There are indeed parallels between the oppression that people of color have experienced and continue to experience in the United States, and the ways homophobia plays out in gay people's lives. But there are differences too. One is that people of color are rarely rejected by their own families because they are a member of a minority racial group.[8] In the following chapters, I explore how widespread, institutionally sanctioned practices of exclusion, rejection, and abuse affect gay children, adolescents, and adults within their own families and communities in the Bible Belt.

Getting a Clue

Shaken by my encounter with Jim, I shared what I called "the abomination incident" with my friends and family, and received confusing responses. The most common reaction my gay friends from Kentucky had was a polite, knowing air of "Duh, where have you been all this time?" This response puzzled me. It lacked what I felt was an appropriate level of outrage on my behalf. I began to understand that although it was horrifying to me to have religiously based insults said to my face, this kind of behavior was not new or particularly shocking to them. Indeed, one of the significant findings from this study is that *growing up* in the Bible Belt regionally shapes an individual's expectations of Christians and Christianity. In contrast, my family members who live in Massachusetts and California, and my gay friends in urban coastal areas *overreacted*. They lambasted southerners as backward hicks and urged us to move immediately. Gay friends from New York City shuddered in horror upon hearing about the abomination incident, and declared they could not visit such a scary place as Thomasville, Kentucky, for fear they would be attacked just for walking down our street.

None of these responses satisfied me. But they did burst my bubble of progressive political feminist self-absorption. I couldn't just up and move—faculty jobs are not easy to get. Also, I liked most of the Kentuckians I met and knew. They are funny, down-to-earth, and smart, and definitely not a redneck stereotype. I did not want to erect a 12-foot privacy fence to keep out devout gardening neighbors. Still, I do not think religious hate speech is something anyone should get used to. If I hadn't paid much attention to homophobia until it walked into my backyard and offended and frightened me, this incident in 2003, coupled with the daily homophobic headlines during the 2004 political season, motivated me to interview gay people raised in Christian homes to explore the insights they have to share about their lives in the Bible Belt.

Geography Matters

What is the Bible Belt? The phrase "Bible Belt" was first coined by the journalist H. L. Mencken around the time of the famous "Monkey Trial," also
known as the Scopes Trial, a legal case that tested the state's stake in the
teaching of Darwin's theory of evolution in public school science classes in
1925 in Dayton, Tennessee. The Bible Belt is a diverse region that consists
of large cities, small towns, and rural areas. A variety of racial and ethnic
groups populate the region as well as a range of religious denominations. For
instance, a visitor finds Roman Catholic churches and Jewish synagogues in
Kentucky. The percentage of people who identify as Catholic in Kentucky is
15%;[9] the percentage of people who identify as Jewish in Kentucky is .3%.[10] At
the same time, protestant Christianity overshadows other forms of religious
expression in the region.

The geographic area of the Bible Belt overlaps with the census regions
of the United States: West South Central (Texas, Oklahoma, Arkansas, and
Louisiana), East South Central (Kentucky, Tennessee, Mississippi, and Ala-
bama), and South Atlantic (West Virginia, Virginia, Maryland, Delaware,
North Carolina, South Carolina, Georgia, and Florida).[11] After doing a cross-
tabulated analysis between census region and the 2006, 2008, and 2010 General Social Survey (GSS) question that taps religious orientation with the
question, "Do you consider yourself a fundamentalist, moderate, or liberal?"
data illustrates that a much larger percentage of respondents who live in the
Bible Belt self-identify as fundamentalist.[12]

Region of the US	% of individuals who self-identify as fundamentalists		
	2006	2008	2010
East South Central*	62.5	63.8	57.9
South Atlantic*	49.7	39.9	41.1
West South Central*	45.5	38.7	40.6
East North Central		27.2	20.1
West North Central	28	24.3	22.3
Mountain	26.7	23.8	15.3
Pacific	18.6	15.5	14.3
Middle Atlantic	12.5	14.5	14.1
New England	11	11.5	7.1

* Bible Belt regions

While the term "fundamentalist" coupled with "liberal" and "moderate" is a weak measure, both because it collapses political and religious orientations and because it is overly broad, GSS data demonstrates that 20–40% of respondents from Bible Belt states compared to other census regions chose "fundamentalist" as their identity. This suggests a high level of conservative religiosity in the region. Further, although it is problematic to make sociological claims about a region as broad and diverse as the Bible Belt, especially given that the majority of the people I interviewed are mostly from two states in the region—Kentucky and Texas—I believe the communicative frame of the Bible Belt offers both lay readers and scholars more than it takes away. The linguist George Lakoff describes frames as "mental structures that shape the way we see the world."[13] The Bible Belt frame swiftly and succinctly references both region and a hegemonic religious ideology, which produce wide-ranging observable consequences in the area. At the same time, this region is not homogenous, encompassing as it does population differences as vast as the urban centers of Houston, Texas, and Atlanta, Georgia, small towns like Thomasville with a population of 16,500 people, and rural areas so remote one might travel a two-lane road for 30 miles before reaching a dirt road into a "hollow" in which three generations of a family live.

U. S. Christian Fundamentalism: A Brief History

The terms "fundamentalist," "evangelical," "religious Right," and "Christian Right" all describe Christians and forms of Christianity sometimes used in confusing, poorly defined, and overlapping ways. It is a fact worth repeating that not all Christians, nor all Christian denominations, denounce homosexuality. Certain denominations, the Episcopal Church for example, have made great strides in recognizing gay people as equal to heterosexuals: all as God's children. Even among evangelical Christians, there is a diversity of perspectives on homosexuality. The word "evangelical" comes from the Greek word meaning gospel or good news. Essential evangelical beliefs include (1) recognizing the authority of the Bible; (2) salvation through being born again in Christ, and (3) spreading the word of Christ.[14] Importantly, self-identified evangelicals may be politically conservative or liberal, although the majority of evangelicals tend toward the political Right, with only a significant minority on the Left.[15] For instance, Randall Balmer's *Thy Kingdom Come, an Evangelical's Lament* opens with the following, "I write as a jilted lover. The evangelical faith that nurtured me as a child and sustains me as an adult has been hijacked by right-wing zealots who have distorted the gospel of Jesus Christ, defaulted on the noble legacy of nineteenth-century evangelical activism, and failed to appreciate the genius of the first amendment."[16] Consequently, while most fundamentalists consider themselves evangelicals, not all evangelicals identify as fundamentalist. Jerry Falwell famously described a fundamentalist as "just an evangelical who is mad about something."[17]

Additionally, in the scholarly literature on religion, there are key differences among conservative Protestant denominations which preach biblical inerrancy.[18] For example, while Baptists and Pentecostals both advocate a literal interpretation of scripture, and both denounce homosexuality as sinful, Baptists believe that all of God's mysteries may be found in the Bible. In her book *Bible Believers: Fundamentalists in the Modern World* Nancy Tatom Ammerman, a sociology of religion scholar, notes that the fundamentalist belief system begins with the understanding that "There are simply no truths for human beings to discover that are not already revealed in the Bible."[19] In contrast, Pentecostal denominations are charismatic. This means that members believe there are still divine prophecies that the devout may uncover. During Pentecostal services parishioners may be filled with the spirit, perform healings, and speak in tongues. Brother Damien, who is 44, Native American, from Central Kentucky, and a religious brother in the Orthodox Church of America, grew up in a Pentecostal church and described it during our interview:

> My mother was Pentecostal. The closest religion to Pentecostal Christianity is Voodoo. Voodoo and Pentecostal are very similar in that the core tenants, of, for instance, Voodoo are possession by the lower spirit, and in Pentecostalism it's the same thing. The core of the religion is possession. They believe in two types of possession: the demonic possession and the holy possession of the Holy Spirit. And everything centers around that. Pentecostals are obsessed with demonic possession. I grew up in that. I kid people, it's like growing up in the *Exorcist*, because people are constantly talking about demonic possession and holy possession and they're speaking in tongues. If you go to a Pentecostal service, people will be possessed by the Holy Spirit and they'll start speaking in tongues, they dance around, they gyrate their bodies because they're being possessed.

The term "fundamentalist" thus most accurately describes a small group of conservative Protestant denominations such as Baptists.[20]

Fundamentalism emerged as a militant wing of Christian evangelicalism, accruing power and cultural influence through crusades, missions, and revivals, throughout the late nineteenth and early twentieth centuries, waxing in popularity until the mid-1920s and the Scopes Trial on the teaching of evolution in public schools. Although William Jennings Bryan, the prosecuting attorney for the Scopes Trial, won his case against biology teacher John Scopes, the decision was later overturned on a technicality and the media coverage of the trial, particularly journalist H. L. Mencken's satirical stories about the "backward hill-billies" who accept "degraded nonsense which country preachers are ramming and hammering into yokel skulls," cast fundamentalists and fundamentalism as outdated, restrictive, and antimodern.[21] After this public ridicule, fundamentalism became "not so much somnolent as invisible to the larger society until the mid 1970s" retreating into its "own subculture of congregations, denominations, Bible camps, Bible institutions, colleges, seminaries, missionary societies, and publishing houses."[22]

Fundamentalists reentered public life with the neo-evangelicals of the 1940s and '50s, most notably Billy Graham, Carl Henry, and the beginnings of *Christianity Today,* a publication billed as a "magazine of evangelical conviction."[23] In the 1970s, Jerry Falwell, who was originally opposed to political activism, became convinced that America was losing its moral center; he joined with other conservative Christian leaders such as D. James Kennedy, Charles Stanley, Timothy La Haye, and Paul Weyrich to form the Moral Majority—"a nonpartisan political organization to promote morality in public life and to combat legislation that favored the legalization of immorality."[24] In the presidential election of 1976, the Moral Majority cast their support for Jimmy Carter, a staunch Southern Baptist, but they quickly became disenchanted with Carter's leftist evangelicalism and progressive policies, and backed Ronald Reagan in 1980. The Moral Majority operated for approximately 10 years, dissolving with the ascendancy of other Christian political organizations including the Christian Coalition and James Dobson's Focus on the Family. Reaching a wide audience through radio, television, and mass mailings, Christian Right groups rally financial and social capital using the politics of fear against an imagined threat or enemy.[25] In the 1970s and '80s, the dual threats most often cited to mobilize funding were those of communism and abortion. With the collapse of the Berlin wall in 1989, a communist takeover ceased to be perceived as a real threat, and Christian fundamentalist leaders replaced the "Red scare" with opposition to homosexuality.[26] Abortion remains a key conservative Christian issue. Throughout the 1990s and during the eight years of the staunchly pro-choice Clinton administration, conservative Christian organizations continued to gather financial steam and broadcast their religious and political agendas. They largely remained out of the national media spotlight until 2000 while advancing a number of anti-gay ballot initiatives in individual states including Oregon, Colorado, Maine, and Idaho.[27]

Conservative Christians had a strong advocate in George W. Bush, the 43rd president of the United States and a born-again Christian. During Bush's presidency from January 20, 2001, through January 19, 2009, faith-based programs and policies were well funded, and homosexuality, particularly fears about same-sex marriage, emerged as a wedge issue for politicians on both sides of the aisle. The 2004 presidential election season was an exceptionally difficult period for lesbians and gay men in many states as Arkansas, Georgia, Kentucky, Louisiana, Michigan, Mississippi, Missouri, North Dakota, Ohio, Oklahoma, Oregon, and Utah all included and passed anti-gay marriage ballot initiatives that year. With the anti-gay marriage amendment on our Kentucky ballot, the homophobic rhetoric in newspapers, television broadcasts, political advertisements, and mailings arriving at our home ramped up. Lurid language and ominous music warned that "family values" were under attack by gay activists determined to destroy marriage as a social institution. Gay marriage was compared to marrying a dog, horse, cousin, or child. Lesbians and gay men were constructed as perverse, polluting people, and homosexuality literally something one could catch by contact with gay people.[28]

Bible Belt Christianity

Conservative Christian, conservative Protestant, fundamentalist, evangelical: none of these designations perfectly captures the climate that Bible Belt gays described in recorded interviews. While there may be great variation in church norms throughout the Bible Belt—some forbid dancing, some expect women to sit in the back pews, wear skirts, and never cut their hair, some sport live bands, some expect member to walk door to door saving souls for Christ—most Christian denominations in the Bible Belt, from Baptist to Methodist to Holiness to Catholic to Jehovah's Witness to Mormon to nondenominational, are uniform in their construction of homosexuality as sinful. And it is this condemnation of homosexual behavior that is most salient for Bible Belt gays. Because the vast majority of places one might worship in the Bible Belt are homophobic, close to 100% of interview subjects logged significant time learning that same-sex attractions are bad, sinful, and disgusting. Thus, from the perspective of lesbians and gay men from the region, the term that best conveys the rampant and widespread presence of homophobia within Christian institutions is "Bible Belt Christianity."

Further, Bible Belt Christianity is not confined to religious institutions and Sunday worship. This particular brand of Christianity permeates the multiple environments in which residents work, socialize, and worship. Christian crosses, messages, paraphernalia, music, news, and attitudes saturate everyday settings. Bible Belt Christianity thus influences a wide range of local secular institutions like schools and workplaces, and Bible Belt Christians exert a powerful influence on city, county, and state political and cultural institutions. For Bible Belt gays then, institutional authority figures openly opposed to homosexuality enforcing homophobic institutional policies and practices affect how families and communities perceive and treat gay people, as well as how comfortable an individual feels being openly gay-identified. The historian John Howard explored this phenomenon in his anthology *Carryin' on in the Gay and Lesbian South*, examining how "a cultural configuration unique to the Bible Belt South" of police, political leaders, media, and churches target homosexuals.[29] This configuration creates a hostile climate for homosexuals in the Bible Belt.

This is especially so in rural areas with small populations in which people know one another and one's family histories spanning generations. In these areas, regardless of any individual's actual church attendance, most people self-identify as "Christian"(meaning conservative Protestant), defer to the assumed righteousness of any "Christian" institution, and are suspicious of and deem inferior anyone who is not Christian.[30] As Patty wryly noted, "The only thing worse than being gay in the Bible Belt is being an atheist." Tara, a 48-year-old white lesbian from Oklahoma, experienced this firsthand at her public high school in suburban Oklahoma City. Although she should have been valedictorian of her class, her Southern Baptist school principal skipped over her to the next candidate who was also Southern Baptist, and Tara received no honors. She believes this is because she lacked any church affiliation and had been raised as an agnostic.

The Study

This book is a "bricolage,"[31] a work creatively constructed from a patchwork of tools at hand, in this case, of qualitative methodologies, to best illuminate the lives and experiences of lesbians and gay men living in the Bible Belt. These methodologies include ethnographic fieldwork, content analysis of media texts, both written and visual, participant observation, autoethnography, and in-depth interviews with Bible Belt gays.[32] In ethnographic fieldwork, a classic anthropological method, the researcher immerses herself in the environment of her subjects to observe firsthand their physical geography, climate, culture, and habitat. Such immersion enables a researcher to produce "thick description"[33] of the research setting and subjects, and thus identify, explore, and interpret the often messy and multilayered phenomenon of human interaction. From the local tire store advertising "Wheels and Bibles" on its front sign, to a radio advertisement for an area church in which the pastor explains "that God will give you not just one chance to redeem your life but many more at the Trinity Baptist Church," to the musical bands who perform at megachurch services, *Pray the Gay Away* engages in thick description of the Christian-dominated environments of Bible Belt gays.

The social worlds within which I observed manifestations of Bible Belt Christianity included environments as diverse as grocery stores, neighborhood homes and shops, parties, public events, doctor's offices, gyms, small businesses, churches, and my workplace. In 2006, the official starting point for this study, I began taking note of every expression of Christianity I came across, from bumper stickers, i.e., "1CROSS + 3NAILS = 4GVN" and "Jesus '08" to pamphlets, music, newspaper columns, yard signs, billboards, charity cups, and references to Christianity in daily conversations. I collected pamphlets and church announcements sent to our home. I jotted down bumper stickers. I counted churches. I noted references to Jesus in casual conversations. I listened to Christian programming. I went to church. In this way, expressions of Christianity—like the velvet painting of Jesus in boxing gloves for sale in a Christian store—intensely sprang into life. Christianity was literally everywhere I looked.

At social events, I chatted about religion with acquaintances over cocktails. I found that most people have strong ideas about religion and sexuality, and most eagerly seized on the opportunity to share theirs with a respectful listener. In my observation, although Christianity plays a starring role in the Bible Belt, most people lack the language and opportunity to discuss their religious experiences and ideas within a critical, analytical framework. Offer such a framework, as is the case when I interview someone, or give a public lecture on being gay in the Bible Belt, or even gently query a colleague about their religious upbringing during party small talk, I found most people eager and grateful for the opportunity to talk openly about religion and homosexuality.

Because Bible Belt Christianity was originally so foreign to me that I feared I was not fully understanding the experiences of Bible Belt gays, I continued, and continue, to informally question the people I come into contact with about their thoughts on religion, as well as pose such questions during formal interviews. While I might argue that I share an insider status with Bible Belt gays because I am a lesbian who has lived in the

Bible Belt for the past 20 years, both my religious background and the fact that I did not move to Kentucky until I was 25 make me an outsider to Bible Belt Christian cultural norms. I grew up Roman Catholic in a politically progressive family. My parents, especially my mother, taught me to believe that discrimination was morally wrong and that acting with prejudice toward a member of any minority group, including homosexuals, was unacceptable. My childhood and adolescent experiences of religion were benign: Liberation Theology Catholicism, sprinkled with an education in Buddhistlike Eastern spirituality, compliments of my father. Northeastern Catholicism, as I experienced it during the late 1970's and '80's, was also in a warm and fuzzy phase. Post–Vatican II,[34] influenced by the social movements of the 1960s and '70s, the priests, nuns, and other religious teachers I interacted with tended to be pleasant, affirming, and socially progressive. Further, there was almost no discussion of hell in churches or my home. I have a distinct memory of being a small child and saying to my mother, "Hell is scary. I don't understand it." Her response was, "Oh honey, you don't need to worry about hell. We Catholics have purgatory. Hell is only for really bad people like Hitler."

Roman Catholics make up a larger percentage of the population in the Northeast than in other regions. The American Religious Identification Survey notes that 39% of Massachusetts residents identified as Catholic in 2008, down from 54% in 1990.[35] I left Massachusetts to go to Ohio for my undergraduate education in 1988. Thus, my personal religious upbringing was as a Catholic in a Catholic area: I was a member of the religious majority. I believe this early religious privilege made it especially difficult for me to *see* Bible Belt Christianity, and unconsciously influenced me to assume that my religious experience was common. For example, Roman Catholic dogma contains many challenging constraints on sexuality and reproduction. Birth control, premarital sex, same-sex activity, even masturbation is still sinful within Catholic doctrine. As a child though, I watched as all the Catholics around me, including my family, regularly attended Mass and simply ignored the elements of Catholic doctrine unworkable in their lives. I observed divorced people receive Communion, knew of adolescents and adults having sex outside of marriage, and assumed most women were using birth control since family sizes were small. I knew no one who went to weekly confession. These transgressions were largely ignored by religious, educational, and familial authorities. When I queried adults about this discrepancy between dogma and behavior, I was told some version of the following: "the institution had not yet caught up with people's real lived experiences, but it will eventually, so you don't need to worry about it."

Most conservative Protestant denominations advocate many of the same restrictions on sexuality and reproduction as Catholicism, and like northeastern Catholics in the 1980s, most twenty-first-century parishioners do not adhere to them. What is different though, and what I believe my early privilege as a religious majority member blinded me to, is that many Bible Belt Christians actively try to conform to the narrow dictates of their churches, and most don't just ignore the elements that inhibit daily functioning as I had observed the Catholics do. At first, I did not believe that any individual would genuinely try to live by what I perceived to be unlivable guidelines (i.e., a literal interpretation of the Bible that prohibits homosexuality), especially when they experienced negative consequences for doing so. Further, as shortsighted as it sounds, I did not think that people really believed they would go to hell for, what was to me, socially constructed "sins." I perceived Bible Belt Christianity through the lens of my northeastern Catholic experience.

While I was coming out and for years after, it was difficult for me to imagine that anyone could, in real life, think less of another because of the sex of one's partner. As an intellectual exercise, like the inevitability of death, I knew such oppression existed, but I could not imagine someone actually doing something intentionally homophobic to me, or anyone else for that matter. It was, quite simply, ridiculous, and not something it occurred to me to worry about. I felt confident that we (Americans) had collectively evolved beyond such irrational prejudice and that I was riding the crest of the next wave of progressive social change. In short, I traveled inside overlapping bubbles of religious, educational, regional, and femme[36] privilege, and like most of us with privilege,[37] the bubbles were invisible to me until they popped.

Bible Belt Gays

For the lesbians and gay men I interviewed who grew up in the Bible Belt, the "irrational prejudice" I perceived was the daily terrain they negotiated. I conducted audiotaped interviews with 59 lesbians and gay men ranging in age from 18 to 74. I found interview participants through a mix of personal contacts, convenience, and snowball sampling,[38] attending a board meeting of the Kentucky Fairness Alliance, a statewide gay rights organization, and an Integrity meeting, an Episcopal gay organization. I also spent a week at Texas A&M in College Station, Texas, as a visiting guest researcher for Coming-out Week in October 2008 and interviewed 7 of my informants there. In total, I have interviewed 36 lesbians and 23 gay men. These include seven Black people, three Native Americans, four Hispanics, two Jewish Americans, and the remainder Caucasians. The 59 participants include 11 couples whom I interviewed together, and one other small group of friends I interviewed at the same time, at their request. In other words, I interviewed 22 people in groups of two, and one group of three friends together. The remaining 34 people I interviewed individually. In addition to these formal interviews, because I participate in several gay rights groups, have gay friends and acquaintances, and give public lectures on being gay in the Bible Belt, I have had informal conversations with hundreds of Bible Belt gays, their straight supporters, and some heterosexual Bible Belt Christians about the issues explored in *Pray the Gay Away*.

The 59 people who compose my sample are oversampled in three ways. First, because much of my recruitment occurred through gay right's groups, activists may be overrepresented. Second, because I work in Eastern Kentucky, live near Eastern Kentucky, and my partner is from Eastern Kentucky, I both found and attracted a large number of gay people from rural Kentucky, and rural Eastern Kentucky in particular. I classified 31 subjects, or 53%, of my sample as rural. The degree to which one is "rural" versus "suburban" or "urban" is difficult to measure precisely. This is because people move. To use my partner Anna as an example, she grew up in a small, isolated town in Eastern Kentucky, moved to Lexington (with a population of approximately one-half million people) in her early 20s, and then in her early 30s moved to Thomasville, another small town. Though she lived several years in Lexington, Kentucky, her roots are rural and much of her family still lives in the country. Anna tends to perceive social life through a rural lens and, for these reasons I would classify her as a "rural informant." Although I do not have access to the same level of biographic detail about all my interview subjects as I do my partner, I used similar criteria to classify the participants in *Pray the Gay Away*. This meant, in some cases, that an individual interview subject might be classified as both rural and urban since he or she spent significant periods of time living in both geographic environments.

Third, I purposely sought out people from strong religious backgrounds and classified the religiosity of participants. I determined religiosity by the interest individual subjects expressed in religious ideas, their overall knowledge about religious phenomenon, the degree of their engagement with religious institutions both in the past and present, and their current spiritual/religious identities and practices. Thirty-one, or 53%, of my sample exhibited high religiosity and another 10, or 17%, medium religiosity. Denominationally, 41 of the Bible Belt gays I interviewed, or 69%, grew up in a conservative Protestant church. Of these 41, 19 people, or 32% of the total sample, identified their religion of origin as Baptist or Southern Baptist; 13, or 22%, grew up Roman Catholic; 9, or 15%, of interview subjects worshipped in Pentecostal/charismatic churches at some period during their lives. Two were Jewish, one was raised Unitarian, and only two people I interviewed had little to no religious background or interest. Because people change churches, many of those I interviewed had been members not only of more than one church but had also tried out different Christian denominations. For example, Sarah who is white, 43, and from Eastern Kentucky, had been highly involved in both Baptist and Pentecostal churches. Summing up, more than two-thirds of the Bible Belt gays I interviewed were well versed in Christianity and expressed that their faith, or their spiritual selves, were important to them

The Undifferentiated Homosexual

It is common for scholars and activists working on gay issues to use the moniker LGBT (lesbian, gay, bisexual, transgendered), and more recently, LGBT-TQQA (lesbian, gay, bisexual, transgendered, two-spirited, queer, questioning, and ally) to refer to a gay and gay-affirming population. Although LGBTTQQA advocates an admirable public commitment to inclusion and recognition of diversity, I deliberately do not invoke this alphabet-string phrase for the following reasons. *Pray the Gay Away* explores what it means to be gay in the context of multiple and overlapping hegemonic Christian environments, which are largely hostile to homosexuals, and what I call the Bible Belt. I found that an *undifferentiated* status of "homosexual," regardless of sex, much less whether one is bisexual or questioning, best frames the experience of Bible Belt gays. For example, most of the people I interviewed attended conservative Christian churches—i.e., Baptist, Pentecostal, and Church of Christ—and grew up in families in which homosexuality was frequently denounced. Consequently, participants' identity struggles more often took place under the shadow of a preacher's voice thundering floridly about "homosexuals," and parents proclaiming that "any child of mine that is gay is dead to me" at the dinner table than in an LGBT center.

Thus, the arguments that I make in *Pray the Gay Away* emerge from Bible Belt gays lived experiences of being stigmatized by those around them. To illustrate, in terms of the oppression we endure, how Bible Belt gays *identify* is less significant than how we are *perceived by others*. The early twentieth-century sociologist Charles Horton Cooley theorized this in his interactional theory: the "looking-glass self."[39] Cooley imagined the social world to be a mirror, reflecting back to us others' perceptions and judgments, which, in turn, shape the way we see ourselves. In the conservative Christian looking-glass, it matters little how an individual identifies. Consider, for example, the case of a bisexual woman in a committed heterosexual relationship. Her bisexual identity is both invisible, unless she shares it, and irrelevant, often even if she does share it. Similarly, if she is in a committed lesbian relationship, her bisexual identity is again invisible and irrelevant. She is engaging in a homosexual lifestyle, which most Bible Belt Christians condemn as sinful.

More Than Victims

Pray the Gay Away draws on theories of domination and oppression[40]—specifically exploring the intersection of religiosity, region, and sexual identity,[41] and, to a lesser extent, class, race, and gender—to analyze the persistence of homophobic attitudes in the Bible Belt, and bell hooks's theoretical concept of "talking back" to give voice to Bible Belt gays. She describes talking back as an essential act of resistance by an oppressed, marginalized group "that heals, that makes new life and new growth possible."[42] It is speech, visibility, and the sharing of stories that transform marginalized groups from objects to subjects in the eyes of the dominant culture. Because Bible Belt gays see and hear constant reminders that we are unwelcome outsiders, many move away from homophobic, conservative areas to more open, or at least more anonymous, urban ones.[43] *Pray the Gay Away* shifts the "center"[44] of analysis to explore the experiences and insights of the ones that stay.

In her research on South African LGBT activism, the feminist sociologist Ashley Currier observed a tendency among those from more progressive parts of the globe to perceive those from less progressive areas as "victims" who have little to add to the conversation on gay rights and social change. Currier argues:

> Such normative ethnocentrism also prevents Northern LGBT activists from recognizing that they can learn from LGBT activists in the global South because Northern activists continue to see Southern activists as always, already victims. This perception is unfortunate because it keeps LGBT activists in the United States, for instance, from approaching activists in South Africa, who secured marriage equality for same-sex couples, for advice about how to persuade lawmakers and the general public to support marriage equality in the U.S.[45]

Likewise, Bible Belt gays are more than victims. Because many of us daily interact with conservative Christians, we have valuable strategies to offer to those who live in more progressive areas. On the front lines of the culture wars in the United States, we have hard-won insights to offer sexuality scholars, activists, and the general public. The Bible Belt gays you will meet in the following pages—for example, Brother Damien who critiques the Christian Right on theological grounds, Linda who engaged in intensive Bible study to reconcile her conservative Christian upbringing with her emerging understanding of her lesbian identity, and Will, experienced in forming allies with progressive local groups—have insider perspectives on Bible Belt Christianity. As Terry, a white lesbian, who is 29 and from Eastern Kentucky, explained, "We speak fundamentalist Christianity. We are interpreters and liaisons. We know that fundamentalists are not crazy. They are wrong. And there is a difference." Bible Belt gays learn early the lesson I was just figuring out: you need to be careful who you let in your home and your backyard when you are gay. You don't give up your privacy and risk insult or injury for the low reward of some freely offered yard work.

1

Welcome to the Bible Belt

Where are You Going to Spend Eternity? Dear Soul, if you were to die
right now, do you *know* whether you would go to heaven or to hell for
all eternity? The Bible, the Word of God, says that you *can know*.
—Fellowship Tract League

There Will Be No FIRE ESCAPE in HELL . . . but you can escape
hell by believing in the Lord Jesus Christ and accepting Him as
your sin bearer.
—Old Paths Tract Society

These tracts each separately appeared on a green mat that Anna and I have
outside the front door of our house in the small town of Thomasville, Kentucky, welcoming guests to our "Home Sweet Home." These are not the only
Christian texts to appear uninvited at our home. We regularly receive flyers
and pamphlets urging us to join one or another of the 52 churches in our
town of 16,500. Moreover, in addition to the usual rounds of Jehovah's Witnesses and Mormons knocking on our door, individuals from local Christian
churches have personally approached our home to invite us to visit Damas-
cus Baptist Church or the Blueberry Hill Church of God.[1] We do not need to
even walk out the front door to experience reminders that we are in the Bible
Belt. In this chapter, I explore manifestations of Christianity in the social
landscape of the region—starting in Thomasville—and demonstrate how
Christian signs, symbols, and social interactions affect residents. I liken this
effect to living in a panoptic prison.

The panoptic-prison design features a centrally located guard station so that one guard can survey many cells at one time and was first introduced in the late eighteenth century. The philosopher Michel Foucault argued that "the major effect of the Panopticon [is] to induce in the inmate a state of conscious and permanent visibility that assure the automatic functioning of power . . . the surveillance is permanent in its effects, even if it is discontinuous in its action."[2] In other words, under a panoptic gaze people feel that they are always being watched, even when they are not, so that they regulate their own behavior according to an imagined, external authority. In the twenty-first century, ubiquitous video cameras documenting our every move in prison as well as at the ATM machine, the convenience store, and the gas station serve this function. Americans from every region of the United States have grown accustomed to local, state, and federal surveillance of our whereabouts and behavior via our vehicle registrations, phone records, credit card purchases, and computer usage. We have some vague sense that we are always being watched, or might be being watched, by federal antiterrorist organizations. This panoptic effect is not regionally specific.

The "Bible Belt panopticon" adds another, more personal layer of potential surveillance for residents of the region.[3] Rather than functioning through anonymous and invisible state authorities, the Bible Belt panopticon, an important element of Bible Belt Christianity, manifests through tight social networks of family, neighbors, church, and community members, and a plethora of Christian signs and symbols sprinkled throughout the region. As Foucault theorized, the panopticon "automatizes and disindividualizes power."[4] To briefly illustrate, Tara, quoted in the introduction, who is 48, white, and from Oklahoma, explained that she no longer had to hear homophobic statements "to evaluate my appearance as too dykey or change my pronouns. All it takes now is to see a hand with a cross ring on it, or a fish key chain." Simply seeing a Christian symbol on another prompts her to be careful about how she does or does not reveal that she is a lesbian. Tara, like most of the Bible Belt gays I interviewed, learned to discipline her self-expression in the presence of Christian symbols. And this is not because she is ignorant about, or particularly fearful of, Christianity and Christians. Although Tara was raised agnostic, when I interviewed her, she worked as a religion professor at a Christian seminary.

Daily Living in the Bible Belt

In the Bible Belt, cross rings, fish key chains, Christian T-shirts, bumpers stickers, tote bags, and verbal references to one's Christian identity are readily observable in everyday life. For example, approximately 20 miles from Lexington, Kentucky, Thomasville has one bookstore in town: a Christian bookstore. In addition to Christian books, this bookstore also sells Christian themed plaques, T-shirts, bumper stickers, jewelry, music, knickknacks, and home schooling materials for kindergarten through middle school. Christian books are also available at the Thomasville Public Library. Designated "inspirational," the books are organized together and comparable in number to those in the mystery and science fiction/fantasy sections. The library also has a long table and bulletin board for the community on which members can advertise and share information. Christian tracts like those quoted in the opening of this chapter, and one I picked up on a recent visit to the library with a photo of a big white man dressed in camouflage holding a rifle next to a dead deer titled "Me Now! God Later?" and invitations and information about local churches are liberally displayed.

Thomasville has three small ballet schools for children and adolescents, one of which is named "Thomasville Ballet School, Praise His Name in Dance." This particular school is very close to my home, and I took one class there in the fall of 2010 and another in the summer of 2011. The other students in the class were all Christian home-schooled adolescent girls. Two girls were graduating high school. One planned to attend a Christian college, the other to do a nine-week Bible course in the fall and go on a mission. The male teacher led us in a prayer before class, we danced to Christian music during the class, and, I later learned, the instructor, most recently from New York City, is in Central Kentucky to attend a local, conservative seminary. In the waiting room of my physical therapist's office, a copy of the Bible and a few ancient magazines, including a *National Geographic* from 1983, are my reading options. At the checkout counter at a local grocery store, I notice a bedraggled cup asking for charitable offerings for the Christian ministry Operation Baby Blessings. In Goody's clothing store I spot a table displaying Christian T-shirts for juniors. These are all in gender-appropriate pastels and have sayings on them, such as "Got Jesus?" and "Saving Myself for Jesus." In the summertime, I hear the ice-cream truck luring young people for sweets with the Christian hymn, "I Know My Redeemer Liveth." A nearby strip club advertises drink specials under the heading "Sin Sunday."

Over the past year, the local adult alternative radio station I listen to while cooking and cleaning began airing advertisements for a Bible study series titled "Truth Unchained" held at a church in Lexington. I overhear one of these "Truth Unchained" teasers at least twice a month. They feature an announcer referencing a commonly held Christian belief in the form of a provocative question such as, "Does your church teach that Jesus is the son of

God?" A preacher (always the same preacher) then corrects this misperception by, in my opinion, deliberately playing on a listener's fear of a wrathful God with something like the following, "If so, you have been learning blasphemy, my child, and such blasphemy will keep you out of heaven. Jesus was born of a human woman, a human child and did not become God until. . . ." This particular announcement played during the Christmas season in 2010, and I heard it at least eight times. These "Truth Unchained" advertisements last at least 30 seconds and conclude with the announcer saying, "Don't *you* want to worship where the truth is told?" I have repeatedly paused, hands in rubber gloves holding a soapy dish to closely listen to each, waiting to hear a theological argument, but at its conclusion, feel baffled. In the case of the previous example, I pondered, "Am I going to hell if I believe Jesus is the son of God, or only if I believe He was *born* the son of God?" The "Truth Unchained" series air on what is otherwise a secular radio station with local DJs, one of whom even brings in a psychic to do phone readings with listeners from time to time.

Where Anna and I get our vehicles serviced, the local auto repair shop bill includes "We thank you for your business. Jesus is Lord. May God Bless You" at the bottom of the invoice. On a fishing trip to a federally funded campground, Anna received a flyer inviting her to a "casual service to worship the Lord, Jesus Christ" with the campground regulations and map. Several times throughout the semester, I walk over a sidewalk chalk message advertising a "Campus Crusade for Christ" going into the university office building. Also, at least once a semester, and sometimes more often, people affiliated with a conservative Christian church stand in the university free-speech area, hold provocative signs with messages such as, "Fornicators, sodomites, partiers, dancers, porn freaks, HELL IS REAL!" and preach about God, sin, and hell. They almost always denounce homosexuality. Men also show up twice a year at my university to distribute miniature Bibles to passers-by, usually students. On a 125-mile stretch of Kentucky country road linking a major city with small towns, there are at least 12 identical signs spaced 5–20 miles apart, 3 x 5 feet each, with blue backgrounds and red borders reading, "Warning: Jesus is Coming!"

People's vehicles sport a variety of Christian messages, including some that I have personally seen and jotted down such as, "Choice is Before the Baby is Made," "Happiness is Knowing Christ," "Our God is an AWESOME God," "If Satan rocks your boat, Jesus is your anchor," "No Jesus, know pain," "Jesus '08," "Victory is Imminent," "As for me and my house, we will serve the Lord," "Don't Follow Me, Follow Jesus," "If you died tonight, would you be in . . . HEAVEN or HELL?" "Jesus Saves, Are you saved?" and "When

America Remembers GOD, GOD will Remember America," as well as fish ornaments, family values license-plate holders, church affiliations, and, perhaps the most striking of all, back windshield appliqués of Jesus wearing a crown of thorns, his face twisted in agony. Some Bible Belt gays also grew up with a plethora of Christian-themed collectibles in their homes, as well as Christian books, movies, and radio programming. Misty, who is white, 24, and from Eastern Kentucky, attended a small, rural fundamentalist church 2–3 times a week throughout her childhood and adolescence, and described the Christian items in her childhood home:

> What I mainly remember is endless bizarre house decorations, crazy end of days books and prophecy pamphlets from grocery stores. The pamphlets were always damning and condemning and warning of end of days, and there were DVDs of screaming preachers rehashing previous tragedies like the flood. Specifically, my mother has a fiber optic Jesus decoration. It plugs into the wall and glows like the toys kids get at the circus. She bought a ceramic Jesus with very dark skin tone once and painted it really light. At one time she had over one hundred ceramic angels in our living room besides the rest in the house. Ceramic manger scenes, large plastic outdoor manger scene, the Lord's Prayer on a big spoon hanging on the wall, things that to some people would just seem almost sacrilegious. To me, it just seems very commercial and irrational. Like making chocolate crosses to eat.

And the church options are prolific. Within a three-block radius of our house, there is a church next to a liquor store, a church on top of a grocery store, and a church next to a dollar store. Some churches also sport messages, lettered on church billboard signs. A few examples include "The strongest position is on your knees," "Big Bang Theory? I don't think so—God," "A lot of kneeling will keep you in good standing," "Talk to God in prayer or you are in trouble," "We really begin to live only when we are born twice," "Stop in the name of love and meet the Supreme!" "If you walk with the Lord you will never be out of step," "The Church—land of the free home of the brave," and "Almost saved is totally lost." Misty emailed me about a church billboard she came across near her home in Eastern Kentucky that read, "Get Right or Get Left" and offered the following analysis:

> Get right means to be saved and get left means to be left behind at the resurrection, but this also conveys a dual message of the church's political affiliation as well. It's very polarizing, and when I read it, it sounds like

a threat. This is an example of how antigay rhetoric, especially to a Bible Belt gay, doesn't have to say anything at all about homosexuality. It's the associations. A Bible Belt gay knows homosexuality isn't included in the right column, and in areas where there are higher concentrations of fundamentalist-type churches which will display messages like these regularly, it comes to the point where seeing anything related to this religion feels like an attack on you because of your training in church on what is and isn't moral, and the aggressive way it is worded. I think many people not from the Bible Belt might be shocked by the types of messages some fundamentalist churches regularly put on their signs.

In the summer of 2011, a good friend of Anna's, and also a Bible Belt gay, stumbled across an openly homophobic church billboard reading, "Wednesday Night Bible Study, Politically Incorrect: 'Gay is not okay.'" This was on a church in Eastern Kentucky near Anna's home town. Not only do these signs sometimes feel like an attack to Bible Belt gays like Misty and Anna, they also serve the panoptic function of policing open expression of a homosexual identity. Simply put, these visual markers in the landscape warn Bible Belt gays to stay closeted.

The symbols, messages, signs, and tracts function as a shorthand for conservative Christian beliefs, opinions, and ideology, and teach the Bible Belt gays I interviewed, like Tara, to be careful about how they present themselves to others. Further, some interview subjects, like Julie, who is white, 51, and from Central Kentucky, described learning to read *all* Christian symbols as potential evidence of homophobic attitudes after the 2004 anti-gay marriage amendment on the Kentucky ballot. Julie shared:

I am scared to death when someone tells me they're Christian, and I hate to say that. Anybody that says they're Christian, or they have a cross around their neck, I say, "oh hell I've got to be careful around this person, because I just don't know." And I guess that's terrible, but I assume that they're going to be antigay and very homophobic, and mean and cruel . . . and after what we've gone through I'm right sometimes.

Julie's partner, Mary, who is white and 61, concurred:

Sometimes when I see these religious bumpers stickers, I feel the way I think a Jew might feel, seeing a swastika displayed on somebody's car. There goes somebody who thinks that I'm less than a full human being, that I can be deprived of my rights. Now granted, these people are not going around collecting us up and putting us in concentration camps, and sentencing us to death by hundreds of thousands, but still, these are people who think we are less human, that we have less in the way of rights than they have. Because of that they are a danger in a great number of ways, and we are harmed by that. And it's not just symbolic harm, we are truly materially harmed.

Thus, within Bible Belt Christianity, under the Bible Belt panopticon, residents, like Tara, Misty, Julie, and Mary learn to associate even presumably value-neutral Christian symbols like a T-shirt reading "SAVED" or a cross over a local grocery store with homophobic social attitudes.

Bill's Story—The Bible Belt Panopticon and Social Surveillance

Not only do the surfeit of Christian signs and symbols embedded in the physical landscape reinforce the Bible Belt panopticon by reminding Bible Belt gays to police themselves, so do routine social interactions. To illustrate, conversations in Kentucky are highly mannered with each party careful to spend an appropriate amount of time situating themselves within a common social network (i.e., So you are from Paintsville, do you know Bob Smith? There's been an awful drought round there lately.)[5] This repetitive small talk establishes trust. This is particularly the case in small towns and rural areas, but can still be a factor in larger cities to the degree that individuals interact in smaller social networks. You are rude to another at your peril in tight-knit social circles. Members of small town communities know one another. They know each other's parents and relatives and neighbors and children. If you say something sharp to Ms. Johnson across the street, cut someone off in front of the convenience store, or neglect to nod at an acquaintance at a local diner, you will be talked about—and not in a good way. It will get back to your mom and your aunt and your cousin, all of whom will fuss at you and warn you, for example, not to offend so-and-so because she is on the school board and your little sister is trying to raise money for the cheerleading squad and do you really want to sabotage her chances? This is one example of how southerners regulate one another's behavior, and an important element of the functioning of the "Bible Belt panopticon."

In the Bible Belt the church community, God, and scripture are powerful external authorities. Under a godly veil of righteousness, preachers interpret scripture for community members and set the moral guidelines that family, friends, and neighbors enforce.[6] One of my heterosexual students, Jake,[7] illustrated this dimension of the Bible Belt panopticon with the story of a young man named "Bill" who was a faithful worshipper at his Baptist church. Jake described Bill as "somewhat feminine," devout, and punctual. When a parishioner spotted Bill in the company of a "known homosexual," he told the church deacon, a special meeting was called, and Bill's fate in the parish debated. Some wanted him to kick him out of the church community immediately. Others felt the claim that Bill was homosexual must be proven before he was shunned. Jake explained that the "whole church" agreed to get rid of Bill if he were indeed gay because homosexuals are evil in the eyes of God. After investigating the matter with a thoroughness that Jake, a criminology major, compared to the state police, they concluded that since they had no hard proof that Bill was homosexual, they would tolerate him as long as they never had any future reasons to suspect he might be gay. The pastor spoke with Bill and warned him to avoid associating with known homosexuals. He explained that the deacons hated to cause a disturbance in the church, but they were willing to do so if it ever emerged that Bill "is thought for sure to be gay." Jake concluded:

> I have observed that the members who were aware of the situation still harbor negativity toward him. Bill felt shame and guilt about the accusations brought against him, although he seemed to brush it off as a simple misunderstanding. I could tell from talking with him that he felt hurt. He never did completely tell me straight out that he was gay, but he knew I knew he was. He felt like he was evil and sick, and that everyone was ready to stone him to death.

Bill's story illustrates the influence and significance of local churches in small towns and rural counties in the Bible Belt. In rural areas, with few public places to gather, church communities serve as both social support and entertainment. Whole families often attend a specific church, including generations of the same family. One's great-great grandfather may have laid the foundation for the church of which one is a member. Because family, church, and community are so interwoven in these areas, Bible Belt gays or Bible Belt may-be gays recognize that there is more at stake than their membership in a specific parish, or even their eternal salvation if they come out or are found out. They must weigh the consequences of their family members rejecting them, as well as the impact of community disapproval focused on the whole family unit. A Bible Belt gay, or may-be gay, who has been kicked out of a parish, loses not only her social network, but the whole community—including of course her family—witnesses the public shame; some family members may even share the disgrace.

Personalism

Further, in the presence of someone espousing conservative Christian attitudes, even those who do not share them may hesitate to say so because of the regional social norm of "personalism." The essayist Loyal Jones describes personalism as a traditional Appalachian value, explaining, "We will go to great lengths to keep from offending others, even sometimes appearing to agree with them when in fact we do not. It is more important to get along with one another than it is to push our own views."[8] Not only an Appalachian phenomenon, personalism—the desire to fit in, get along with one's neighbors, to not offend, to present the social façade of harmony and good humor—influences social interactions throughout the Bible Belt.[9] In this environment, regardless of one's opinions on a particular topic, whether it be teen sex, abortion, going to church, women's role in the household, gay marriage, or even where the pond you used to swim in is located, people typically do not contradict one another, and especially do not disagree with authority figures like parents, preachers, and teachers. Doing so invites censure and isolation.

In *Out in the Country*, Mary Gray, a communications professor, writes, "Powerful individuals wield a disproportionate amount of power in setting local agendas and, therefore, the conditions for LGBT visibility. This leaves little recourse or incentive to risk one's local acceptance by registering dissent."[10] In her study, Gray primarily identified local politicians as "powerful individuals," but the same argument can be made about local clergy. When you couple personalism with the Bible Belt panopticon—again, the symbols, signs, and social interactions that make one feel watched and thus police oneself—and a dearth of gay public space, bigoted ideas about homosexuals are normalized. Misty explored this in a follow-up email to me after our interview:

> So, to put it into context begin first by imagining yourself in a rural area, the nearest gay establishment is 50 or 90 miles away. So right off the bat there is no, what I call "gay space" that non-gay people may have to pass and be aware of at all. So, there aren't necessarily ever any encounters with gay culture by straight people in this area. This can allow learned, false, negative beliefs to continue for years without having an experience which contradicts these beliefs. So isolation and seclusion are a factor. What you are exposed to on a fairly regular basis, however, are preachers teaching that gay people are an abomination, sinners, unnatural, and that sodomites were struck down by a wrathful and vengeful god. While this

might be a main topic of a sermon on occasion at church, the twice yearly evangelical visiting pastor always devoted a whole night to it, sometimes a night at these revivals might last two and a half hours. So homophobia is institutionalized in religion.

Further, Bible Belt Christianity trains members of the region—those who are heterosexual *and* those who are gay— to repeatedly present their Christian identity to others in routine social interactions. Not to do so invites attention and marks one as an outsider. Some people go to church at all only so that they won't be talked about by other members of the community. They certainly aren't going to challenge the preacher, whose high regard most are seeking, to speak out for homosexuals, an almost universally despised group in the region. Indeed, in fundamentalist churches, like the one Misty attended, pastoral authority is ordained by God.[11] When there is little to no impetus to stand up for gay rights, homophobia persists unchallenged. Misty continues:

> This, for me, is a major way religion and my family colluded to keep me or anyone in the toxic closet. You see your whole immediate family, not agreeing so much like they are sitting and nodding their heads as he speaks, but you see them in no way disagreeing. They listen intently, shake the preacher's hand on the way out with a smile and the belief system has been reinforced.

Such personalism supports the Bible Belt panopticon by creating the impression that "everyone" (meaning good Christian folk) seamlessly agrees that homosexuals are an "abomination," even when some may not. Under this Bible Belt panoptic gaze, with one's Christian identity constantly on display and one's Christian practices judged by neighbors, friends, and relatives, modeling the appearance of submission to God's authority is expected. This makes, at least the *presentation* of complicity with Bible Belt Christianity compulsory for most in the region. In this way, the Bible Belt panopticon is a tool that furthers the politics of domination.[12]

Going to Church

In addition to conducting audiotaped interviews with Bible Belt gays, I also visited area churches to better understand Bible Belt Christianity. One of the first churches I attended was "Vision," a nondenominational Christian mini megachurch (approximately 3,500 members) oriented toward young people and located in Lexington, Kentucky. In style and substance it resembles one of many new megachurches springing up across the United States, and which the sociologists Richard Flory and Donald Miller describe as "appropriators" in their book *Finding Faith*.[13] "Appropriator" churches seek to create compelling individual spiritual experiences for members by re-creating the products, trends, and music of popular culture within a Christian framework. I had heard about Vision from Patty, who does technology support for the church. Patty was impressed both by the amount of technology Vision used (five screens and a light show!) and the friendliness of the parishioners that she met there. I chose to visit Vision because I was interested in finding out if the youth-oriented congregation and pastors translated into any kind of progressive politic. I hoped that their "vision" included accepting gay people. I knew many Pentecostal and Baptist denominations preached hellfire for homosexuals, but perhaps Vision was different. I wanted to be fair in my assessment of Bible Belt Christianity.

Vision markets itself as hip, welcoming, and casual. First-time visitors enjoy a free drink at their coffee shop. I invited two good friends, a white gay man, Jeff,[14] and an African American heterosexual woman, Stephanie, to accompany me on my visit. I suggested that we arrive early so we could peruse the bookstore and get our free drinks. Unsure what to wear, we all put on business casual (after all, we were going to church) and were the best-dressed folks there. As we approached the building, we saw several groups of young people in prayer circles. They had all just returned from a leadership retreat. Almost everyone was dressed in jeans and T-shirts that advertised a music concert that Vision was promoting for the following week. Because the building had housed a huge video complex before Vision took it over, walking in the church we all felt like we were entering a mall, complete with its own Starbucks clone.

Perhaps because we were overdressed, or maybe because we were reading through the printed materials about Vision in the bookstore with the avid curiosity of social scientists, the "Envisioners" (this is what they called themselves) immediately pegged us as newbies. We were warmly welcomed and asked how we had found Vision. I responded that I was interested in exploring the area churches. Standing in line for our free drinks, we chatted with the woman taking our orders, and she made much about the fact that this was our first visit to Vision, writing "first timers" on our cups in a black Sharpie. Having overheard that we were new, a young (20ish) woman standing in front of us in line and wearing jeans and a black T-shirt turned around to smile at us. She bobbed her head in that way some young people do these days, eyes slightly squinted, and said, "That's cool."

While we were waiting for the service to begin, I struck up a conversation with a longtime member of Vision, "Allison." When Allison learned that I was attending my first service, she eagerly shared her thoughts about the church, her experiences there, and like the other Envisioners we had met, made heroic efforts to make me feel welcome and at ease. She described Vision as an environment in which everyone was accepted, of every age, class, race, and ability level. She shared that she had been raised by atheists, but that when Jesus had spoken to her here at Vision, her whole life changed. Allison spoke rapturously about Jesus, Vision, and her life. After about 15 minutes of nodding, smiling, and listening, I finally inserted a comment. I said, "This seems like a great place. I have some gay friends who are interested in Vision, and am wondering if gay people are welcome here too."[15] Allison did not miss a beat. She said, "Send them here. We want everyone—gay, straight, black, white, pink or purple." I felt a rush of hope. Then she continued, "Don't be surprised though if they start to change once they come here. Jesus works on people all the time." I wondered what she meant. Before I could inquire, Allison launched into a story about a young lesbian in her Vision sponsored support group.

As a longtime (since 1999) Envisioner, Allison leads one of the many weekly church support groups. These groups meet to discuss a variety of issues: relationships, weight loss, addiction, and grief, for example. In charge of one of the women's groups, Allison described a member who had defiantly declared that she was a lesbian at one of their meetings. Allison explained that she had responded, "So? But," Allison continued, "Jesus worked on her heart." A few months later, this same young woman had sheepishly confessed to Allison that she was ready to have children and, of all things, with a husband. "Jesus knows we are all sinners," Allison concluded, "We all struggle with things like anger and drug addiction, but he can change us." Deflated and disturbed by this interaction, I thanked her for her time and tea, collected Jeff and Stephanie, and made our way upstairs for the service.

The physical environment of Vision included none of the usual visual indicators of a Christian church. There were no crosses, no stained glass, no candles, no pews, no flowers, and no altar. Services took place in an auditorium seating approximately 700 on the second floor in a room resembling a movie theater or conference center. My companions and I found comfortable seats facing the proscenium stage and placed our free drinks into conveniently placed cup holders. I started craving popcorn. The service opened with a live band, dressed in retro '80's tight jeans and black T-shirts, playing loud Christian rock. I spotted the young woman who had been in front of us in line at the cafe who had said it was "cool" that we found our way to Vision.

Christian childhood. Joshua went to Christian schools, watched Christian programming, and listened to Christian music. He served as the chaplain of his school council and as a youth minister. He began to fall out of alignment with his Southern Baptist upbringing when he started experiencing same-sex attractions at age 14. These feelings created great emotional distress because he worried they meant he was not saved. He explained:

> Because of these feelings toward other men, I doubted the legitimacy of my salvation, and I was convinced that it didn't take, so to speak. When you are saved, your name is written down in the Lamb's Book of Life. Jesus was the sacrificial lamb, and so the Lamb's Book of Life is where all the names are kept of those who have accepted Jesus as their savior. So from childhood I imagined it as a big, open book and there's some scribe, and every time somebody says their prayer of salvation, their name goes down in the Lamb's Book of Life. And I honestly had this mental image of my name not being written down, because I doubted that I ever did it sincerely, or that I ever accepted Jesus correctly because I thought if I had, I wouldn't be having these doubts. And I wouldn't be having these feelings. So I tried over and over and over to pray. I wasn't telling anyone that I was doing this because it would have been some sort of acknowledgement of failure or weakness or sin if I told people that I privately wasn't even sure if I had become a Christian.

Ammerman theorizes about the importance of salvation among her research subjects at a fundamentalist church "Southside." She writes:

> The people at Southside, in fact, are eager to tell anyone who will listen that they are different than the rest of the world. At the heart of the matter is the fact that they are saved and the rest of the world is not. They have their names "written in the Lamb's Book of Life" and can look forward to an eternity in heaven. The rest of the world is lost, separated from God, and headed for eternity in hell's torments. For believers this difference is like that between light and darkness; it affects how they identify themselves and how they relate to everyone else.[20]

Fundamentalists believe that "the Bible prophesies the end of the world, followed by the Second Coming of Christ and the arrival of the 'millennium.'"[21] Some fundamentalists think that they can exactly predict Christ's return through carefully de-coding scripture.[22] Fundamentalist doctrine includes teachings on premillennial dispensationalism, in other words, the

She sang with the band, her hands cupping the microphone in prayer, singing ecstatic Christian grunge music for our worship. Close-ups of individuals on stage were projected onto several large screens angled in a way that parishioners in every part of the auditorium had a good view of the stage. The camera work was impressive. As the band played, the words to the music scrolled along the bottom of each screen for the parishioners to sing along. People stood during the praise music, waving their hands and swaying while a trippy light show of stars, squiggly lines, and moons projected on the ceiling and walls hypnotized the crowd.

After the music, the band exited, the set changed, and two young people (a woman and man) performed a theatrical skit related to the theme of the service "keeping up with the ball." The actors were good, the theater piece funny, and except for a part in which the young woman exclaimed over how fat she was and the young man agreed she needed to get into shape, I was mostly entertained. I did not, however, feel like I was in church. After about 30 minutes of music and theater, "Pastor Dan" emerged, casually dressed in slacks and a button-down shirt, and began to speak. He framed the content of his sermon within an elaborate and extended football metaphor, comparing the barriers to God that we all face (which sounded like the devil though he never openly identified this negative force as "Satan" or the "devil") to the kinds of plays an opposing football team makes to confuse, frighten, and batter the other team.

The sermon dragged on for more than an hour. Trying to follow the elaborate football analogy—complete with the plays diagrammed onto a chalkboard with little x's and o's—became tedious. It was an extremely masculine message, all about winning, not dropping the ball, and being one of the team. Pastor Dan urged us to keep our "eyes on the prize of heaven" because "Jesus knows everything. He knows when you will fail him, and he loves you anyway." Like our community expectations for the University of Kentucky basketball team to make it to the "Final Four,"[16] Pastor Dan urged us to develop a culture of "winning" against sin, and "take our commitment to the Lord to the next level by continuing to advance the ball and giving 100%." The service wrapped up with an offering and more praise music, but no communion. A little worn out, we quickly left.

Vision is lower key about their homophobia than many Christian churches in the Bible Belt. They don't threaten their members with hell, although they do talk a lot about sin. They don't tell one another that they are bad. But the message I received from Allison was clear: Jesus is not cool with gay people. Reflecting upon the service, I recognized that even if it were gay-friendly and feminist, *and* I wanted to join a Christian church, it would not be Vision. I like the liturgy, the sacred garments, the candles and incense ("the smells and bells") of the Roman Catholics and Episcopalians. But I can see the appeal of Vision for others, especially young people. You go, you hear live music, people are laid back, they are friendly, you get saved, and you have 3,500 new friends. Vision, like most megachurches across the United States, offers prospective members an instant community—unless you are gay and don't want to, or can't, pray the gay away.

Thus, the individual seeking spiritual guidance and succor from Vision must accept these terms: same-sex attraction equals drug addiction, alcoholism, domestic violence, adultery, gluttony, and gossiping. It involves concurring with the premise that there is something inherently flawed with you if you are gay. So, alongside the threat of damnation and in addition to the psychological struggle to feel good about being gay when others believe that homosexuals are diseased and perverse, for a hypothetical gay youth whose heterosexual friends are all excited about joining Vision, being gay also means not being welcome as one is to serve the Lord and connect with others in this dynamic new social environment. The young self-accepting gay Christian who enjoyed the "cool" atmosphere at Vision and wanted to become an Envisioner would swiftly face a mind-warping process of framing his same-sex attractions as one of many sins for which he should pray to Jesus for help. Either the gay Envisioner colludes in her own oppression or she doesn't get to join the club.

Theological Foundations for Bible Belt Christianity

I will boast in the Lord, My God. I will boast in the one who is worthy.
—lyrics to a Christian song played at a megachurch

In a public lecture at the Episcopal Church of St. Michael the Archangel in Lexington, Kentucky, New Hampshire Bishop Gene Robinson, the first openly gay ordained bishop in a major Christian denomination, explained that Christians have two main narratives for understanding their faith and interpreting the social world: the sin/fall narrative, and the creation/liberation narrative. Christians operating within a sin/fall narrative (which includes most conservative Christians) perceive humans as innately flawed and one's human existence a battle over one's sin nature. In contrast, Christians whose faith originates within a creation/liberation narrative express and experience their connection with the Divine intellectually, mystically,

and politically with personal sin rarely featured. Bishop Robinson, a Kentucky native, also likes to say that many people consider themselves on the "selection committee" (judgmental) when they should be on the "welcoming committee" (accepting). When I started going to church in the Bible Belt and really paid attention to the sermons, the most striking textual element of the sermons was this focus on sin and submission to God. The boiled down message I repeatedly heard went something like this: "You are a sinner. You will always sin. Only God can save you from your sin. Even if you are saved, you will still sin. You need to pray to God for help on your sinning tendencies. God loves you even when you are bad. You must submit to him to be saved from the eternal consequences of your sin. You, human, are weak, flawed, and unworthy. Boast only of God and his word."

The fundamentalist world that subjects like Misty and Joshua grew up in not only spotlighted sin but also legitimated a patriarchal hierarchy in which the Triune God (Father, Son, and Holy Spirit) is on top, followed by religious leaders, and husbands and fathers.[17] Members of each group are expected to submit to those above them and exert dominion over those below. Those in authority are automatically "right" in their ideas about the social world because they are closer to God. Several informants explained that questioning someone in authority about a passage from the Bible is not only discouraged but seen as evidence of a sinful state. At the same time, love, responsibility, and compassion in companion with hierarchy, sexism, and sin are a central to fundamentalist theology. So, while a conservative Christian may be quick to identify a sinful behavior, she may be equally quick to forgive believing that since Adam ate from the tree of forbidden fruit, all humans struggle constantly with sin. Moreover, those higher up in the Christian hierarchy are expected to assume greater responsibilities. Husbands are to love their wives "as Christ loved the Church" and serve as head of the family. Christian fundamentalists appreciate adhering to a clear system of enjoy the stability that such rules provided, and feel pity toward those their conviction.[18] Compared to the chaos of the world, their fundamentalist doctrine provides order and some relief from the anxiety caused by and confusion. Finally, those who are saved are taught that they are better" than those who are not. As Nancy Tatom Ammerman notes, convinced that their differences from others make them superior because they have something better but because theirs is the only

While not everyone is attracted to the spiritual and psychological that fundamentalism offers its adherents, it is fair to note that fundamentalist life can be a rich, positive experience. Joshua, who 29, and from suburban Atlanta, explained that he enjoyed his fun

Rapture. Fears about the Rapture figured prominently in Joshua's psychological dilemma. He shared, "I actually became quite fearful that the Rapture would happen and I would get left behind."

Unlike Joshua, Misty always felt uneasy with the doctrine her small church preached, especially the emphasis placed upon ensuring one's salvation before the end-times. Misty shared that the members of her church, who were mostly family members, believed that the world would end on midnight on December 31, 1995:

> I was literally terrified for a year or two of the coming of the resurrection. There was this extreme fear and urgency built into this idea that you were working against the ticking clock to get saved before Jesus came back to earth, because if you didn't get saved before then it was too late, and you were damned to hell, which they loved to vividly describe. Yet you were also told that the time had to be right for you to get saved, Jesus had to call you, to touch your heart to get saved and without a personal relationship with Jesus and the Holy Spirit compelling you to get saved, it wasn't your time. This creates a vague area of, am I worthy to be saved, and fear of what would happen if you didn't find your way in time. Why am I not feeling this Holy Spirit? What is wrong with me?

By the time she had left home and before she identified as a lesbian, Misty had rejected the fundamentalist doctrine in which she had been raised. Misty credits the severe depression and the complete repression of sexual feelings she experienced in adolescence with her fundamentalist upbringing.

Those who use scripture to condemn homosexuality do not perceive themselves as "homophobic" and "discriminatory." Rather, they believe they are brave warriors battling to save another soul for Jesus. In fact, they worry that they are letting God down, and threatening their own salvation, when they defer to secular norms and do not witness to unbelievers.[23] Indeed, some conservative Christians, including Fred Phelps of the infamous "God Hates Fags" Westboro Baptist Church, claim that it is their love for gay people that gives them the strength to enforce God's heterosexual standards. For the Bible Belt gays I interviewed, the expectation that good Christians submit to God's authority regardless of their own needs or those of loved ones—as represented in the infallible Bible—prevents a gay child, sister, or cousin from making an effective argument based on the inviolability of kinship responsibilities. By this I mean, a gay relative cannot reasonably argue that their well-being within the family system is more important than what God thinks about homosexuals.

To illustrate, in one of my earliest interviews I asked Celia, who is white, 40, from Eastern Kentucky, and executive director of a statewide gay right's organization, what might happen if she said to her Pentecostal aunt who had rejected her, "I love you and care about what you think, and it makes me sad that you won't accept that I am gay and include my partner in family events." Celia paused for a long time and looked confused. She said that it had never occurred to her to say any such thing. She explained, "God's feelings on the matter are really the only ones that matter. And yours don't, mine don't." Celia suspected that if she asked for some verification of her aunt's acceptance, her aunt would respond, "Celia, I love you, but you know what the Bible says." Thus, conservative Christians construct "morality" as objectively determined by God and scripture, and enable a usually loving aunt to not only reject her niece but to deny responsibility for that rejection. Celia's aunt gets a free pass from reflecting upon the emotional, psychological, and social consequences of ostracizing her niece because she is following God's law, and doing his will. This way she can hedge her bets on her *own* entry into heaven. To one reared with such beliefs, gay or straight, this is an obvious finding, part of the fabric of their culture: God's law trumps everyone and everything.

The insight that I seamlessly share here did not emerge so neatly during my research. I was still puzzled after my interview with Celia. I continued to feel confused and did not believe that such familial rejection was commonplace among Bible Belt gays, so outside of my paradigm was it of both religious experience and family life. The forcefulness, the determination, and the commitment that individuals feel and make to such a belief system, in spite of what I perceived to be their own best interest, finally became real to me in fall of 2007 when I received a virulently homophobic student essay in a gender class I was teaching. The assignment was to analyze the intersections of sexuality and activism in the documentary *The Education of Shelby Knox*.[24] One of my students, "Emily," turned in a 5-page diatribe for sexual purity and against homosexuality. When I first read the essay, I felt sick to my stomach and angry. I could barely read it, so unnerved was I by the language she used in it to justify her beliefs. I had to face the undeniable truth that one of *my* students, whom I had taught all semester, wrote this essay to me, her out lesbian professor *grading* her.

I come out in all of my classes, often on the first day of class, and almost always by the end of the first week. I believe that I teach best when I easily and comfortably reference relevant personal experiences and that it is important to model for all the students, but especially the gay ones, relaxed same-sex expression. When I was a less experienced teacher, I came out by rather awkwardly stating that "I am a lesbian." Now, I just bring up Anna, my partner, and discuss her and/or something we did, observed, or experienced as a couple in the context of the material, and continue to do so throughout the semester whenever I think it is relevant. To clarify, I reference my same-sex status and mention Anna as often I would a heterosexual partner were I married. The students typically respond well. Some look a little confused and alarmed the first time I mention a partner and say "she," especially in the large introductory sociology classes, but after I keep on doing so, they appear to get used to it.

While most students respond well to my disclosure in the classroom and, in my opinion, the benefits of coming out far outweigh the costs, I have received some negative teaching evaluations because of it, dealt with some combative questions, and endured Emily's frankly hate-filled essay. The fact that Emily, relatively quiet up until then in the classroom, turned in an essay that was likely to both offend me and receive a failing grade made visible to me how real the threat of hell feels to many conservative Christians. Consider the implications. What kind of church community must Emily have grown up in if, at the age of 20 she chose to tell her 40-something lesbian professor that homosexuality is an abomination in a written essay? Her willingness to commit academic *seppuku* (a form of Japanese ritual suicide by disembowelment) for God illustrates her priorities.

Bible Belt gays grow up, live, and work with people like Celia's aunt, Emily, and people who "wish to construct a conception of the world that is secure, unambiguous, where there are good people and bad people, and where they are clearly on the side of the good and true".[25] Among the central questions *Pray the Gay Away* explores is how it affects Bible Belt gays to be classified as *bad people*, inferior outsiders in their own families, home towns, schools, and churches. And the short answer is that it is confusing, and psychologically and physically damaging. Conservative Christian theology on homosexuality divides families, poisons relationships, fosters resentment, encourages violence and abuse, inhibits civic engagement, squanders talents, and overall causes great psychological, material, and spiritual harm.

At the same time, viewing conservative Christians singularly as hateful bigots is not useful. In fact, the more I observed such individuals at churches and interacted with them in my daily life, the clearer I became that these seemed to be mostly nice people intent on doing good even if our definitions of what that meant differed. For example, I'd rather vote for a politician who promised to put more money into social programs for the poor than house 18 homeless men once a week in a church building. This homeless project is one of many missions that the members of a certain Christian church charge themselves with in their efforts to do good work in the Lord's name. For Bible Belt gays, being excluded from such well-intended fellow-ships in church communities solely because of their same-sex attractions is confusing and distressing. But gay people are not the only ones who suffer from homophobia. In the next chapter, I explain that heterosexuals also suffer when families splinter, children attempt suicide, or any family member or friend is attacked and bullied.[26]

2

"My Parents Disowned Me"

Family Rejection

My mother came at me with a butcher knife!
—Angie, white, college student in Western Kentucky

Angie, young, vibrant, the president of the student gay/straight alliance at her university, and the other members of the GSA group were sharing a meal with me a local restaurant. They had brought me to campus to give a public lecture on being gay in the Bible Belt. After asking the conversation opener, "So, would you like to all share your coming out stories with me?" Angie, seated to my right immediately burst out, "My mother came at me with a butcher knife!" The young woman to my left whispered, "You don't want to hear my story, it's too violent." More violent than your own mother attacking you with a butcher knife, I wondered, how is that possible? I thought, "your mother is the one that's supposed to protect you from the person holding the butcher knife, not be the person wielding it. What kind of psychological damage does this do?" It emerged that Angie's 14-year-old younger sister had outed her to their mother. How scary for the younger sister to witness such a dire reaction to a petty act of tattling. This mother's violent, homophobic response to Angie psychologically harmed both girls.

Meanwhile, the GSA students, although attentive and respectful to Angie and one another, did not act disturbed or even very surprised by the butcher knife story or the ones that followed. Their general demeanor suggested that these kinds of stories were simply business as usual in their lives. We all got up, filled our plates, and upon our return to the table, they continued to share:

> "My mother didn't speak to me for three months."
> "My partner and I had to fake a break-up so I could keep my car."
> "My father called me an abomination and quoted scripture."
> "My parents disowned me."
> "I haven't come out to my parents because they couldn't handle it."

With rare exception, no opinion is more important, no rejection more painful, and no support more sought than those from the families, and especially the mothers, of the gay men and lesbians I interviewed. History and culture instruct us that relationships with family members mean something different than those with the rest of the world. We learn that "family is always there for you," and "you can't divorce your family." We are told to "take care of family" and that "a mother's love is unconditional." Family "takes you in when no one else will have you." Home is a "haven." Regardless of the validity of these cultural narratives in any particular family, they function as an ideological backdrop against which most of us measure our family relationships.

Unfortunately, home is not a haven for many gay youth in the Bible Belt. A gay child with the bad luck to be born into a homophobic family risks becoming one out of the three gay youths who attempt suicide.[1] She might also choose, or be forced, to leave home as teenager. As I stated in the introduction, research indicates that gay youth are overrepresented among homeless youth. The Family Acceptance Project based in San Francisco is among the first groups to conduct a large-scale study examining the relationship between family reactions to their child's coming out as lesbian, gay, or bisexual, and the mental and physical health of LGB youth. The results are grim, if unsurprising. The researchers found that "higher rates of family rejection were significantly associated with poorer health outcomes."[2] Specifically, those youth whose families responded negatively to their sexual identity were 8.4 times more likely to report attempting suicide, 5.9 times more likely to be depressed, 3.4 times more likely to use illegal drugs, and 3.4 times more likely to report engaging in risky sexual practices.

My data finds that heterosexual family members who exclude and abuse their gay relatives, especially their children, are following a homophobic script modeled over and over again by elected political representatives and institutional authorities at churches, schools, and workplaces in the Bible Belt. Not only do local officials and local institutions fail to protect gay children and adolescents from child maltreatment, but in their worst manifestations they teach homophobic families how to abuse their gay children. At the same time, not all gay children and adolescents experience such harmful reactions from family members. Many come from warm, accepting families. Further, since every person I interviewed was 18 or older, the stories that follow are memories and hence potentially distorted by the lenses of time and reflection. Finally, I deliberately sought out individuals who grew up in homophobic families and churches to best explore their consequences. All caveats aside, I observed that it required little effort to find interview subjects from homophobic families as well as those who attended homophobic churches. Three out of four lesbians and gay men that I contacted, or who contacted me, fit this profile.

Acts of Commission—Threats, Violence, and Ostracism

Definition of child maltreatment: "Any act or series of acts of commission or omission by a parent or other caregiver that result in harm, potential for harm, or threat of harm to a child."
—Department of Health and Human Services

The Center for Disease Control with the Department of Health and Human Services distinguishes between "acts of commission and omission" in defining child abuse. Acts of commission include physical, psychological (emotional and mental), and sexual abuse, specifically language and actions that cause harm, potential harm, or the threat of harm to a child. Acts of omission refer to all forms of child neglect: a "failure to provide" for the physical, emotional, medical, and educational well-being of a child. The lesbians and gay men I interviewed described suffering both these dimensions of abuse. In this chapter, I explore some "acts of commission" subjects shared. Chapter 3 spotlights subjects' socialization into Bible Belt Christian churches and doctrine, and in chapter 4, I examine some of the more subtle consequences of growing up in homes that "fail to provide" a gay-affirming childhood and adolescence. Overall, Bible Belt gays typically learned, as Robert, age 24,

African American, and from Houston, Texas, succinctly expressed, "If you are gay, you are not part of us."

Robert grew up in an authoritarian Baptist home. His parents taught him that being gay is against the Bible and nature. Robert explained that his parents subjected him to intense scrutiny as an adolescent, fearing their son was a homosexual. He shared the story of the first big confrontation he had with them about homosexuality:

> My dad was out doing an errand and I was on the phone with a friend of mine. It was just a friend, no one I was interested in or anything like that. We had been on the phone for over an hour. I hadn't realized that my mom had picked up on the phone and she heard that I was talking to this guy and that it was going on for a very long time. At the same time, my dad had a flat tire. So, he's calling home. He can't get through on the main phone, so he calls my mom on her cell phone. Mom proceeds to tell him, "the reason you can't get in on the phone is because Robert has been on the phone with some guy for over an hour." So my dad comes home, rushes through the door, comes to my room and starts swirling all these things about how I need to stop being gay, how I am doing all these gay things and how I need to stop doing debate and drama because those things are gay. And this is what finally got me in trouble when I finally said, "What if I am? What if I'm gay? I'm still the same son you raised. I just happen to like guys." My dad took a swing at me. Thankfully, I know my dad so I ducked. I had a feeling. He didn't hit me, but he did tell me I would be out of the family if he found out I was gay or participated in gay things. My mom was watching. She was saying, and agreeing with the same things. The next morning when I woke up, my mom came into my bedroom and reiterated everything, saying it was against God, we didn't raise you to be that way. You would be out of this family if we ever found out you were gay. And at this time, I was 18.

Robert eventually did come out to his father after he left home, and their relationship is strained. His mother died before he could come out to her.

In interview after interview, subjects shared similar tales of rejection, abuse, and violence. John, a white, 18-year-old first-year student from Eastern Kentucky, sought me out to talk about being gay when he read about my research, which had been featured in our university newspaper. He emailed me, came to my office for our interview and said, "I saw it in the newspaper and decided that being part of that would be important to me. It bothers me how people just think so stereotypical about things that I went through, and

She sang with the band, her hands cupping the microphone in prayer, singing ecstatic Christian grunge music for our worship. Close-ups of individuals on stage were projected onto several large screens angled in a way that parishioners in every part of the auditorium had a good view of the stage. The camera work was impressive. As the band played, the words to the music scrolled along the bottom of each screen for the parishioners to sing along. People stood during the praise music, waving their hands and swaying while a trippy light show of stars, squiggly lines, and moons projected on the ceiling and walls hypnotized the crowd.

After the music, the band exited, the set changed, and two young people (a woman and man) performed a theatrical skit related to the theme of the service "keeping up with the ball." The actors were good, the theater piece funny, and except for a part in which the young woman exclaimed over how fat she was and the young man agreed she needed to get into shape, I was mostly entertained. I did not, however, feel like I was in church. After about 30 minutes of music and theater, "Pastor Dan" emerged, casually dressed in slacks and a button-down shirt, and began to speak. He framed the content of his sermon within an elaborate and extended football metaphor, comparing the barriers to God that we all face (which sounded like the devil though he never openly identified this negative force as "Satan" or the "devil") to the kinds of plays an opposing football team makes to confuse, frighten, and batter the other team.

The sermon dragged on for more than an hour. Trying to follow the elaborate football analogy—complete with the plays diagrammed onto a chalkboard with little x's and o's—became tedious. It was an extremely masculine message, all about winning, not dropping the ball, and being one of the team. Pastor Dan urged us to keep our "eyes on the prize of heaven" because "Jesus knows everything. He knows when you will fail him, and he loves you anyway." Like our community expectations for the University of Kentucky basketball team to make it to the "Final Four,"[16] Pastor Dan urged us to develop a culture of "winning" against sin, and "take our commitment to the Lord to the next level by continuing to advance the ball and giving 100%." The service wrapped up with an offering and more praise music, but no communion. A little worn out, we quickly left.

Vision is lower key about their homophobia than many Christian churches in the Bible Belt. They don't threaten their members with hell, although they do talk a lot about sin. They don't tell one another that they are bad. But the message I received from Allison was clear: Jesus is not cool with gay people. Reflecting upon the service, I recognized that even if it were gay-friendly and feminist, *and* I wanted to join a Christian church, it would not be Vision. I like the liturgy, the sacred garments, the candles and incense ("the smells and bells") of the Roman Catholics and Episcopalians. But I can see the appeal of Vision for others, especially young people. You go, you hear live music, people are laid back, they are friendly, you get saved, and you have 3,500 new friends. Vision, like most megachurches across the United States, offers prospective members an instant community—unless you are gay and don't want to, or can't, pray the gay away.

Thus, the individual seeking spiritual guidance and succor from Vision must accept these terms: same-sex attraction equals drug addiction, alcoholism, domestic violence, adultery, gluttony, and gossiping. It involves concurring with the premise that there is something inherently flawed with you if you are gay. So, alongside the threat of damnation and in addition to the psychological struggle to feel good about being gay when others believe that homosexuals are diseased and perverse, for a hypothetical gay youth whose heterosexual friends are all excited about joining Vision, being gay also means not being welcome as one is to serve the Lord and connect with others in this dynamic new social environment. The young self-accepting gay Christian who enjoyed the "cool" atmosphere at Vision and wanted to become an Envisioner would swiftly face a mind-warping process of framing his same-sex attractions as one of many sins for which he should pray to Jesus for help. Either the gay Envisioner colludes in her own oppression or she doesn't get to join the club.

Theological Foundations for Bible Belt Christianity

I will boast in the Lord, My God. I will boast in the one who is
worthy.
—lyrics to a Christian song played at a megachurch

In a public lecture at the Episcopal Church of St. Michael the Archangel in Lexington, Kentucky, New Hampshire Bishop Gene Robinson, the first openly gay ordained bishop in a major Christian denomination, explained that Christians have two main narratives for understanding their faith and interpreting the social world: the sin/fall narrative, and the creation/liberation narrative. Christians operating within a sin/fall narrative (which includes most conservative Christians) perceive humans as innately flawed and one's human existence a battle over one's sin nature. In contrast, Christians whose faith originates within a creation/liberation narrative express and experience their connection with the Divine intellectually, mystically, and politically with personal sin rarely featured. Bishop Robinson, a Kentucky native, also likes to say that many people consider themselves on the "selection committee" (judgmental) when they should be on the "welcoming committee" (accepting). When I started going to church in the Bible Belt and really paid attention to the sermons, the most striking textual element of the sermons was this focus on sin and submission to God. The boiled down message I repeatedly heard went something like this: "You are a sinner. You will always sin. Only God can save you from your sin. Even if you are saved, you will still sin. You need to pray to God for help on your sinning tendencies. God loves you even when you are bad. You must submit to him to be saved from the eternal consequences of your sin. You, human, are weak, flawed, and unworthy. Boast only of God and his word."

The fundamentalist world that subjects like Misty and Joshua grew up in not only spotlighted sin but also legitimated a patriarchal hierarchy in which the Triune God (Father, Son, and Holy Spirit) is on top, followed by religious leaders, and husbands and fathers.[17] Members of each group are expected to submit to those above them and exert dominion over those below. Those in authority are automatically "right" in their ideas about the social world because they are closer to God. Several informants explained that questioning someone in authority about a passage from the Bible is not only discouraged but seen as evidence of a sinful state. At the same time, love, responsibility, and compassion in companion with hierarchy, sexism, and sin are also central to fundamentalist theology. So, while a conservative Christian may be quick to identify a sinful behavior, she may be equally quick to forgive, believing that since Adam ate from the tree of forbidden fruit, all humans struggle constantly with sin. Moreover, those higher up in the Christian hierarchy are expected to assume greater responsibilities. Husbands are to love their wives "as Christ loved the Church" and serve as head of the family. Christian fundamentalists appreciate adhering to a clear system of rules, enjoy the stability that such rules provided, and feel pity toward those lacking their conviction.[18] Compared to the chaos of the world, their fundamentalist doctrine provides order and some relief from the anxiety caused by doubt and confusion. Finally, those who are saved are taught that they are "better" than those who are not. As Nancy Tatom Ammerman notes, they "are convinced that their differences from others make them superior not only because they have something better but because theirs is the only truth."[19]

While not everyone is attracted to the spiritual and psychological order that fundamentalism offers its adherents, it is fair to note that for some, a fundamentalist life can be a rich, positive experience. Joshua, who is white, 29, and from suburban Atlanta, explained that he enjoyed his fundamentalist

Christian childhood. Joshua went to Christian schools, watched Christian programming, and listened to Christian music. He served as the chaplain of his school council and as a youth minister. He began to fall out of alignment with his Southern Baptist upbringing when he started experiencing same-sex attractions at age 14. These feelings created great emotional distress because he worried they meant he was not saved. He explained:

> Because of these feelings toward other men, I doubted the legitimacy of my salvation, and I was convinced that it didn't take, so to speak. When you are saved, your name is written down in the Lamb's Book of Life. Jesus was the sacrificial lamb, and so the Lamb's Book of Life is where all the names are kept of those who have accepted Jesus as their savior. So from childhood I imagined it as a big, open book and there's some scribe, and every time somebody says their prayer of salvation, their name goes down in the Lamb's Book of Life. And I honestly had this mental image of my name not being written down, because I doubted that I ever did it sincerely, or that I ever accepted Jesus correctly because I thought if I had, I wouldn't be having these feelings. And I wouldn't be having these doubts. So I tried over and over and over to pray. I wasn't telling anyone that I was doing this because it would have been some sort of acknowledgement of failure or weakness or sin if I told people that I privately wasn't even sure if I had become a Christian.

Ammerman theorizes about the importance of salvation among her research subjects at a fundamentalist church "Southside." She writes:

> The people at Southside, in fact, are eager to tell anyone who will listen that they are different than the rest of the world. At the heart of the matter is the fact that they are saved and the rest of the world is not. They have their names "written in the Lamb's Book of Life" and can look forward to an eternity in heaven. The rest of the world is lost, separated from God, and headed for eternity in hell's torments. For believers this difference is like that between light and darkness; it affects how they identify themselves and how they relate to everyone else.[20]

Fundamentalists believe that "the Bible prophesies the end of the world, followed by the Second Coming of Christ and the arrival of the 'millenium.'"[21] Some fundamentalists think that they can exactly predict Christ's return through carefully de-coding scripture.[22] Fundamentalist doctrine includes teachings on premillennial dispensationalism, in other words, the

Rapture. Fears about the Rapture figured prominently in Joshua's psychological dilemma. He shared, "I actually became quite fearful that the Rapture would happen and I would get left behind."

Unlike Joshua, Misty always felt uneasy with the doctrine her small church preached, especially the emphasis placed upon ensuring one's salvation before the end-times. Misty shared that the members of her church, who were mostly family members, believed that the world would end on midnight on December 31, 1995:

> I was literally terrified for a year or two of the coming of the resurrection. There was this extreme fear and urgency built into this idea that you were working against the ticking clock to get saved before Jesus came back to earth, because if you didn't get saved before then it was too late, and you were damned to hell, which they loved to vividly describe. Yet you were also told that the time had to be right for you to get saved, Jesus had to call you, to touch your heart to get saved and without a personal relationship with Jesus and the Holy Spirit compelling you to get saved, it wasn't your time. This creates a vague area of, am I worthy to be saved, and fear of what would happen if you didn't find your way in time. Why am I not feeling this Holy Spirit? What is wrong with me?

By the time she had left home and before she identified as a lesbian, Misty had rejected the fundamentalist doctrine in which she had been raised. Misty credits the severe depression and the complete repression of sexual feelings she experienced in adolescence with her fundamentalist upbringing.

Those who use scripture to condemn homosexuality do not perceive themselves as "homophobic" and "discriminatory." Rather, they believe they are brave warriors battling to save another soul for Jesus. In fact, they worry that they are letting God down, and threatening their own salvation, when they defer to secular norms and do not witness to unbelievers.[23] Indeed, some conservative Christians, including Fred Phelps of the infamous "God Hates Fags" Westboro Baptist Church, claim that it is their love for gay people that gives them the strength to enforce God's heterosexual standards. For the Bible Belt gays I interviewed, the expectation that good Christians submit to God's authority regardless of their own needs or those of loved ones—as represented in the infallible Bible—prevents a gay child, sister, or cousin from making an effective argument based on the inviolability of kinship responsibilities. By this I mean, a gay relative cannot reasonably argue that their well-being within the family system is more important than what God thinks about homosexuals.

To illustrate, in one of my earliest interviews I asked Celia, who is white, 40, from Eastern Kentucky, and executive director of a statewide gay right's organization, what might happen if she said to her Pentecostal aunt who had rejected her, "I love you and care about what you think, and it makes me sad that you won't accept that I am gay and include my partner in family events." Celia paused for a long time and looked confused. She said that it had never occurred to her to say any such thing. She explained, "God's feelings on the matter are really the only ones that matter. And yours don't, mine don't." Celia suspected that if she asked for some verification of her aunt's acceptance, her aunt would respond, "Celia, I love you, but you know what the Bible says." Thus, conservative Christians construct "morality" as objectively determined by God and scripture, and enable a usually loving aunt to not only reject her niece but to deny responsibility for that rejection. Celia's aunt gets a free pass from reflecting upon the emotional, psychological, and social consequences of ostracizing her niece because she is following God's law, and doing his will. This way she can hedge her bets on her *own* entry into heaven. To one reared with such beliefs, gay or straight, this is an obvious finding, part of the fabric of their culture: God's law trumps everyone and everything.

The insight that I seamlessly share here did not emerge so neatly during my research. I was still puzzled after my interview with Celia. I continued to feel confused and did not believe that such familial rejection was commonplace among Bible Belt gays, so outside of my paradigm was it of both religious experience and family life. The forcefulness, the determination, and the commitment that individuals feel and make to such a belief system, in spite of what I perceived to be their own best interest, finally became real to me in fall of 2007 when I received a virulently homophobic student essay in a gender class I was teaching. The assignment was to analyze the intersections of sexuality and activism in the documentary *The Education of Shelby Knox*.[24] One of my students, "Emily," turned in a 5-page diatribe for sexual purity and against homosexuality. When I first read the essay, I felt sick to my stomach and angry. I could barely read it, so unnerved was I by the language she used in it to justify her beliefs. I had to face the undeniable truth that one of *my* students, whom I had taught all semester, wrote this essay to me, her out lesbian professor *grading* her.

I come out in all of my classes, often on the first day of class, and almost always by the end of the first week. I believe that I teach best when I easily and comfortably reference relevant personal experiences and that it is important to model for all the students, but especially the gay ones, relaxed same-sex expression. When I was a less experienced teacher, I came out by rather awkwardly stating that "I am a lesbian." Now, I just bring up Anna, my partner, and discuss her and/or something we did, observed, or experienced as a couple in the context of the material, and continue to do so throughout the semester whenever I think it is relevant. To clarify, I reference my same-sex status and mention Anna as often I would a heterosexual partner were I married. The students typically respond well. Some look a little confused and alarmed the first time I mention a partner and say "she," especially in the large introductory sociology classes, but after I keep on doing so, they appear to get used to it.

While most students respond well to my disclosure in the classroom and, in my opinion, the benefits of coming out far outweigh the costs, I have received some negative teaching evaluations because of it, dealt with some combative questions, and endured Emily's frankly hate-filled essay. The fact that Emily, relatively quiet up until then in the classroom, turned in an essay that was likely to both offend me and receive a failing grade made visible to me how real the threat of hell feels to many conservative Christians. Consider the implications. What kind of church community must Emily have grown up in if, at the age of 20 she chose to tell her 40-something lesbian professor that homosexuality is an abomination in a written essay? Her willingness to commit academic *seppuku* (a form of Japanese ritual suicide by disembowelment) for God illustrates her priorities.

Bible Belt gays grow up, live, and work with people like Celia's aunt, Emily, and people who "wish to construct a conception of the world that is secure, unambiguous, where there are good people and bad people, and where they are clearly on the side of the good and true".[25] Among the central questions *Pray the Gay Away* explores is how it affects Bible Belt gays to be classified as *bad people*, inferior outsiders in their own families, home towns, schools, and churches. And the short answer is that it is confusing, and psychologically and physically damaging. Conservative Christian theology on homosexuality divides families, poisons relationships, fosters resentment, encourages violence and abuse, inhibits civic engagement, squanders talents, and overall causes great psychological, material, and spiritual harm.

At the same time, viewing conservative Christians singularly as hateful bigots is not useful. In fact, the more I observed such individuals at churches and interacted with them in my daily life, the clearer I became that these seemed to be mostly nice people intent on doing good even if our definitions of what that meant differed. For example, I'd rather vote for a politician who promised to put more money into social programs for the poor than house 18 homeless men once a week in a church building. This homeless project is one of many missions that the members of a certain Christian church charge themselves with in their efforts to do good work in the Lord's

name. For Bible Belt gays, being excluded from such well-intended fellow-
ships in church communities solely because of their same-sex attractions is
confusing and distressing. But gay people are not the only ones who suffer
from homophobia. In the next chapter, I explain that heterosexuals also suffer when families splinter, children attempt suicide, or any family member or
friend is attacked and bullied.[26]

2

"My Parents Disowned Me"

Family Rejection

My mother came at me with a butcher knife!
—Angie, white, college student in Western Kentucky

Angie, young, vibrant, the president of the student gay/straight alliance at her university, and the other members of the GSA group were sharing a meal with me a local restaurant. They had brought me to campus to give a public lecture on being gay in the Bible Belt. After asking the conversation opener, "So, would you like to all share your coming out stories with me?" Angie, seated to my right immediately burst out, "My mother came at me with a butcher knife!" The young woman to my left whispered, "You don't want to hear my story, it's too violent." More violent than your own mother attacking you with a butcher knife, I wondered, how is that possible? I thought, "your mother is the one that's supposed to protect you from the person holding the butcher knife, not be the person wielding it. What kind of psychological damage does this do?" It emerged that Angie's 14-year-old younger sister had outed her to their mother. How scary for the younger sister to witness such a dire reaction to a petty act of tattling. This mother's violent, homophobic response to Angie psychologically harmed both girls.

Meanwhile, the GSA students, although attentive and respectful to Angie and one another, did not act disturbed or even very surprised by the butcher knife story or the ones that followed. Their general demeanor suggested that these kinds of stories were simply business as usual in their lives. We all got up, filled our plates, and upon our return to the table, they continued to share:

> "My mother didn't speak to me for three months."
> "My partner and I had to fake a break-up so I could keep my car."
> "My father called me an abomination and quoted scripture."
> "My parents disowned me."
> "I haven't come out to my parents because they couldn't handle it."

With rare exception, no opinion is more important, no rejection more painful, and no support more sought than those from the families, and especially the mothers, of the gay men and lesbians I interviewed. History and culture instruct us that relationships with family members mean something different than those with the rest of the world. We learn that "family is always there for you," and "you can't divorce your family." We are told to "take care of family" and that "a mother's love is unconditional." Family "takes you in when no one else will have you." Home is a "haven." Regardless of the validity of these cultural narratives in any particular family, they function as an ideological backdrop against which most of us measure our family relationships.

Unfortunately, home is not a haven for many gay youth in the Bible Belt. A gay child with the bad luck to be born into a homophobic family risks becoming one out of the three gay youths who attempt suicide.[1] She might also choose, or be forced, to leave home as teenager. As I stated in the introduction, research indicates that gay youth are overrepresented among homeless youth. The Family Acceptance Project based in San Francisco is among the first groups to conduct a large-scale study examining the relationship between family reactions to their child's coming out as lesbian, gay, or bisexual, and the mental and physical health of LGB youth. The results are grim, if unsurprising. The researchers found that "higher rates of family rejection were significantly associated with poorer health outcomes."[2] Specifically, those youth whose families responded negatively to their sexual identity were 8.4 times more likely to report attempting suicide, 5.9 times more likely to be depressed, 3.4 times more likely to use illegal drugs, and 3.4 times more likely to report engaging in risky sexual practices.

My data finds that heterosexual family members who exclude and abuse their gay relatives, especially their children, are following a homophobic script modeled over and over again by elected political representatives and institutional authorities at churches, schools, and workplaces in the Bible Belt. Not only do local officials and local institutions fail to protect gay children and adolescents from child maltreatment, but in their worst manifestations they teach homophobic families how to abuse their gay children. At the same time, not all gay children and adolescents experience such harmful reactions from family members. Many come from warm, accepting families. Further, since every person I interviewed was 18 or older, the stories that follow are memories and hence potentially distorted by the lenses of time and reflection. Finally, I deliberately sought out individuals who grew up in homophobic families and churches to best explore their consequences. All caveats aside, I observed that it required little effort to find interview subjects from homophobic families as well as those who attended homophobic churches. Three out of four lesbians and gay men that I contacted, or who contacted me, fit this profile.

Acts of Commission—Threats, Violence, and Ostracism

Definition of child maltreatment: "Any act or series of acts of commission or omission by a parent or other caregiver that result in harm, potential for harm, or threat of harm to a child."
—Department of Health and Human Services

The Center for Disease Control with the Department of Health and Human Services distinguishes between "acts of commission and omission" in defining child abuse. Acts of commission include physical, psychological (emotional and mental), and sexual abuse, specifically language and actions that cause harm, potential harm, or the threat of harm to a child. Acts of omission refer to all forms of child neglect: a "failure to provide" for the physical, emotional, medical, and educational well-being of a child. The lesbians and gay men I interviewed described suffering both these dimensions of abuse. In this chapter, I explore some "acts of commission" subjects shared. Chapter 3 spotlights subjects' socialization into Bible Belt Christian churches and doctrine, and in chapter 4, I examine some of the more subtle consequences of growing up in homes that "fail to provide" a gay-affirming childhood and adolescence. Overall, Bible Belt gays typically learned, as Robert, age 24,

African American, and from Houston, Texas, succinctly expressed, "If you are gay, you are not part of us."

Robert grew up in an authoritarian Baptist home. His parents taught him that being gay is against the Bible and nature. Robert explained that his parents subjected him to intense scrutiny as an adolescent, fearing their son was a homosexual. He shared the story of the first big confrontation he had with them about homosexuality:

> My dad was out doing an errand and I was on the phone with a friend of mine. It was just a friend, no one I was interested in or anything like that. We had been on the phone for over an hour. I hadn't realized that my mom had picked up on the phone and she heard that I was talking to this guy and that it was going on for a very long time. At the same time, my dad had a flat tire. So, he's calling home. He can't get through on the main phone, so he calls my mom on her cell phone. Mom proceeds to tell him, "the reason you can't get in on the phone is because Robert has been on the phone with some guy for over an hour." So my dad comes home, rushes through the door, comes to my room and starts swirling all these things about how I need to stop being gay, how I am doing all these gay things and how I need to stop doing debate and drama because those things are gay. And this is what finally got me in trouble when I finally said, "What if I am? What if I'm gay? I'm still the same son you raised. I just happen to like guys." My dad took a swing at me. Thankfully, I know my dad so I ducked. I had a feeling. He didn't hit me, but he did tell me I would be out of the family if he found out I was gay or participated in gay things. My mom was watching. She was saying, and agreeing with the same things. The next morning when I woke up, my mom came into my bedroom and reiterated everything, saying it was against God, we didn't raise you to be that way. You would be out of this family if we ever found out you were gay. And at this time, I was 18.

Robert eventually did come out to his father after he left home, and their relationship is strained. His mother died before he could come out to her.

In interview after interview, subjects shared similar tales of rejection, abuse, and violence. John, a white, 18-year-old first-year student from Eastern Kentucky, sought me out to talk about being gay when he read about my research, which had been featured in our university newspaper. He emailed me, came to my office for our interview and said, "I saw it in the newspaper and decided that being part of that would be important to me. It bothers me how people just think so stereotypical about things that I went through, and if it fixes one person's ignorance about the subject, then it's important to me." John is very young. He had not had a boyfriend, nor even met an openly gay person before I shared that I was a lesbian during our interview. He had heard that being gay is wrong and bad from many people and institutions. His own mother told him she'd have preferred that he stay in the closet. He explained:

> My family, they're pretty much strict Christians, they don't go to church, but they're very stuck in their ways. My dad, he don't know, but I told my mom. At first she didn't believe me, and she actually attacked me quite a bit, and there was a lot of tension between us for about three months. There still is. She won't talk about it at all. She just refuses to acknowledge that I'm gay or anything like that. She thinks that I'm just confused. She said things like, I made her sick. She said that God destroyed a city over that, and that it was evil, and that the devil was in me. She said that the Internet did it to me. At one point, the most hurtful thing to me was that she said, "you took a knife and stabbed me in the heart and turned it." It was very emotional. And I asked her, "would you have wanted me to lie to you?" And she said, "yes, I would rather you have lied to me."

The theologian and Episcopal priest Horace Griffin argues that some families perceive their own gay relatives as inferior because they not only expect homogeneity within the family unit but are unnerved by the presence of a family member who is a sexual minority. In contrast with race, Griffin noted, "black parents produce black children, whereas there is not as strong a link with sexual identity. Heterosexual parents can and do produce gay offspring and gay parents typically produce heterosexual offspring."[3] Rather than provide resources to help families combat homophobia and support their gay family members, conservative Christian institutions exacerbate tension within families by framing homosexuality as sinful behavior, and homosexuals as responsible for destroying traditional family values.

Narrowly Defined Family Values

In February 2009, the American Family Association (AFA) attempted to air *Speechless: Silencing the Christians*, an hour-long television special on homosexuality via two television stations: one in Grand Rapids, Michigan and one in Columbus, Ohio. Concerned that the Obama administration would pass ENDA, the Employment Non-Discrimination Act, many conservative

Christian groups went on the offensive. Hosted by Janet Parshall, a right-wing, Christian spokesperson, *Speechless* frames Christians as the victims of homosexual activists—whose gay-straight alliances and demands for equal protection under the law—threaten the very fabric of society.[4] Because the television stations received so many calls of protest about the material, the program did not air. It is available online, and I watched it in its entirety several times. With a somber expression and tone, Parshall concludes *Speechless* with the following statement:

> Same-sex marriage means that school children are going to be taught that homosexuality is normal, moral and the equivalent of a marriage between one man and one woman. Hate crimes laws mean that Christians, even pastors, will be prosecuted for teaching what the Bible says about homosexuality. And the passage of the Employment Non-Discrimination Act, well, that means that churches, ministries and Christian businesses are going to be forced to hire homosexuals and create a non-offensive work environment for them. I pray that you really get the magnitude of the impact of all of this and the impact that it's going to have on your families and on our nation. Our children, and our cherished freedoms of speech and religion, are very much at risk. The American Family Association made this program possible and they have been fighting for the family for 32 years. They hope that this program has motivated you to do something to protect the traditional family in America. You know, the family is the most important institution for a strong and prosperous nation, but it's also the weakest of our institutions, and unless you and I, we come together and speak out against their agenda, homosexual activists are going to destroy the family as we've always known it.

The AFA, like other conservative Christian groups, regularly employs such rhetoric to denounce homosexuality and position Christians as the real victims of homosexual activists, the liberal, secular media, and an invasive government. To cite another example, I received a copy of the following political action and fund-raising letter from the Family Research Council (FRC), a conservative Christian lobbying organization set up by James Dobson and a sister organization to Dobson's Focus on the Family. This letter, dated November 2009, urges readers to fight against ENDA. The author, Tony Perkins, says, "Truthfully, it should be called the **'Discrimination Against Christians in the Workplace Act'**" (boldface in original). The 5-page document includes a number of improbable claims, including that the passage of ENDA "would trigger a cascade of anti-Christian laws attacking faith, marriage, freedom, and our families." The letter concludes that this "brief outline" of "disastrous" consequences "is a call to Christians who have an obligation to God and society to keep the doors open for a witness to the truth that humanity needs."

These kinds of homophobic messages from organizations like the AFA and the FRC encourage prejudice, confusion, and fear in the parents and relatives of gay people. They also socialize gay youth that there is something wrong with them that they must hide, and foster internalized oppression. This conservative Christian antigay platform trickles down into churches and homes across the country. A large percentage of people in the Bible Belt listen to conservative Christian programming and really do believe that homosexuality is destroying the family. In their book *The Anointed: Evangelical Truth in a Secular Age*, Eastern Nazarene College professors Randall Stephens and Karl Giberson describe the American evangelical community as a "'parallel culture,' that, in its extreme forms, aims to establish its own beliefs as the only worthwhile ones."[5]

Bible Belt gays not only encounter this kind of homophobic hate speech from major religious media outlets, like the FRC, but also in the intimacy of community churches and family kitchens, next to parents, friends, and peers. Terry, who is white and 29, grew up listening to weekly Focus on the Family broadcasts in her Eastern Kentucky home. Thus, for the Bible Belt gays I interviewed, the ominous tone Parshall takes, and the faux arguments she presents were, and continue to be, the background noise of their lives. And, by repeatedly constructing gay people as inferior and an abomination to God, conservative Christian organization like the AFA enable and encourage abusive behavior toward sexual minorities.

"You'd Be Better Off Sleeping with the Whores!"

Will, who is white, 46, and a gay rights lobbyist from Kentucky, came out to his family when he was a grown man of 41. When he arrived at his parents' home to discuss his homosexuality, they immediately turned off the University of Kentucky basketball game (something rarely done in a state in which people brag about "bleeding blue"), dragged out and dusted off the thick family Bible, and confronted him with several verses condemning homosexuality. Will shared that he was surprised by how negatively his family, especially his mother, responded:

> My mom yelled some very hateful things and she was emotional. She was crying as she yelled this, "had you walked in here and told us you'd

murdered someone we would have handled that better than we can do with this!" She says, "You'd be better off," and I can remember her voice almost like a growl, "You'd be better off sleeping with the whores!" It's like a demon possessed my mom's voice for a second.

As distressing as it was for Will to have his own mother tell him she'd rather he be a murderer than a homosexual, it was not the worst part of his coming out to her. Will grew wistful when he explained that what he misses most in his relationship with her since he shared that he is gay are the day-to-day pleasantries that used to occasionally exasperate him:

I'd drop into their house two or three times a week. If we hadn't seen each other during the week my mom would always call on Saturdays. Every once in a while we'd get into real menial discussions, I'd say, "well mom, how are you doing, what's going on . . . how are you and Dad today?" And she'd say something like, "your dad and I had scrambled eggs and sausage for breakfast and the sausage was a little spicy, and it's bothering my stomach a little bit." I remember one conversation that I was thinking, "Mom, just hit the high points, if you're having an ulcer let me know, I'll come and take you to the doctor, if you've just got an upset stomach don't tell me." I didn't ever say that to her, and now I miss those conversations because we don't have those regular conversations any more.

Will's mother is so uncomfortable with the fact that her son is a gay man, she has almost no contact with him any longer. This included terminating not only the weekly updates on the gastrointestinal effects of spicy sausage but also her responsibility to keep Will abreast of important family news. In this way, ostracism from his nuclear family unit impacted Will's relationships with his extended family as well. Will explained:

We still see each other at family gatherings, but we never call each other just out of the blue to say, "Hi, how are you doing?" It used to be whenever somebody was sick, or went to the hospital and when there was a death, I could always count on my mom for a phone call so that I would know to send a card or send flowers. Now I have to count on my aunt to give me that notice. I told her that my mom has stopped some forms of communication and that really hurts.

Will shared that the little communication he did have with his mother was strained:

Then there are times when my mom will force herself to call, and I can tell in her voice even when she leaves a voicemail, she's like timid, she doesn't even want to really be calling me. There's always just a little stutter, not the warm and fuzzy messages and conversations that we had years ago.

Many lesbians and gay men stay in the "toxic closet" just to avoid the terrible consequence of being treated like an unpleasant stranger by one's own parent. This is simply a potential cost too high to pay for many Bible Belt gays.

Burning a Bible

Like John whose mother told him, "you make me sick and God destroyed a city over that," and Robert whose father physically attacked him and whose mother threatened him with expulsion from the family if he were gay, and Will who was shut out of the family circle when he did come out, Sarah, white and 43, also suffered abuse from her family for her suspected homosexuality. Sarah grew up in an extremely rural area of Eastern Kentucky where as a child and adolescent she attended a number of Baptist and Pentecostal churches. Her grandparents belonged to a Baptist sect in which women sat in the back of the church, did not hold positions of leadership, and could not participate in the choir.[6] Sarah also attended a Pentecostal church where "women had to wear dresses, didn't cut their hair, and they spoke in tongues." Both of these churches, like many in rural Kentucky, preached biblical literalism, encouraged wifely submission, and adhered to a theology that condemned homosexuality.

Sarah met Grace when she was 16. Grace was a year older than Sarah, and seemed wiser and more experienced. Sarah felt a "weird connection" to Grace, including strong feelings of sexual and romantic attraction that she did not understand at the time. She had literally never heard the word "lesbian" before. Sarah explained:

I didn't know anybody that was gay. It was a little bitty town, everybody that I knew was kind of like me or richer. I worked all the time, and I was in sports. My mom didn't graduate high school because her father wouldn't let her go. Boys go, but he wouldn't let her go thinking she was a whore, that's her background. So, my mom was very intelligent, but as far as knowing things, you know what I'm saying? Worldly, other cultures, they didn't do the news, we never had newspapers. Current stuff was not discussed. I just wasn't exposed to things that most people would think I would be.

By the time Sarah met Grace, she not only knew nothing about homosexuality but knew nothing about sexuality at all. They snuggled, they kissed, they hugged, they were emotionally involved with one another. Sarah framed this relationship as "best friends" even while she feared that kissing Grace was "wrong." Teenage girls frequently have intense friendships, and for a while Sarah, their families, and community were content to perceive them as such. This all changed when Grace's mother found a letter that Sarah wrote to Grace alluding to a sexual experience. Grace's mother called Sarah's mother, a notoriously strict and controlling person and, as Sarah remarked, "the shit hit the fan." Sarah and Grace were summoned to a meeting with both mothers. She explained what happened:

> And so I was crying, but I was trying not to cry. Mom was like, "You're seventeen, damn your soul!" And this is a crazy thing, but I still really didn't know what all this was. I still hadn't heard the word gay yet. It felt good, but it didn't feel right at the time because of all the church stuff I did. It didn't feel just right because I couldn't be open about it. Mom took everything that Grace had bought me including the Bible and made me burn it. And that made me think, "Oh my God! I think I'm going to Hell." I was damned. So mother had me burn everything, and she wouldn't let me do anything except work, and I worked very hard in the family business. I could play my ball, and I could go to school and that was it. I was to come home, have no phone calls, no anything. I could date boys, but that was it. I got real scared when she was giving me all this stuff, and so that night I decided I had disappointed her so much that I just couldn't stand it, so I ran away.

In what sounds like a state of shock, Sarah took her father's pistol and walked into the woods with only the clothes on her back. She felt that she had disappointed her parents, disgraced herself, and therefore must leave. She wandered into a neighbor's barn and stayed there alone crying. After some time, unclear how and unwilling to use the gun, she left it in the barn. Just a teenager walking in the woods with no plan, no money, and no driver's license Sarah ended up at the home of someone who had always been nice to her:

> And so I was walking in the woods, I didn't want to take the main road, I didn't want people to see me, and so I was in the woods. It was probably ten or twelve miles by foot, and I found my way to this one girl's house. I had been to her house, and I didn't know it then, but I must have had

some kind of sense of stuff, because now she is a gay woman, a Major in the military, she has children. Anyway, I went to her house and nobody was there. I went around back to see if nobody was sitting on her back stoop and nobody was there, but at that time everybody drank those tall sixteen ounce Pepsi bottles, you know those? There was one there that was broken and so I took that little sliver and I went up my wrist and I was just thinking, "Well I'll just do it." So I went to do my wrist, and it wouldn't cut me, and it wouldn't cut me, and I was trying, and I was digging and I was trying and it wouldn't do it, and by this time it was probably about twelve thirty, one o' clock, I was a little cold. I didn't have a coat, and I thought well, "This ain't going to work." I had a gun and I didn't kill myself with that, and this ain't going to let me cut. In my mind and in all my church stuff, God didn't want me to die yet, and I didn't feel totally alone that day either. There was a presence there. So, I decided to come back home, so I got back on the main road, and I started walking home. Mom had had a posse out.

Although this was a hard time for Sarah, in comparison to some other gay youth she was relatively fortunate. While Sarah's mother—authoritarian, stern, and controlling—subjected her to a type of house arrest following this incident (and later forced her to marry the man who got her pregnant), she did not disown Sarah. Even as Sarah is among the many gay youth who attempted suicide, she was not, at least, among the homeless.

"I Am Dead to Them"

Not so for Kelly, a 21-year-old Hispanic college student from Houston. Just ten days before our interview, Kelly's Roman Catholic family disowned her for admitting she was a lesbian. I interviewed her in the LGBT center at Texas A&M, a much-used and needed haven for students and gay community members in College Station, Texas. Kelly was thin, pale, a little punchy and shaky. She looked like someone who had just endured a deep trauma and had yet to make much sense of it. Upon learning that she was a lesbian, Kelly's maternal grandmother had told Kelly that she was ashamed of her. Kelly also said of her family that "they really are ashamed of who I am."

Kelly never intended to tell her family that she was a lesbian. She knew better than to hope such a revelation would be well received. Kelly's mother had threatened all her children during a family dinner announcing, "Any of my children, if they come out gay, I disown you. You are dead to me. I'll kill you myself." Kelly came out to her mother, inadvertently, during a violent confrontation between her mother and Kelly's younger sister, Ella.

Kelly was on a weekend visit at home when Ella stormed into her room terrified because their mother had caught Ella in bed with another girl. Kelly explained what happened:

> After she got caught, she comes blazing through my door and is like, "Oh God, Mom knows!" When I saw my mom grab my sister by the hair and throw her to the wall, I jumped in. Mainly because my mom had just had heart surgery. She's not supposed to be moving that much and, two, my sister was getting thrown into a wall. So, I jumped in and before I knew it, it turned on me. It was, "Why are you defending her so much? Are you gay, too?" So, I was just like, "yeah."

Kelly and Ella fled in opposite directions after this confrontation, and haven't spoken much since then. Kelly shared what followed:

> I am cut off. I am disowned. My family wants nothing to do with me. I'm dead to them. They called once they figured out we were gone and wanted me to come home, and I was like, "No. Oh, no." They were like, "Oh, you'll see when you get here." I was like, "No thank you." So, then that's when they told me, "We don't want you to ever call this house again. Don't talk to anybody in the family. Don't try to contact your sisters. Nobody. We want nothing to do with you. You will not have a penny from us."

The most confusing part of this episode for Kelly was that the family did not disown Ella, just Kelly. She speculated that this was because Ella identified as bisexual and the family had hopes that her attractions to the same sex could be suppressed. I asked Kelly if she was upset with Ella for the way this incident unfolded. Kelly responded:

> In the beginning I was, because that wasn't the first time she had been caught with another girl. So, I was really kind of angry for a little while. How is it that she got busted, with them giving all that talk—disown you and that kind of stuff, and God doesn't approve of this—for me to hear all that all these years, that she would get caught on more than one occasion and still be able to be in the house? No restrictions on her, no house arrest, but if it's me, I'm out of the house.

But, Kelly elaborated, she had gotten past her anger at her sister, her parents, and her family. She prayed after the incident and forgave them. During their last communication, she apologized to them for having to put up with her being gay. She was grateful they let her keep the title to her truck. Kelly, even in our interview, even after such an enormous betrayal, persistently defended her family's homophobic actions. She blamed herself for dishonoring her family. When I questioned her (and apparently I was not the only one) about apologizing to her family for being gay saying, "You shouldn't have to apologize for that, Kelly. You didn't do anything wrong," she responded:

> I want to say I know where they're coming from, and the only reason I say that is religion. Just because of the way I was brought up. Their belief is that it's wrong, it shouldn't exist. I knew this was going to happen. A lot of people ask me, "Well, why did you apologize?" I apologized because, like I said, I never wanted anybody to be hurt and it's all I can do. When it all happened, especially last week, the only thing I could think of was what do I do next?

Kelly's heroic and tragic tale continues to haunt and puzzle me. A sense that this was fated, that Kelly knew "this was going to happen" and that she was cursed, hovered in her tone and body language.

"You Will Kill Me if You Tell Me You Are Gay!"

Most of the people I interviewed expressed learning, through language and actions, that to be gay was the worst thing one could be or "do." They received the impression that to be a homosexual was more terrible, more destructive, more deserving of censure than being a drug addict, a domestic abuser, a rapist, a pedophile, a criminal, or a pregnant teen. For example, Mary, who is white, 61, living in Central Kentucky, and raised Irish Catholic, never came out to her mother. As a teenager, her mother made statements that gave Mary the impression that her life would be in danger if it turned out that she was homosexual. Mary said, "I remember thinking that, at the time, my mother would kill me." Mary continued:

> Some years ago, somebody from rural Kentucky, we were in some group and we were talking, and I can remember him saying that he thought his father would indeed shoot him if his father found out. It's interesting to try to find out how much of this kind of interfamily terror exists.

Reflecting on whether her mother would have actually killed her, Mary concluded that, while "the fear wasn't justified, it was very real to me." She believes this fear pressured her to stay closeted longer than she would have had her mother been less homophobic.

Laura, who is 37, Native American, Melungeon,[7] and white, from Southeastern Kentucky, *did* come out to her mother and it did not go well. She explained:

> I was on the telephone with my mom and we were talking and I was telling her that Allison's mother hated me, and my mom was like, "Why? She doesn't think you're a queer or anything does she?" And I was like, "Well, what would be wrong with that?"
>
> "Oh God, don't tell me you're gay! Just please don't tell me you're gay! You will kill me if you tell me that you're gay!" "Okay mom, I won't tell you." So, she cried. I didn't go home for three months because every time I would talk to her it would end up in an argument. One of us would always end up crying before we got off the phone. She didn't want me to tell my dad.

Laura's mother's response was fairly typical among the Bible Belt gays I interviewed who came out to their parents. Most parents responded negatively, tried to deny it was true, and sought to conceal the information from other family members. Among my informants, only two shared that their parents responded positively to their coming out.

Steven, who is white, 42, and from Eastern Kentucky, revealed that his mother attempted suicide by taking pills and throwing herself off a bridge when she learned he was gay. Steven explained:

> What happened next took me years of therapy, soul-searching, and prayer to comprehend and finally forgive. My mother, in anguish, went to her medicine cabinet, took a full bottle of Valium and decided to die. She walked out the front door of her home wearing her nightgown, crunched through the leaves down onto the boat dock in front of her home, and in the mist and under the moonlight of the autumn night, she threw herself into the river to drown. She remembers feeling empty, hopeless, angry. She tried several times to allow herself to slip under the water, but says that she couldn't because her own parents were still living and she couldn't do that to them. So she swam back to shore, caused herself to vomit up the pills, and walked along the bank in the dark. She went to the home of my aunt who helped her through the rest of the night.

Thomas, who is white, 38, and also from Eastern Kentucky, is friends with Steven. Thomas shared that he and his mom had been discussing Steven being gay and Steven's mother's distress over it when Thomas came out to his own mother. As they were preparing Thanksgiving dinner, Thomas and his mother had the following exchange:

> My mom's very extreme and intense. She was saying that day, on Thanksgiving, that the burden of knowing that she had a child that was gay, and that child's going to go to hell, she could not live with knowing that. We were talking about my friend Steven who was gay. And his mother had had a really hard time, and she said that she understood why. And I said, "Mom that's crazy." And she said, "I mean it. When I was a little girl growing up one of my greatest fears is that I would have a child that was gay." That's what she told me. And I just said, "Mom, you would have to live with it. I'm gay."

Thomas explained that after this revelation his mother started crying, "busted all the dishes on the floor," locked herself in the bathroom, and left Thomas to sweep up the cracked plates and explain to the twelve arriving guests that they were not having Thanksgiving dinner that year. This kind of extreme familial response—"you'd be better off sleeping with whores," "the devil is in you," "one of my greatest fears is that I would have a child that was gay," not to mention the butcher knife incident—vividly instills in Bible Belt gays like Laura, Kelly, Mary, Will, Steven, and Thomas the sickening awareness that their parents can and will reject them for being a homosexual.

Sticky Stigma

Such intensely negative parental responses suggests that having a gay child or relative shames the entire family within a conservative Christian community. Homosexuality has, what the sociologist Erving Goffman dubbed, a "sticky stigma." One need not be gay oneself to experience the stigma of homosexuality. One may only need to be associated with a gay person by blood, marriage, or friendship to suffer homophobia. To illustrate, at a public talk on this research at the University of South Carolina–Spartanburg, the mother of a gay child and a PFLAG (Parents, Families and Friends of Lesbians and Gays) member shared with me that not only was her child kicked out of their church when they learned her daughter was a lesbian, she herself was given the cold shoulder at church for having a homosexual child. She explained that this incident raised her consciousness about the discrimination lesbians and gay men suffer, and motivated her to become more active in the struggle for gay rights. To me, this is a story with a happy ending. Instead of responding to her church's bigotry by rejecting her child, this mother rejected the church and its homophobic ideology. But this story could easily have ended the other way and, in the case of many other Bible Belt gays, did so.

Goffman theorized about stigma in his classic work *Stigma: Notes on the Management of Spoiled Identity*. Goffman distinguishes between two types of stigma: "discredited"—a visual stigma like a limp, scar, or skin color, and "discreditable"—behaviors such as sexual practices and criminal activity. In our culture we are supposed to learn that it is morally wrong to judge people and discriminate against them for "discredited" reasons like one's race or sex because these are seen as something one is born with, and thus, something the individual has no control over. But we can and do judge others, and reject them, for "discreditable" stigma because people perceive this stigma arising from an individual's own actions as a consequence of the choices one has made.

All forms of rejection are painful: the friend who stops talking to you, being last chosen for the kickball game, not getting an invitation to the big neighborhood barbecue. In my mind, the distinction between being rejected for problematic behaviors versus circumstances beyond one's control are clear. The former you helped manifest, the latter is out of your control. For example, if you steal your grandmother's pain pills or take dad's car without permission, your family may not be happy to see you at Sunday dinner. If you sleep with your best friend's boyfriend, she probably won't want to be your friend anymore. Being fired for stealing from the company is different than being laid off when the location of production moves from Oklahoma City to Mexico. While 95% of my informants perceived their own sexual identity as something ascribed, immutable, out of their control and hence "discredited" according to Goffman, most conservative Christian institutions teach that homosexuality is "discreditable," and thus a choice. Framing homosexuality as a "bad, shameful choice" creates an enormous amount of ignorance and unnecessary suffering not only in the lives of individual gay men and lesbians but in their families as well.

Conservative Christian Family Values Hurt the Whole Family

Why did the majority of Bible Belt gays I interviewed experience an almost uniformly negative response from their families, even in this time of greater awareness of gay issues and increasing acceptance of homosexuality among Americans? It's noteworthy that although the Bible Belt gays I interviewed span a fifty-year period in their coming-out stories, the tone and content of their stories is oddly ahistorical.[8] I speculate that the family rejection high-lighted in this chapter is a consequence of institutionalized homophobia in the Bible Belt. Discourse describing homosexuals as "broken," sinful, and "dangerous to the well-being of the family and America" is repeated over and again by such national leaders in the Christian Right as James Dobson and Pat Robertson, conservative politicians in the Bible Belt, and local pastors throughout the United States. And in the Bible Belt, unlike more progressive areas of the country, support for gay youth is sparse, and institutional voices condemning homosexuality are loud.

For example, in spring of 2011 the Texas House of Representatives passed a budget bill that "would require any public college with a student center on 'alternative' sexuality to provide equal funding to create new centers to promote 'traditional values.'"[9] This bill was introduced in response to LGBT centers on the college campuses of Texas A&M and the University of Texas–Austin. In an article in *Inside Higher Ed*, one University of Texas law student, affiliated with the Young Conservatives of Texas, replied:

[I]t is actually traditional students who lack power. If I were to walk through UT law school with a shirt on that said, "Homosexuality is immoral," if I were to do that, there would be an uproar. People would be upset, and it would be considered out of place and not acceptable to do that. I'd probably get a talking to. But if you go through campus to promote homosexuality, that is the norm.[10]

The groups who proposed this legislation did so with the expressed goal of de-funding support centers for LGBT students on public universities in Texas. While this bill did not pass through the senate and has not been enacted, discussion of it in the highest political body in the state created tension and, of course, threatened all the individuals invested in and involved with support centers for LGBT students. It also, once again, sounded an institutional message that homosexuality is "not something Texas taxpayers should spend their money on."[11]

Although gay people across the country suffer from the consequences of homophobic hate speech, Bible Belt gays are more likely to be surrounded by individuals and they interact within institutions, which condemn homosexuality. People in the Bible Belt, gay and heterosexual, learn that homosexuals are bad, diseased, perverse, and inferior within a number of social institutions. Like a creepy, mirrored fun house, abusive language about and threatening actions toward homosexuals on the playground, from the pulpit, in the bar, at work, and during family dinner amplify and reinforce one another. Parents who exclude gay youth and family members who ostracize gay relatives learn these behaviors and responses from institutional officials. In terms of child maltreatment, while an institutional authority such as a public school teacher, nurse, or Bible study leader would not condone ostracizing, disowning, threatening, withholding love, exorcising, yelling at, hitting, and/or attacking a heterosexual child for being straight, they may turn a blind eye to, or actively participate in doing so, with a gay youth.

Thus, many conservative Christian families, especially those who have been socialized that homosexuals are a despised lot, lack the psychological and spiritual tools to integrate and support the gay child or relative in the family unit. Instead, they are told that the homosexual is the problem and is dangerous to the family well-being. In the homophobic family then, the gay member is the minority, the "other." Experiencing minority status within one's primary family group is part of what makes the oppression a gay person endures unique. It's one thing to be perceived of as a second-class citizen in the broader culture—denied legal rights, bullied at school, caricatured in the media, and demonized by religious institutions. It's another thing to be a second-class citizen in one's own family—forbidden to bring your partner to family gatherings, unable to share both the mundane (what we did last weekend) and traumatic (how upset you are that your partner has breast cancer) life events—to hear that homosexuals are an abomination to God, and finally, to observe that Mom and Dad really do seem to love your brother and sister more. Treated as inferior, silenced, perhaps ostracized altogether, the gay relative may stop participating in the family altogether. The most convenient narrative heterosexuals use to explain the absence of "Uncle Chris" or "your sister, Barb," the one they learn from conservative Christian leaders who blame homosexuals for the breakdown of the traditional family, is that "gay people just don't like families." "Once Barb got involved in that queer thing she stopped caring about her family," some might say. The homophobic family blames the homosexual or homosexuality for the family rift, not the homophobic ideology they consciously or unconsciously reproduce that causes them to mistreat their gay relatives.

Disowning and excluding gay relatives not only hurts the individuals ostracized from the family but, indeed, the whole family unit. I advocate a model of family that is inclusive, resilient, and which cultivates the talents of *all* its members because our families and communities are stronger the more we pool our resources. Perhaps your sister Barb's partner, Rhonda, is a building contractor who'd be happy to fix Mom's leaky roof. Perhaps Uncle

Chris's boyfriend Gerald is an accountant who will file all the family tax returns for free. Maybe everyone's life would be a little easier if Barb and Rhonda and Chris and Gerald were around to help put in Grandma's storm windows, till Aunt Katie's garden plot, babysit the girls, and pick up groceries for Cousin Bob who just had gall bladder surgery. A politics of inclusion benefits everyone.

3

"God Would Tell on Me"

Losing Their Religion

Somewhere along the line I just decided that they were spiritually raping me because they pushed me into a corner, literally, and they were ... every Bible verse in the book, every guilt trip in the book, all of the evangelical rhetoric that I didn't even think I was that vulnerable to anymore, because I had been consciously trying to renegotiate what this meant for me. Because, up until that point, I was privately trying to renegotiate a Christian gay identity. I'd been going to a Metropolitan community church, a small little chapter there in Athens by myself. But whatever happened to me that night shattered any chance of me ever wanting to identify as a Christian ever again.

—Joshua, 29, white, from Georgia

I first encountered Joshua when I was a guest speaker in a graduate level communications methods class in the fall of 2009. Joshua sat in the front row, his eyes alight, demonstrating great interest in the issue under discussion. The following year we again crossed paths at a holiday party and eagerly renewed our acquaintance. Joshua shared compelling bits of his story among the buzz of cocktail party small talk surrounding us. He said he felt that he had been spiritually raped by his experience of Christianity and wondered if I thought, as a Women's Studies professor, that the analogy of rape was problematic. I did not. Two weeks later Joshua met me in my office for a formal audiotaped interview, and the words poured out of him with seamless clarity and purpose.[1] He explained:

I want to be a part of the discussion because, I think it's very important, and it's not something that everyone understands. Unless you're in it, some of the shades of this issue are lost on a lot of people.

a practice that emerged within some charismatic churches, involves closely monitoring the behaviors of church members to maintain accountability. In this practice, individual parishioners agree to shepherd—to guide and mentor—each other in the best way to please God, and disobeying one's shepherd is tantamount to disobeying God. Members at Brandy's church, which she repeatedly called "the crazy church," expected parishioners to publicly confess every sin and submit to community sanctioning and guidance. Brandy quit this "crazy church" after she had sex with a woman because she said, "I was not going to get up in front of the church and confess that to everyone." She described how church members had treated her heterosexual sister when she was sexually involved with a man in the parish:

> The crazy church made my sister, when she was involved sexually with a gentleman in the church, made both of them get up in front of the church and tell everybody that they were involved sexually. And then he was supposed to hang around with the men and try to become a whole person, where she hung around with the women. She was their maid and their babysitter. She was trying to learn from the older women of the church. That was the old biblical thing, older women should teach younger women.

Puzzled, I asked Brandy why she felt she *had* to confess, couldn't she just attend services and not tell anyone what she had done? Brandy responded, "I didn't feel like I could. I felt they would know." When I pressed her as to how and why they would know, she illustrated a further dimension of the Bible Belt panopticon. Brandy said, "Because I felt like God told them. That's how I felt at the time." Laughing, she continued:

> I mean I probably wouldn't feel that way right now, you know what I mean? But at the time, I felt that they communicated with God so well, that God would tell on me. That's freaky isn't it? I mean, hearing myself say that, that's weird, but that's how I felt at the time. I knew everybody would know what happened, so I quit going to church right then and there.

The stakes are high when even one's thoughts threaten one's eternal soul, and one believes that those who are the most devout in their Christian practices will automatically know one's secret sins. Fear of hell is a powerful motivator for those who believe in it. It keeps women in abusive relationships,[5] it encourages people to deny the evidence of evolution, it makes whole groups of nameless strangers into the "enemy," and it terrifies young people who cannot control for whom they feel a romantic and sexual attraction. In this chapter, I explore how participation in conservative Christian churches and dogma affected the Bible Belt gays I interviewed. They explained that their earnest and heartfelt attempts to reconcile the irreconcilable: God's love, their eternal salvation, and their identities as good, moral Christians with the unchangeable fact of their same-sex desires caused them enormous psychological, spiritual, and material harm.[6]

Can't Pray the Gay Away

The Bible Belt gays I interviewed echoed each other in explaining how they experienced and managed (or did not manage) this crisis of faith and identity. Derek, who is white, 39, and a Lexington, Kentucky resident shared, "I spent years doing everything I had been led to believe would allow God to change me into a straight man, and God did not answer that prayer." Susan, who is white, 41, and from Southern Kentucky, explained that she repressed her spiritual self for years because "I had been told my entire life that I couldn't have God in my life and be a lesbian." Misty, white, 24, and from Eastern Kentucky, said, "I had been filled with so many awful ideas about homosexuals that I couldn't even comprehend gay as having anything to do with love and desire. Homosexuality was viewed in religion so much like a pestilence or plague." Many Bible Belt gays I interviewed shared that they had heard that homosexuals were sinners and homosexuality an abomination week after week in their churches. Jennifer described the environment in her Pentecostal church:

> The preacher would preach on homosexuality. He would always group us
> in with the so-called perverts, like child molesters and just awful people.
> Of course, since I was having feelings about me being different, I felt like
> I needed to go to the altar and just pray and ask God to forgive me every
> Sunday. And every Sunday I would get on my knees and just cry and pray.

In the comfort of their secluded home in rural Kentucky with Caroline, her partner of 3 years, Jennifer explained that she struggled with depression and suicide, dated men, tried the ex-gay reparative Christian-based program Exodus, and feared that she was "unlovable." Like Misty, Jennifer said specifically that her early in-depth socialization with Bible Belt Christianity negatively affected her self-esteem. Because of what she learned in church, Jennifer confided, "I never thought I would be good enough to go to heaven. I never thought I would be good enough to please another person. I thought no one would ever love me." Jennifer tried to "pray the gay away," entered counseling, and participated in ex-gay ministries for more than ten years. None of it worked, and she reported becoming more depressed and suicidal. Jennifer directly attributed her feelings of depression and her continuing struggles with low self-esteem to the combination of fire, brimstone, and homophobia she absorbed in her church. Jennifer explained:

> I had my first lesbian experience at a summer camp. After that, I wasn't sure if I was gay or what. Because of my background growing up Pentecostal, I just knew that I was going to roast in hell, and had been taught this all my life. I became depressed, even suicidal at times. I didn't want to go to hell and I was just stuck.

Unlike Joshua, the Bible Belt Christian impact on Jennifer's self-esteem was independent of overt familial religiosity. Jennifer's parents were indifferent churchgoers themselves and, while they could have been more actively supportive of their daughter's struggles with sexual identity, they did not outright condemn or disown her because of it as did the parents of many of my other interview subjects.

The problem was that Jennifer's parents, like many in the Bible Belt, deferred to the authority of local churches and preachers in matters of social and moral issues. This prevented them from connecting Jennifer's depression with the messages she was receiving in church. The Bible Belt gays I interviewed explained that there is a shared understanding within families and communities that attending church is good, it "keeps you right with the Lord" no matter what actually happens there. Because there is a collective expectation that church is a safe and holy place, and parishioners and community members are socialized to defer to the authority of church leaders, there is little critical scrutiny on the content of sermons, the actions of parishioners, or the possible sexism, racism, and homophobia preached and practiced. Laura (see chap. 2) attended an 80-person parish in which a church deacon and an elder both sexually abused the girls *at the church*. This abuse continued partly because membership in the community required upholding a patriarchal fundamentalist standard that devalued females as persons and overvalued male church authorities.

What this combination of Bible Belt Christian indoctrination and parental passivity added up to in Jennifer's life was an ongoing struggle with low self-esteem based on the belief that because she was gay, God did not love her, no one would love her, and that she was, literally, unlovable. In desperation, Jennifer tried an ex-gay program hoping they would have some secret formula to "fix" her. Ex-gay groups like the Exodus ministry with Focus on the Family (see chap. 5) are a conservative Christian response to the argument that sexual orientation is something one is born with and therefore a status that should be protected under law. Ex-gay groups argue that sexual orientation is a choice and, hence, changeable, and they minister to those trying to change from homosexual to heterosexual. When the Exodus therapy failed to eliminate her romantic and sexual feelings for women, Jennifer resigned herself to being damned and alone. It took two decades of suffering, counseling with a lesbian therapist, and meeting her partner Caroline for Jennifer to emerge partway out of the wasteland of depression, anxiety, and hopelessness within which her religious upbringing had stranded her.

Thomas, white, 38, and from Eastern Kentucky, was so unhappy about his same-sex attractions he agreed to let his parents invite church parishioners to their home where they all laid hands upon him to "pray out a demon of lust and homosexuality." Thomas also struggled with alcoholism, an addiction he directly connected with the ongoing feelings of shame he experienced because of his conservative Christian upbringing. He explained:

> Growing up fundamentalist, you hate yourself. You're taught to hate yourself I think. I think that's why the addiction was there. I think that's why there's such a high rate of alcoholism, and drug addiction, and sex addiction in the gay lifestyle. It's because there's so much self-loathing, from the earliest memory, you believe that there's something wrong with me, there's a secret. And that's reinforced, you sit in church and you hear . . . it is a deadly, deadly sin. You're going to burn in hell. And, to me, when you're small, you believe what the people that take care of you tell you.

After a long day of drinking, Thomas had a panic attack. His parents called 911 and after the paramedics explained that there was nothing physically wrong, his parents decided to "bring in the spiritual." At 2:00 a.m. they called members of their church to come to the house to lay hands on Thomas. Thomas said that "I was so upset and wigged out that I crawled on top of the coffee table." And also, "I was very drunk." Unlike Chris, whose story we read in the introduction, Thomas consented to his exorcism. Three church members showed up and they, along with Thomas's parents, began to pray. He narrated:

> I crawled on top of the coffee table, and they all laid hands on me, and were praying. To me it was a very intense moment. And I could feel, and I don't know if it's my nerves or just the intensity of everyone's body movements, but I remember that the table was shaking, and the more it would

shake, the louder everyone would get. And I remember that I just wanted it to go away, whatever it was. I was willing to do whatever if it would help me, because nothing else had helped me. And they prayed and prayed and prayed. And I remember I was crying, and finally I relaxed and I think the panic attack went away.

Thomas felt some temporary relief after this:

I had gone to psychologists, I had gone to therapists, I couldn't quit drinking, I was feeling suicidal. Now when I look back, I know it was my addiction. It was alcoholism. And just emotional turmoil. But as I calmed down, they sort of calmed down and they prayed and coaxed me and they said, "it's gone. It has left." And after that for a couple of weeks I went to church with them. I remember I had gay porn and I threw away all the porn. I was trying to convince myself, this is gone, I don't want this anymore. I'm not attracted to women, but maybe my role in life, and that's what I had been told too, is to be celibate and to do God's work.

A commitment to celibacy is difficult to sustain. Thomas explained, "It lasted for a couple of weeks, and I went back to drinking and I went back to feeling that I was gay. I decided to kill myself." Thomas had a suicide plan:

I'm going to leave the house. I'm going to go out one last time. I'm going to go to a bar. I'm going to hook up with a guy. I'm going to have sex. I'm going to get a nice hotel room. I'm going to take this whole bottle of Valium and I'm going to just end it. I don't want to live this way anymore. So I went out, and it just kept going through my head, "God, I don't want to die, I'll miss so much, what I am going to go to?" What if there is a hell, what if I go to hell?

Thomas did not kill himself that evening. He credits God for the life-changing events that happened that evening:

From 11 o'clock in the morning till three in the morning I had 52 beers and six Valiums. And I still felt so broken. I decided not to kill myself, but I'm like, I just need to go home and I need to get a cab. I don't know what I'm going to do, but I'm going to deal with it tomorrow. So I leave the bar and this guy walks up to me and he's like, "what's going on?" I'm like, "I'm trying to find a cab to go home." And he's like, "do you want me to suck your dick?" And I'm like, "no." I said, "I just need to find a pay phone, I need to call a cab and go home." And he's like, "I'll show you where a pay phone is." So he's kind of leading me down this alley and I said, "well there's a pay phone over there on the corner." I saw it out of the corner of my eye under a streetlight. So I go over there and I dial the phone and he puts a gun to the back of my head and he says, "give me your wallet, give me your watch, or I'll blow your brains all over this wall." And right then and there I said, "God help me." And I felt a spiritual experience. I felt this intense rush of warmth and peace complete my body and then come out of my body and I knew it was over. I was finished drinking. And I've not drunk since then and that's been probably four years ago. And the very next day I left my parent's house and I've not gone back there except to visit.

This violent threat was life-changing because it not only gave Thomas the ability to manage his addiction to alcohol but also because it gave him a new clarity in his perception of God. He stated, "For the first time I thought, not through my parents, not through a church, but through my own experience of what I perceive God to be, I felt for the first time it's okay that I'm gay. God still loves me."

"If You Are Gay, You Are Not Part of Us"

During our interview, Robert, 24, African American, and from Houston, Texas, explored a turning point in his understanding of homophobia in Black churches. Robert grew up Baptist and attended a predominately Black church most of his life. The message that he received about homosexuality was that it was evil. This message was reinforced when his childhood church declined to hold the funeral of its own minister of music because he died of AIDS. Robert explained:

This particular Minister of Music, and I swear, our choir was never the same before this man came and after, because during his time was the glory days of our church. We had increased attendance. Multiple people would just come to our church to hear our choir because it was a really good sound that he was producing. But he died of AIDS and the church refused to have his funeral at the church because of that. He had been the music director for at least 5 years. The family said the church is not letting us have the service here because he had AIDS. The Minister wasn't saying why. He just said, "it's not being done here" without any explanation, but the family clearly stated, "this is what we were told and this is why we are not having it here."

By refusing to lead the funeral of a once-active church member because he died of a "gay disease," this institution sent a clear message to parishioners that gay people are essentially unworthy no matter how much service they do, and sacrifice they offer, to heterosexual religious organizations. Robert continued:

> I was stunned because this man had done so much greatness for this church and we can't even honor him in the church that he helped cultivate for the last 5 years just because he has AIDS? To me, it was disheartening. If you are gay, you are not part of us ...

Robert still considers himself a Christian, but not a Baptist because of their position on homosexuality. He attends a nondenominational Christian church that is both racially diverse and accepting of gay people.

None of my Black informants discussed any individual member officially kicked out of Black churches. Rather, suspected or known Black gays existed in a "don't ask, don't tell" relationship with the parish, were ignored, or withdrew. Black churches have traditionally served as a source of support and a haven from oppression and discrimination for members.[7] Institutional racism results in unpredictable and volatile consequences in the lives of racial minorities. A vibrant Black church must be a forgiving and welcoming place for community members—even when they violate social mores—*except* if the individual in question is homosexual. You can bring your schizophrenic brother, your alcoholic uncle, your unmarried teenage sister, your neighbor who abuses his wife and children, but as Cathy, who is African American, 35, and from Central Kentucky, observed, "you can't bring them to church and say, 'this is my gay brother.'" Being gay is worse than being promiscuous, abusive, mentally ill, having unprotected sex, or being a convicted felon in the eyes of most Black churches.[8] Cathy elaborated:

> People having babies out of wedlock when they are 15, 16, the Black church is okay with that. I mean it's upsetting, they don't want to see it, but they will rally around, they will give you baby showers, they will pray for you. But if you are gay, then they look at you completely different, like that would be the absolutely worst thing that you could have ever done. My brother is a convicted felon. He's a drug dealer. Back when I was younger, I saw my mom take him to church, and they acted like he was just the greatest thing ever because God saved him.

Cathy has been back to her family church only a few times since she came out because she feels as if she is treated with injustice. The political scientist

Cathy J. Cohen explores why the Black church frames homosexual activity as "worse" than a host of other arguably more problematic and destructive behaviors in her book *The Boundaries of Blackness: AIDS and the Breakdown of Black Politics*. Cohen explained that clergy distinguish between the "sick" behavior of drug users in contrast to the "sinful" behavior of homosexuals. Cohen writes,

> Neither behavior or lifestyle is condoned by the church, but drug use is seen as a temporary "condition" that black clergy can acknowledge, talk about, and most importantly, develop programs for. Homosexuality, on the other hand, is viewed as sinful behavior, not to be acknowledged or accepted.[9]

Interestingly, this analysis also suggests that some Christians may perceive homosexuality as worse than other "behaviors" because it is seen as more immutable, that is, not temporary and harder to change, than criminal activity. Such reasoning is implicitly in tension with the conservative Christian argument that homosexuality is a choice.

Unlike Cathy, Mark, who is 48, African American, and from Central Kentucky, continues to find solace in a Black church in spite of its homophobia. Mark found what he called a "progressive Baptist" church with a minister he respects. This minister does not preach against homosexuality, but Mark also is not fully out at the church. He tried attending MCC (Metropolitan Community Church)[10] with a boyfriend and, although the experience was pleasant, Mark explained that "when I leave I don't feel like I've been to church." For Mark, his racial identity trumps his sexual identity in matters of religion, and he is content with a "don't ask, don't tell" status in a traditional Black church:

> Because it's just a tradition for me. It's being Black, there's all the discrimination that you face and you just keep going and doing what you need to do for yourself, and that's the same thing with the church in the Black community. It's a big part of me. I'm Black. Even though some people, not all, condemn and look at you funny, I'm who I am and I'm not going to give up my spirituality and what makes me comfortable and gets me through the week just to please other people. Because even though I may get those stares I still feel okay with my connection with whatever the message is. Or there may be a song or two that is sewn into the message that I get. It's that whole ceremony.

In her book *Black Sexual Politics*, the sociologist Patricia Hill Collins noted this "curious effect"—Black churches that allow homosexuals in the choir and pews as long as they consent to existing in a "don't ask, don't tell" status. Collins quoted the Reverend Edwin C. Sanders, a founding pastor of the Metropolitan Interdenominational Church in Nashville, about this phenomenon: "the unspoken message . . . says it's all right for you to be here, just don't say anything, just play your little role. You can be in the choir, you can sit on the piano bench, but don't say you're gay."[11] Like Cohen, Sanders observed that this limited the church's efficacy in dealing with HIV/AIDS. Collins quoted Sanders who said, "six Black musicians within Black churches died of AIDS, yet churches hushed up the causes of their deaths."[12] Cathy, who is a social worker, expressed concern that the Black church's unwillingness to discuss homosexuality and accept Black homosexuals has negative consequences for the entire Black community:

> I feel like that's part of the reason why there's such a rise in HIV and AIDS cases in the Black community is partly because the Black churches has attached an even bigger stigma to being gay than what's already out there, in general mainstream society.[13]

When I first embarked on this project, I conceptualized race, in addition to region and religious background, as important in understanding Bible Belt Christianity. I imagined that racial minorities, having endured oppression and discrimination, might be more empathetic to the suffering of gay men and lesbians. This was not the case among my informants. Even those individuals like Cathy and Mark, who had relatively accepting families, observed that their minority group seemed less accepting than some of their white counterparts. The author and political consultant Keith Boykin wrote in his book *One More River to Cross: Black and Gay in America*, "Despite the growing number of black congregations that value their lesbian and gay members, religion is often the most frequently cited factor in black homophobia."[14] Boykin clarifies, "It is not so much the church community but, rather, church doctrine that ostracizes homosexuals. This distinction helps explain why the Black church is alternately cited as the most homo-tolerant and the most homophobic black institution."[15]

"You Are Consciously Spitting on the Blood that
Jesus Shed for You"—Joshua's Story

One of three interview subjects whose family tried to exorcize the demon of homosexuality from him, Joshua, quoted at the beginning of this chapter, felt so shattered by the violence done to him in the name of Christianity that he compared it to rape. And, like a rape victim wanting nothing to do with his abuser, Joshua repudiated Christianity. In this section, I share a detailed account of the rift that Joshua's coming out created in his family. It is significant to note that while Joshua narrated more painful details—specifically a blow-by-blow account of his traumatic ostracism—than did most other interview subjects, the complex dynamics he described help explain why gay youth are over represented among the homeless. Were he not already in college when his parents learned he was gay, Joshua would have been homeless himself. As it turned out, Joshua's parents literally took everything short of the clothes off his back from him once they were certain he had embraced a "sinful homosexual lifestyle."

Although Joshua began having same-sex attractions during adolescence, he suppressed them until college. He had wanted to attend a private Christian college like Liberty University, but the University of Georgia had offered him a full scholarship, and his family did not have the funds for a Christian college. Joshua explained that everyone, including himself, was worried about him attending a "liberal, secular university." To combat this influence Joshua immediately immersed himself in Christian organizations at the University of Georgia. He related:

> I quickly joined Bulldog Christian Fellowship, quickly joined a church, Prince Avenue Baptist Church in Athens, quickly surrounded myself with a little collection of Christian friends, continued to listen to my Christian radio, wore Christian T-shirts. I put a Christian poster on my dorm room door. I wanted to advertise that I was a Christian. I wanted to let people know that those were my values. Coming out of the closet or dealing with the fact that I was gay was not on my radar at all.

Things began to change when Joshua met David through a mutual acquaintance at their dining hall. David assumed that Joshua was gay and out (probably, as Joshua shared, laughing, "because I think I was going on and on and on about Celine Dion, and have you heard Celine Dion's new single, something like that, so he just assumed this boy is gay and it didn't occur to him that I'd be closeted"). David wanted to ask Joshua out on a date and asked a mutual friend to let Joshua know he was interested. Intrigued and alarmed, Joshua called David to explain to him that he was not gay, but that they could be friends. He had convinced himself that this was appropriate because it offered him an opportunity to minister to David. Joshua explained:

I honestly thought that that was what I was going to do at first. Because I decided had the Lord not given me the strength, or had Satan ensnared me, I could've been gay too. But all of that quickly devolved into me realizing I had a crush on him, and I was flattered that he had a crush on me, and within three weeks of us being introduced we wound up in my dorm room alone and he kissed me.

The fact and rightness of his homosexuality crystallized during that kiss:

Through that physical kiss, something instantly shifted, and I never second guessed it. I knew, "okay this is what's right, and I'm going to have to figure out how to calibrate the rest." So after that very first kiss, I never, ever doubted that I was indeed a gay man and that that was what was right. It's strange how instantaneously it changed. Now, the trappings, if this makes any sense, the security in knowing I am gay, that happened instantly. Now figuring out what to do then with the rest of it, took years.

The "rest of it," the biggest barrier Joshua faced coming out, was his family. Back at his childhood home, Joshua juggled many identities the following summer: he attended a Metropolitan Community Church and began reading gay literature on Christianity in order to nurture a positive gay Christian identity, he secretly maintained a relationship with David, and worked as the Youth Intern at his home church in charge of planning Bible study and the summer mission.

Joshua explained that his plan was to keep all these identities compartmentalized, and certainly hide that he was gay from his family, while he tried to process the revelation of his homosexuality. This plan derailed when Joshua's mother found an email he wrote to David, confronted him, and insisted he see a Christian therapist. Joshua said, "She basically blackmailed me. She said that she would out me to the rest of my family and certainly to the church, and I would lose my job, that I had to have this therapy." Joshua complied, saw a local Christian therapist three times, and then, skillfully employing Christian rhetoric, persuaded his mother that he was cured. The following November she learned his relationship with David was still ongoing, told Joshua's father and, after a chain of traumatic events, Joshua's parents disowned him. The unraveling of Joshua's relationship with his parents began while he and David were visiting Joshua's grandmother, his father's mother. She was supportive of Joshua's homosexuality and had prepared a celebratory dinner for the couple. Somehow, Joshua's mother found out about the dinner and called. Joshua recollected:

> Grandmother had just put the dinner on the table and the phone rang. And it was my mom, and she said, "I know what you're doing." And grandmother played dumb and said, "what are you talking about?" "I know that Josh and David are at your house and I'm not going to allow this to happen. And I'm on my way." David and I instantly fled back to the University of Georgia. We didn't even take a bite of food. Because I was scared of my mom and I knew my dad would be in tow, arriving at grandmother's.

Afraid of Joshua's father, David literally hid in his dormitory closet in his locked dorm room as Joshua prepared to face his parents. Concerned, Joshua's grandmother had called the university police. Joshua continued:

> We fled grandmother's house, got back in David's car, drove back to the University of Georgia. Grandmother, in the meantime, called the university campus police and said, "my grandson is gay, he's with his boyfriend, and his parents are in pursuit and they are driving to the University of Georgia to take him." We got to the dorm. David hid in his dorm room with the door locked, and then hid in the closet. I got to my dorm room and then my parents arrived. By this point, my resident advisor came to me, before my parents had even got there, and said, "Josh the police called, they said that your parents were chasing you, is this true?" I said, "yes, they're on their way, they've just found out that I'm gay, and I don't know what they've got in store, but it's going to be dramatic."

The resident advisor assured Joshua that he did not have to allow his parents in his dormitory room, but Joshua decided to let them in. At first, his mother expressed more anger than his father did. Joshua said, "I never really recovered from the things that she said to me that night. She said, 'you've lied to me since April. You are not the son that I thought you were, you disgust me.'" Joshua's father still believed the situation was manageable and tried to calm her down. Joshua continued:

> Dad was like "Sandra, shut up, shut up Sandra." It was very ironic. I would have not thought that it would unfold that way. Daddy was the one trying to say, "Josh, don't you understand that we love you, that we can help you." Whereas Mom was like, "no Bill, he's past that. The devil has him." Momma was just like this angry snake, seething with betrayal and venom.

And Daddy was the one trying to comfort me and plead with me, however misguided, but from a position of love and concern. And that went on for I don't know how long, but it was a long protracted conversation there in my dorm room. It eventually got to the point where Daddy and Momma, somehow in combination basically made this ultimatum: "You've got to come back; we've got to take you home." And I said, "no I'm not leaving." Eventually Daddy said, "Josh, are you trying to tell me that you really think that you're gay, and you're really trying to lead some gay lifestyle." In that moment I realized it's now or never, and however brokenly I managed it, I made them understand I am gay. That is not changing. You have to understand that. When Daddy realized that I wasn't really going to get broken down and that I wasn't going to have that moment where they could sweep in and give me mercy and grace and forgiveness and the Lord could heal me, he switched. He instantly became as angry as my mom. And I remember Michael, the RA, was on the other side of the door knocking, "Josh are you okay?" because at this point my dad was yelling. And I think they were concerned for my physical safety.

Joshua's parents insisted that he come home, a two-hour drive, that night with them if he ever hoped to see his little brother again. Further, they decided to take all of Joshua's possessions with them, explaining that they would not equip Joshua with anything that supported a sinful lifestyle. Joshua described their thought processes:

I think they were trying to connect this to some sort of prodigal son parallel. If you're going to go out and live in sin, and consciously reject your savior and consciously reject the values and everything we have invested and sacrificed to raise you . . . they're thinking, "how many thousands of dollars did we spend on these private schools to keep them safe and teach them the values that they need to be strong Christians in the dangerous sinful world?" They felt that I was in that moment betraying all of that. And I was very mindful of the fact that they thought that was what I was doing, which killed me. They took the bed sheets, the toaster, the refrigerator, all the clothes.

To make sure I understood this accurately, I asked Joshua, "Your parents took these things from your dorm room?" Joshua responded:

From my dorm room. They took all of that. They explained to me, they said, "understand, because this is your moment to get to choose. If you are sitting here telling us that you are going to stay here and be a queer, then you're not doing it with any support from this family." And they started parading out. By this point I'm curled up in the fetal position in the corner of my dorm room. The door is now open, and little heads looked in I was later told. Because people would later recount to me how they remembered that night. People were watching in the hallway, "What the heck is happening in room 212 to Josh?" And they paraded out my computer, the lamp on my desk, my toaster, anything that had been the family's.

While the RA continued to insist to Joshua that this did not need to happen, that his parents had no legal right to take his belongings from a state institution, Joshua said, "No, my parents are going to do what they are going to do, so stand back." Joshua even helped them carry out his things, got in the car and drove back home with them. They had threatened to never let Joshua see his younger brother again unless he left with them, right at that moment. Joshua explained, "They said if you don't come tell him yourself, we'll have to tell him and you'll never see him again. Much less, will you ever see us again. My parents made it clear that until I came back to Jesus this family relationship was over."

Back at the house, Joshua's parents had arranged for their church pastor and Joshua's former Sunday school teacher to meet them to spiritually counsel Joshua. They both locked and blocked the front door. Realizing he was cornered, the first thing Joshua said was that he was going to jump out the window and run to the police station. All assembled interpreted Joshua's threat to jump out of the window as evidence that Joshua was under the spell of the devil. Joshua recounted what ensued:

The pastor had set me down and was hurling Bible verses at me. I realized it was stinging more than I thought it would. There was like this tiny, tiny sliver of a moment where I almost believed what he was saying. And there was my Sunday school teacher praying in tandem with him preaching at me. My parents are over in the corner bawling hysterically watching this happen. And I can sense that my brother is hiding in his bedroom listening to it happen. And for a fraction of a second I almost felt vulnerable to it, but it was a very passing moment. And something snapped and I basically said to myself, "fuck all of this. I'm done. If this is what it's going to lead to, if this is what they're doing, then no." I mean it really just shattered my soul.

This was the moment, Joshua explained, when his "capacity or desire for Christianity was forever extinguished." However well-intentioned were his parents, pastor, and childhood Sunday school teacher, and Joshua fully acknowledged that they were, for Joshua the intervention/exorcism was a violent, destructive, emotional, psychological, and spiritual violation that shattered his relationship with Jesus Christ. Their hysterical repudiation of Joshua's homosexuality twisted all that he held sacred, intimate, and meaningful in Christianity into something perverse, dangerous, and intimidating. Joshua continued:

> It was so invasive, and so humiliating, and so consciously intentionally wounding. I think they were consciously playing on, "you should know better. You do know what you're doing. You do know what a sin this is in God's eyes. You are consciously and willfully as a Christian that's been saved, you are consciously spitting on the blood that Jesus shed for you." They would use all of the rhetoric that they knew I should be responding to, because they knew that I knew it. Does that make sense? They knew that I knew how this should work. And so there was some sort of very deliberate and conscious effort to make this hurt as bad as it possibly can because he appears to be so far gone that we've basically got to use every strategy we have available. I know that they saw it as some sort of valiant rescue mission, or spiritual intervention, but it basically just shattered me.

This went on for several hours. Joshua never felt like he could just get up and walk out the door because either his father or the pastor, both of whom were twice his size, blocked his way. With no lessening of intensity by 2 a.m., Joshua eventually realized that this barrage of spiritual abuse was not going to stop until he submitted. He said, "I got really quiet and lied straight through my teeth, and said, 'will you please pray for me?'" Joshua consciously decided to manipulate his parents to bring an awful day to conclusion. He continued:

> I didn't say I was renouncing my homosexuality. I thought, "if I give them an inch, it will be enough." And I said, "could you please just pray for me? Because I feel so broken." And that's a code word in the Christian community. There's a language that we have, and I knew that the connotations to that word would be such that it would imply more to them then I meant, but I did that consciously. I thought, "I'll tell them that I'm broken, and that I need their prayers. I'm not renouncing anything." I

knew that it would be enough to get them to feel like they had had some sort of small measure of victory. I knew that's what they were after. So I let them do it. I said, "pray for me." That was the culmination, some sort of victory, some sort of conquest that they needed. I knew it wouldn't stop until they were satisfied. And so I let them pray over me, and went through the motions, some sort of feeling, some sort of gratitude, that they had done that.

Joshua felt that he had no physical advantage in the situation. His best choice was to submit to what he perceived as a spiritual rape in order to survive it, after which they all finally went to bed. The next morning Joshua woke before the sunrise, went into his parents' bedroom and said that he needed them to take him back to the University of Georgia. There had been a plan afoot to send Joshua, at the church's expense, to an ex-gay hospital, affiliated with Exodus International, in Florida. The following morning Joshua recognized that he had given them what they wanted the night before, but he could not continue to do so. After a little more negotiation, his parents gave up and drove him back to UGA. They went back in a different car than the one they had used the evening before because the other was full of Joshua's belongings, which they would not return. The family barely spoke during the two-hour trip. Joshua described their parting:

This was on November the 15th. My dad pulled into a Krystal, the hamburger place, and said, "are you hungry?" And I said, "yes." And they ordered me some food from Krystal's and said, "this is the last thing you'll ever get from us until you realize what you've done." They said, "like the prodigal son, you're going to come back." I had graduated valedictorian from my high school class. I had been maintaining a 4.0 at UGA. They said, "you have talents and those all come from the Lord, and you're going to lose all of that." By this point we were at the corner of my dorm. They opened the door and said, "Get out." And I stood there holding a bag of Krystal's as they drove off. And we didn't talk for about a year.

Joshua explained that he is still trying to heal from all of this:

Last November 15th, I've been a vegetarian for a long time, I went back to Krystal's and I ordered the same thing that they gave me and I ate it. It was sort of a weird ritual. I don't know why I did, but I did. Almost as a validation of myself, like I'm still here. I graduated from UGA summa cum laude. I got a scholarship to go to Canada and study French. I'm at

Morehead State University in a master's program. I have succeeded, and they swore to me that I wouldn't. And I went to Krystal, and I hadn't eaten meat in forever, for years, but I ordered exactly what they ordered me that night and I ate it.

There is much to unpack in Joshua's harrowing and haunting story. Before he came out, Joshua had had a relatively close and loving relationship with his parents, particularly his mother. Further, they were a middle-class family, not straining under the stress caused by extreme financial hardship. As "shattered" as Joshua understandably was by their rejection, he did not demonize them nor did he share any stories of childhood abuse. Disowning their son was not the last of a long list of other abuses his parents committed. They had supported Joshua in all his other pursuits. Strikingly, their rejection of Joshua's homosexuality, and the violent rift it caused, sounds singularly tied to a fundamentalist interpretation of Christianity, which places active homosexuals outside of God's love and unworthy of salvation. Joshua's parents believed that by embracing homosexuality, Joshua had rejected Jesus and thus the family. This forced them, according to their belief system, to denounce their son.

The Importance of Institutional Support

I think it is important to recognize the role that staff, faculty, and students of the University of Georgia played in helping Joshua cope with this trauma. There has been much recent public discussion about the connection between peer bullying behavior, homophobia, and gay youth who attempt or commit suicide. I am thinking, in particular, of Tyler Clementi, a first-year student at Rutgers University who committed suicide by jumping off the George Washington Bridge in Manhattan in October 2010 after his roommate streamed live video footage of Tyler's sexual encounter with a man. Such stories of gay youth bullied into attempting suicide need to be told as they raise consciousness about homophobic norms in our culture. At the same time, stories of institutional support, even in the Bible Belt, also need to be shared, and Joshua's story is one such tale. Not only were the campus police, his RA, and dorm mates supportive of Joshua during this difficult transition, a faculty member in the University of Georgia's French department swooped in and organized a network people to help Joshua replace his belongings including his bed sheets, computer, clothes, even his car. He was offered an academic leave from the university, which he did not take, and a student job, which he did. In short, a caring network of university community members helped Joshua survive emotionally, psychologically, and materially.

The fact that the University of Georgia is a public institution, with an expressed commitment to diversity, eased Joshua's journey. Such is not the case for students at private Christian schools. More than 200 Christian colleges and universities have policies prohibiting homosexuality or homosexual behavior.[16] In the student handbooks of these institutions, homosexuality is framed as sexual misconduct, and identifying as a homosexual or engaging in homosexual acts are grounds for expulsion.[17] One of my interview subjects, Jason Johnson, was expelled from the University of the Cumberlands, a Christian college affiliated with the Southern Baptist Church and located in Williamsburg, Kentucky, for sharing that he was gay on his MySpace page. Jason explained what happened:

> I had a meeting with the vice president and the director of Student Services. They showed me a printout of my MySpace page. Under where it said the orientation I said, "gay." They showed it to me, and they asked, "Is this your page?" And the thought in the back of my mind was, "I could say no. I could say that someone made that up about me." But that would be lying and I told myself that I wouldn't lie about this. This was just one of those things that flashes through your brain really quickly, because my immediate answer was, "Yes, yes, that is mine. I'm not going to lie about this." They said, "Okay." The vice president left and another lady came in. She was there to bear witness. She read me the policy in the handbook and she said, "You violated the policy because of this and this and this. Because you are gay, you are being suspended."

Jason transferred to a state university. Fortunately Jason's family supported their son through this ordeal. Kimberly, 32, white, and from Texas, worried that she would be both disowned by her family *and* expelled from her Christian college when her mother discovered that Kimberly was a lesbian:

> My mom found out. She caught me kissing my first girlfriend, which was real tragic. It was Christmas break. She made me leave. She made us both leave. She made me take everything I wanted and told me never to come back. She didn't talk to me for several weeks afterwards.

During this period, Kimberly dealt not only with the trauma of her mother's rejection, she feared losing her athletic scholarship and expulsion from her private Christian college should school authorities learn that she was a lesbian. Kimberly explained:

She threatened to call the dean of my college. I also played softball and I was the mascot at the college. I went to a private Christian school, and, of course, it [homosexuality] was forbidden. It was in the handbook if you were caught you would be dismissed, so I was worried that she would call.

Kimberly's mother did not follow through on her threat, and Kimberly graduated. What all these stories illustrate is the damaging consequences of a *cumulative* lack of support, something that makes Bible Belt gays more vulnerable to harm than peers in regions of the United States more accepting of homosexuality.[18] If these institutions—one's family, school, church, peers, workplace, and neighbors—are all adamantly in alignment that homosexuality is an abomination to God, a rejected gay youth may literally have nowhere to turn.

Driven Away from Christ

Forced out of the heavenly family—and in many cases flesh-and-blood families as well—and facing eternal damnation, gay Christians struggle with fear of hell, depression, suicidal thoughts, ex-gay programs, feelings of worthlessness, and self-destructive behaviors. Depending on their religious backgrounds, Bible Belt gays' responses to experiences of oppression within conservative Christian denominations varied from atheism/agnosticism to exploring non-Christian beliefs like Buddhism and Wicca to believing in a Christian God but eschewing organized religion to participation in gay-affirming Christian churches (Episcopal, MCC, Unitarian Universalists, United Church of Christ, Orthodox Catholic Church of America). Some, like Jennifer who tried a number of Baptist and Pentecostal churches before converting to Roman Catholicism, and Mark, still remain closeted members in Christian churches.

Brother Damien, quoted in the introduction, argued that conservative Christian churches that exclude gay people not only from individual congregations but from membership in the Body of Christ, cannot rightly call themselves Christian. Brother Damien believes such people are doing the work of Satan:

I believe that they're not Christians. I will come out and state that. What the religious Right has done, what the ultra-conservative Christians have actually done is what Satan wants to be done. And that is driving people away from Christ. And Jesus had something to say about that.

He [paraphrased], "For those who drive His children away from Him, it would actually be better if they had a millstone tied around their neck and were thrown in the sea rather than face His wrath."

Joshua is an obvious example of someone "driven away from Christ," and he is not the only one. Celia, who is white, 40, and from Eastern Kentucky, observed that her experiences with conservative Christianity created "a lot of bitterness toward religion":

It's unfortunate that my religious experience is completely tainted. I don't have the first desire in the world to ever go into another church. And I think that spirituality is an important part of every human. It's an important part of me that, frankly, I have abandoned, for all intents and purposes, because it's brought so much pain, and that's unhealthy.

Misty confided that she was still struggling with feelings of anger and resentment because of her religious upbringing and certainly did not identify as Christian:

I totally can't stand Christianity at all. When I was a child, they would preach acceptance, peace, and passivism, and love Jesus, and be kind to your fellow neighbor, and then they would do the exact fucking opposite. So it was obvious to me that they were hypocrites. I have actually come to the point in the past year of being able to accept that people are Christians, I'm not joking. Since I was about thirteen until I was about 21, I was so mad and pissed off about everything that had been done to me, everything that I had been taught, everything that I had been led to believe, that I became the most vicious, sarcastic opponent to Christianity you've ever met.

Linda, whose father is a preacher with the Disciples of Christ and whose mother is a Bible scholar, grew up in churches. She said, "As preacher's kids, we were expected to be there all the time." She considers the Bible the inspired Word of God but does not regularly attend church any longer, something she misses:

You can only keep yourself spiritually nourished in so many ways for so long. It can be difficult, especially in this part of the country. You wish that you could go to church sometimes, and not be afraid of just being told what a horrible person you are. Even if they don't realize that they've got a gay person sitting in their pew, just to hear that over and over again. You want to stand up and scream, "You've got it so wrong! Where did you go to seminary?"

After years of prayer, psychological distress, low self-esteem, and an extremely abusive heterosexual marriage, Linda finally came out at the age of 27. For her, this took wrestling with the scriptures by herself.

> I went through a whole struggle with God over it because of the way I was raised. God's very important to me. I started doing research. I realized I need to stop looking at the Bible the way people told me to look at it, and start looking at it as though I've never seen it before, and make my own interpretations of what I see there. Let God talk to me, he doesn't need any human beings' help to tell me what he has to say. So I started doing research, and I had at least two copies of the Bible next to me at my computer at all times, and I would spend hours and hours and days and days and days just pouring over linguistic, theological, cultural research to find out what exactly the texts were saying, and what was the context of those texts, and I discovered that . . . God doesn't condemn homosexuality, at all. He has nothing negative to say about it.

The process Linda describes here of biblical study and research is one other researchers have noted among their informants.[19] The sociologist Jodi O'Brien calls this process of integrating a gay and Christian self "living the contradiction."[20] Melissa Wilcox, a religion scholar, framed the effort Linda described as "religious individualism," an intense, personal, often lonely journey integrating socially constructed conflicting identities.

Some of my interview subjects, like Linda, Thomas, and Brother Damien, managed to erect a gay Christian identity, in spite of the abuse and rejection they had suffered in the name of Bible Belt Christianity. Others, like Joshua, Misty, and Celia, found not only was their understanding of themselves as Christian irrevocably shattered but they had lost all interest in contemplating the divine. They even felt angry with the *idea* of religion and hence cut off from inner spiritual resources. Joshua said, "I feel like because of what happened I wouldn't know healthy spirituality if it hit me in the head. I could feel my blood pressure going up if I even saw a church." To put this in the context of food, imagine contracting a violent case of food poisoning from a fast food restaurant like Burger King and deciding not only that you will avoid this restaurant chain in the future, but that you no longer want to eat.[21]

In *Religion Gone Bad*, Mel White makes a grim case that prominent leaders in the Christian Right—including Jerry Falwell, Pat Robertson, D. James

Kennedy, and James Dobson[22]—are deliberately attempting to influence public policy to restrict and deny gay rights to generate money for their organizations. Such conservative Christian leaders, those who control the dissemination of homophobic doctrine, refuse to include people in same-sex
relationships among the "saved" no matter how much LGBT folks beg to be
invited to the table, and no matter how much we debase ourselves trying
to share the meal. The physical, psychological, and spiritual violence done
to a lesbian or gay man threatened with eternal damnation and ostracized
from local and familial communities in environments socially constructed
as "Godly places of worship and fellowship" is horrific in itself. But White
argues that an even more disturbing possibility is that leaders in the far Christian Right might advocate the end of homosexuality by any means. Although
most conservative Christian leaders stop short of promoting direct violence
against homosexuals, it appears to be the logical endpoint of their ideology.
For, if homosexuality is found or believed to be immutable, and conservative Christians judge that the presence of homosexuals so angers God that
he rains natural disasters, death, famine, and disease among us because of it,
the next step might involve easing God's wrath by eliminating homosexuals.
Thus, by repeatedly constructing gay people as inferior and an abomination
to God, conservative Christian theology plays a starring role in the passage
of discriminatory legislation,[23] frightens gay people so that they stay in what
I call the "toxic closet" and encourages abuse, violence, and ostracism toward
sexual minorities everywhere.

4

"They Don't Know Who I Am"

The Toxic Closet

I've been there for thirty years and nobody really knows me.
—Caroline, 52, white, from Kentucky

I'm holding myself in this little box and I wasn't allowed to grow.
—Annie, 23, African American, from Cincinnati

Among the biggest battles gay people living in conservative areas struggle with is whether, when, and how to come out. To come out is to risk rejection, abuse, abandonment, and loss of one's job, friends, even, in some extreme cases, one's life. And, unlike most members of other minority groups, for example women and people of color, many gay people can "pass" as members of the dominant group—heterosexuals. Even those gay people who are gender non-normative, for example a "butch" woman or a "femme" man will be treated by others as heterosexual in many circumstances out of politeness. Especially in the Bible Belt, a region in which expressions of homophobia are rampant and widespread, to assume that someone is gay based on their appearance is perceived as rude and insulting. Even people who look, sound, or act stereotypically "queer" may be spoken to and interacted with in ways that maintain a presumption of heterosexuality, and questions about relationship status are carefully avoided.

At the same time, passing, hiding, pretending, and evading also cause problems; staying in what I call the "toxic closet" creates its own set of long-term emotional and psychological issues. The costs of closeting have been well explored by historians, literary scholars, theologians, social scientists, and journalists.[1] In this chapter, I add to the scholarship of the closet through an examination of the toxic closet primarily as a condition of inarticulation about the gay self. By this I mean that the closet is toxic not only because it is a place that encourages secrecy and shame but also because closeting inhibits effective communication with others about oneself, and then this lack of language potentially compromises one's social interactions. We learn in the toxic closet to hold back, to not express ourselves, to accept that we do not deserve the taken-for-granted social courtesies, legal rights, respect, care, and support that heterosexuals enjoy without thought. We deserve better.

Yet sexual minorities have many reasons to stay closeted in the Bible Belt, a place of little institutional support for gay expression and same-sex relationships, when coming out may mean negotiating violence, job loss, and ostracism by family, friends, and neighbors. It is the right of each individual to choose her own path and decide when or if she wishes to reveal information that could cause potential negative consequences. To make coming out even more complicated, a gay person can also experience negative consequences for *not* coming out, i.e., friends, family, and co-workers who ask, "Why didn't you trust me? or "How could you keep such a matter secret for so long?" In each case the burden of change, of expressing or presenting a gay identity in a heterosexist culture, is all placed upon the gay person. Thus, the one experiencing the oppression is perceived as "causing" any consequences that ensue. This is a paradox.[2] As Tony E. Adams describes in his article, "Paradoxes of Sexuality, Gay Identity, and the Closet," living a fully out life is paradoxical because doing so, or attempting to do so, creates "an interactional situation constituted by contradiction."[3] I explore illustrations of this paradox—how coming out can be difficult, ongoing work fraught with potential complications, yet staying in the toxic closet is also laborious and limits a gay person's ability to connect with others—throughout this chapter.

Coming Out and the Closet

The closet is a cultural trope we use to refer to areas of a person's life we do not disclose. The phrase "skeletons in the closet" instantly conjures up a whole host of possibly stigmatizing secrets—extramarital affairs, drug addiction, felony convictions. If something is in the closet in our culture, it is there for a reason and those who probe into such secrets do not generally do so with the best of intentions. For gay people, the dominant experience of the closet is silence and the dominant emotion is shame.[4] In interviews, almost 100% of Bible Belt gays discussed coming out and closeting in these terms: "It's just not been discussed at all," and, "I remember having a feeling that this was going to be my dark secret that I had to shoulder and hide from the world." Claiming a homosexual *or* heterosexual sexual orientation involves expressing and integrating the following three elements: attraction, behavior, and identity.[5] To illustrate, a lesbian feels attraction for women, engages in sexual behavior with women, and identifies as a lesbian. Sexual attraction, behavior, and identity do not always align in a person's life. For example, most people experience attractions for others upon which they do not act. On the other hand, sex workers, for example, may engage in sexual behavior with those to whom they are not attracted.[6] Further, some individuals internalize negative cultural, familial, religious, and community messages about homosexuality so that they do not assert a gay identity, even while they may act on their attraction to the same sex. To measure this group of people, public health specialists constructed a behavioral category of "men who have sex with men" (MSM) to describe men who engage in sexual activity with men but do not identify as gay or bisexual. Ted Haggard, the former head of the National Evangelical Association and pastor of the New Life Church, confessed to engaging in sex with a male prostitute but continues to assert that he is 100% heterosexual. This is a public example of an individual who falls into this category.

Coming out starts with one's self.[7] The sociologist Peter Davies describes this as "individuation, an internal, psychological process whereby I come to recognize my gayness."[8] This involves acknowledging that one has same-sex attractions, accepting that this is unlikely to change, and integrating this realization in future life choices.[9] Ninety percent of the Bible Belt gays I interviewed discussed going through a period of time in their childhood, adolescence, and/or adulthood in which they realized they were having same-sex attractions and felt concerned that this was a problem. By the time of our interview, most had adopted a gay identity, although some made comments that illustrated that they were still struggling with self-acceptance. For example, Thomas (see chap. 3) explained, "I had a very hard time accepting my sexuality because of my religious upbringing. There was a great fear of being punished by God. There's still remnants of that with me. I think there may always be." Self-acceptance entails recognizing and, at least partially, rejecting the homophobic attitudes of others while working through issues related to internalized homophobia. Annie, who is 23, African American, and from Cincinnati, quoted in the epigraph, came out at the age of 19. She explained that she did not want to accept that she was gay at first. In her Pentecostal church, gay people are not among the saved. She explained, "When I was closeted I had a lot of self-issues":

> I wasn't growing as a person. I wasn't being able to experience things that I thought I should be able to experience. I wasn't happy. I was going around with this mask on. And then in any kind of setting, especially if I was at church, if I would see somebody that I thought was attractive I would immediately tell myself that that's wrong and you know you can't think things like that. And it would be my own little inner war going on in my head.

Looking back, Annie recognized that this self-censorship caused her to treat other gay people poorly:

> I'd see someone that I was attracted to, and I knew they'd be gay, but I was like, "no, I'm not like that." I caught myself a lot of times treating people that I thought were gay very poorly because I didn't want to be associated with them.

In our interview, Annie compared being closeted to being an alcoholic. For her, the first step to recovery was admitting she was a lesbian to her college roommate, who subsequently became her first girlfriend. Annie spoke at length about her work to resolve this inner conflict that still emerges around certain members of her family and church community. Annie, like many Bible Belt gays settled for a "don't ask, don't tell" family policy. For example, even though Annie's grandmother knows Annie is a lesbian, and Annie lives with her when she is not in school, Annie explained that "It's pretty much a taboo topic in the house. She knows I have a girlfriend, and I bring her home, and she likes her and she says she loves her and then we just don't talk about it." Annie, like many Bible Belt youth, lacked role models and support for exploring her same-sex attractions, and this disadvantaged her compared to her heterosexual peers. This lack constitutes another form of child endangerment, what the Department of Health and Human Services defines as child neglect: a failure "to provide for the physical, emotional, medical, and educational well-being of a child."

A Condition of Inarticulation

The seeds of the toxic closet begin growing in childhood. In homophobic environments, all children learn from an early age that same-sex affection is inappropriate and subject to sanctioning by both adults and peers. Most of the Bible Belt gays I interviewed heard, like Henry, who is white, 51, and from Illinois, that it was wrong to be homosexual:

> People said they're queers and faggots, and they're just evil people, it's just from the society that I was in that stirred that in me. The church did it too. The Baptist church that I went to—it was a man and woman and that's all it is. So there was this whole society around me that made me feel that way, and I didn't have any gay friends. I didn't know anyone that was a positive role model for me.

Similarly, Donald, who is white, 52, originally from Indiana but a long-time resident of Louisville, Kentucky, said, "it was ingrained in my mind through my family and through the church that all gay men are pedophiles. They played with little boy's buggers. My Aunt Miranda said that to me a hundred times, 'Watch out for those men, they play with your bugger.'" As the personal experiences explored in previous chapters illustrate, suspected or out gay members may be ostracized, excluded, and generally treated as inferior within the family unit. The consequences of one's family knowing definitively, without a mask of denial, that one is gay can be grave. But the ones who are not out, those in the toxic closet, also suffered a type of endangerment within their families: they lacked the developmental support that enables a child to thrive.

In a homophobic family, gay youth learn early to stay in the toxic closet or risk violence, ostracism, and homelessness. My data indicates that many adapt to hostile homophobic familial environments with linguistic strategies of evasion and, sometimes, guarded attitudes that repel intimacy. Katie, who is 26, Black, and raised Roman Catholic, whom I interviewed in Texas but was originally from New York, started having feelings for other girls in sixth grade. Her only framework to interpret these feelings was that she was a bad person. She said, "I felt like I had this fire in my belly that I was trying to keep down because I could not say that I had feelings for another girl." In Katie's childhood and adolescence, the toxic closet also created behavioral and academic issues. Katie believed that hiding her sexual orientation caused the latter, having experienced a period of time in which her inability to openly express her sexuality inhibited her from writing anything at all:

> I distinctly remember a time. It was 11th grade English, and I couldn't write. I couldn't write anything and I found it was because of that. I remember a

teacher saying to me, "write whatever you feel. Write whatever comes to mind. It will help you." At that time, because I was just holding back, it felt like I was on the edge of a cliff. I was barely holding on, and I remember, we had an assignment to write and he told me, "you are going to fail the class unless you write this assignment." He's like, "I know you are capable." I remember wanting to write about how I felt about myself, how I felt about the situation but not being able to write it and starting a paragraph, crumbling up a piece of paper and throwing it away. I remember I did that for 3 hours. Then I chose to fail the class because I just could not write. I couldn't write anything because the one thing I wanted to come out and say, I couldn't say and it blocked me from doing anything.

Katie went through a period in which she was classified as a special needs student because she wasn't doing any of her homework. Katie explained that it was easier to be labeled a poor student and a "bad kid" than a gay student. Then she acted out like a bad kid and got in trouble:

It's easier to be someone who just doesn't listen, as to someone who's struggling with being gay or lesbian. There are many times when I would get in trouble and I would go to the office and they would ask me why I did the things I did and I would just cry. They didn't know what to do with me. [In] 12th grade, I trashed the art room. I broke everything in the art room. I trashed other people's artwork. I put pottery in the kiln and turned it up to 300. I threw clay onto the walls. I was just so angry. It was my last year in high school and I felt so unfinished as a person. I was leaving this institution and still not getting what I needed out of it. I saw everyone else so happy to move on to the next level of their life and basically, I was wondering whether I had to keep this a secret or not.

Katie did not grow up in the Bible Belt. She attended high school in the Bronx. Obviously, the negative consequences of homophobic attitudes in the lives of gay youth extend beyond the Bible Belt. Katie moved to Texas partly to attend college and partly to get away from her homophobic family. She explained that before moving to Texas she had only ever lived 10 or 15 minutes away from them. Under these circumstances, she felt she could not be out, date, or even walk down the street with a woman without it potentially getting back to them and having to face difficult questions. Katie thinks they suspect she is a lesbian but believes her family is "happier living in denial." Katie confided that she has had many opportunities to tell them she is gay but has not out of fear:

I was afraid of my family just saying, "Hey, we're done with you. We just can't speak to you ever again." I felt like they have that right because, being as religious as at least my mother is, she would have every right to have nothing to do with me because the Bible says that I am an abomination. I'm afraid of them being so disappointed in me that they would just never talk to me again. I don't want them to hate me.

Again, Misty is still not out to her parents. She explained that her childhood socialization literally prevented her from perceiving and interpreting her same-sex attractions, i.e., that her fantasies about women might mean she was a lesbian. It was not simply that she was afraid to identify as a lesbian, but that the fear was so big it created a kind of white noise in her head that drowned out all thought. She said, "conditioning from religion, family, and society suppressed the feelings completely into the subconscious until a time that it could be safely looked at." Like Katie, Misty was paralyzed, incoherent, and depressed:

At about age 17, I came to a point in high school where I suffered major depression and was somewhat suicidal. It wasn't that I wanted to kill myself, but the thought of no longer being alive and having to deal with my life was appealing. I would cry for hours at night in my room on a regular basis until I fell asleep. I completely avoided my family by either being gone, in bed all day in the dark and I only left my room to go to school. I was like this for the better part of a year. I wouldn't interact with my parents for days at a time. I had absolutely no idea why I felt this way. No one in my family expressed concern or even seemed to notice.

The pain and confusion Katie and Misty experienced as teenagers illustrate the consequences of growing up in a home or in a school system that provides no support for developing a positive gay identity. In this absence, gay youth lack the appropriate tools, especially language, to combat oppression, and be happy, healthy, and self-actualized. They had no linguistic framework to explore their identities and sexual feelings. These consequences are not confined to the Bible Belt, as Katie's story illustrates. They exist everywhere a gay youth faces homophobic barriers to her or his growth. But this toxic-closet condition of inarticulation is more concentrated in the Bible Belt because of the wide-reaching influence of conservative Christian doctrine about homosexuality and the lack of other institutional support for same-sex relationships.

"Denial Is a Strong Force in My Family"

The lesbians and gay men I interviewed spoke at length about negotiating the closet with family members. Several, like Misty, Jose, Darlene, and Katie were not out to their families. Misty explained why:

> I fear the consequences. I've had a lot of people tell me that coming out is not as bad as I might think it would be. I have really wondered if it would be as bad as I thought it would be or if I was just over anxious about it. I wonder if my family doesn't already know and I'm not really sure. Even if I did tell them about it I would think that they wouldn't want to talk about it. It would upset them, in the first place, any member I told, and it would make every future discussion uncomfortable about anything for a long period of time until they got it back out of their minds again. They would deny it. Denial is a strong force in my family.

Jose, who is Hispanic, 19, from Texas, and from a Roman Catholic family, came out to his sister but not the rest of his family. His sister, in fact, cautioned him against telling their parents and older brother. Jose was a sophomore in college at the time of our interview and, thus, financially dependent on his parents. Jose had no plans to tell them until he was self-supporting because he felt certain they would disown him when they found out. When I asked why he believed that they would cut him off, Jose responded:

> Because, in my mind-set about Hispanics, it's about family. It's about raising a family and having grandchildren. For them, since I am the youngest, "we have put so much effort into making you perfect." I am the first one to go to college, too, making so much progress, it would be hard. They would be heartbroken basically.

He explained that hiding his identity from his parents is difficult: "Every single time I go back, I have to either tell them I am going somewhere I am not. Pretend to be more, I guess, heterosexual in my way of acting. It's difficult, but I can't really do much about it." In addition to managing the stress of lying about his whereabouts and withholding his true thoughts and feelings, Jose felt that the biggest cost of closeting was his disengagement from his family. He said, "I see their sadness, as I don't want to spend time with them as much." Like Jose, Joshua (see chap. 3) hid his emerging gay identity from his parents, lied about where he was going, and managed to live an entire double life for several months. Joshua recounted:

I remember that I would go to the mall and buy this whole secret wardrobe that I only wore when I was with David, like I somehow felt the need to wear these tight T-shirts and these flashy colorful shoes. I wanted to dress like what I thought a gay man who was 19 should be dressing like, if that makes sense? I would hide these clothes in the trunk of my car because I didn't want my parents to see them. That whole summer I was secretly meeting David and I would drive to his house, or I would drive to meet him at the mall on the other side of town, and I was hiding all of this from my parents.

It's hard to conceal something as big as one's sexual orientation from the people who have known you all your life. Most parents are keen observers of their children. Many know when their children are being evasive or deceptive. My mother can tell if I am upset by my tone of voice when I say hello on the phone. Similarly, Joshua's mother quickly figured out that Joshua was behaving peculiarly. While it's possible to hide a one-time mistake or indiscretion from someone you love, from something small like an excessive night of partying to something big like a one-night stand, it's much more difficult to hide an ongoing element of one's life. For example, imagine hiding from your own mother, day in and day out, everything related to your dating and relationship status, for an entire lifetime, like Donald did. Donald did not tell his mother he was gay until she was literally on her death bed. When I asked how she responded, he said, "She was not responsive at that point." In and out of ex-gay programs for 15 years, Donald was adept at keeping secrets from his homophobic mother and skilled in the art of vague articulation. When she heard rumors that her son was gay and asked him if it were true, Donald told her to tell those people "to mind their own damn business and get a life." He recounted another episode of evasion;

> One day in the Wal-Mart parking lot in Clarksville my mother was having a nicotine fit. She needed a cigarette. And I was trying to joke around with her, and tease her, and I gave her a kiss on the cheek real loud, and she says, 'You're not one of those gay queers are you?' And I thought, "Oh shit, this is my moment." And I said, "Absolutely not, I am a lesbian." And she had a good laugh and I went in and got her cigarettes and she was fine.

The primary way a gay child, adolescent, or adult can stay hidden about something as big as their sexuality is if the parents are disengaged, in other words if they are indifferent, poor parents, or they just don't want to know, like Donald's mother.

"I Get a Lot of Migraines"

While many of my interview subjects were closeted to their families, most had spent enough time working on this first stage that they had come to some peace about how they perceived themselves. But not Darlene. Among the lesbians and gay men I interviewed, Darlene, who is white, 37, and from Kentucky, struggled the most with self-acceptance. As the sociologist Steven Seidman defined, for Darlene, the closet functioned as "a life-shaping pattern of homosexual concealment."[10] Trapped in the toxic closet, bullied by her homophobic parents, Darlene could not fully commit to her on-again, off-again relationship with Linda, the preacher's kid quoted earlier. Darlene explained that if she were to share that she was in a same-sex relationship, her parents would disown her. Darlene said, "Every time we break up, it has to do with my family. My parents are totally homophobic. I told Linda, I told her over and over, I'm always going to choose my family." In Darlene's case, her family's tireless opposition to homosexuality resulted in a number of damaging consequences throughout her life, primarily deception, conflict, and abuse.

After Darlene bounced some checks when she was living with Linda, Darlene's family decided that Linda was taking advantage of their daughter financially; they drove to Darlene's apartment and insisted that Darlene kick Linda out on Christmas day. Darlene described this incident:

> My parents came with me. They came with me to ensure that I told Linda to leave. It was awful. I mean, it was like, "Linda, you have to leave." And I told her she had ten minutes to get out of the house and go to her family's house. She was crying and then, it was just a mess. We were both a mess. Until she saw me in March and I had started seeing a guy in January. He asked me to marry him immediately and I said, "yes," because I thought it would make my parents happy. He treated me horribly, horribly bad. He put his hands around my throat once. When I saw Linda in March, she thought that I looked thinner. I had dropped like 30 pounds just because I wasn't eating, but, I looked sick because I was sick. I was sick because I was not eating. I wasn't taking care of myself. I was very depressed.

Darlene has dated men, been married once, and engaged at least twice. Most of the men she has seen romantically have not treated her well. Some were emotionally and physically abusive. Darlene explained that she either dated these men in desperation, hoping that one would "fix her," or she used them as a smokescreen to conceal her relationship with Linda from her family. Darlene's parents would rather their daughter be with any man, even an abuser, than in a same-sex relationship, and they loathe Linda because they suspect there is more to her connection with Darlene than Darlene will admit. After the incident at Christmas, Darlene's family forbade her from seeing Linda. Even talking with her was "taboo." Nonetheless, 37-year-old Darlene continued to secretly maintain a relationship with Linda:

> I was trying to keep it secret from the family. My mom would always tell me, "I'm not stupid. I know you're seeing her. I always know when you're seeing her. You dress different. You act different." My sister said, "I know when you're seeing her. You talk different. You act different. You wear your hair different. You wear your make-up different. You dress different." So, it kills me because I don't want to hurt my family but I love Linda and so, well, what do I do?

Hiding, sneaking around, lying, and feeling internally conflicted drain emotional and physical energy that could be put to more productive uses.[11] Such behaviors also create a great deal of stress and tension in same-sex relationships. Darlene continued:

> I get a lot of migraines. It causes a lot of stress on me. It causes a lot of stress on our relationship even. It's very difficult because I told her, "Right now, my thing is, I want to date because if I date I can at least look like I am having a normal life to my parents." Because, I know my mom well enough to know that if I am not dating, she is going to assume that I'm with Linda. If I say that I am not talking to Linda, she will assume that I am not talking to Linda because I am going out with men. So, it's a façade, and Linda's like, "well, I don't have a problem with that as long as you don't bring them back to the house and make out with them." No, she's like, "if you go out to dinner or whatever I don't have a problem with that." I'm like, "well, I don't want to bring them back to the house and make out with them, I just want to go out with them so I can call and say, 'yeah, I got a date tonight Mom.'"

It's easy to look at these dynamics and see a lot of dysfunction. In a homophobic society, we are trained to blame the homosexual or the same-sex relationship. But what happens if we remove the homophobia from Darlene's life? How then might Darlene's childhood and adolescence evolved differently? She could have dated both girls and boys, without internalizing the idea that she was innately flawed because of her same-sex attractions. She might still have controlling parents, they would likely still try to regulate her sexuality according to sexist gender norms, and they might still dislike Linda, but it wouldn't be because Linda is a lesbian. Eliminating homophobia would free Darlene from the toxic closet and its accompanying deception, secrecy, and manipulation. Overall, this would mean less drama, less pain, and less abuse as well as more support, more love, and more clarity. While giving Darlene a whole new life free of homophobic oppression would not solve all her problems, it would likely make substantial inroads on the worst of them. In Darlene's case, the toxic closet serves the selfish comfort of her family members.

"I Got Really Tired of Hearing How Wrong It Is, so I Just Quit Bringing It Up"

To fully examine how the toxic closet constrains communication, it's important to clarify what it means to come out and be out as a gay person in a homophobic family, workplace, or church. As other scholars have noted, coming out is far messier, complicated, and ongoing than any one individual's coming-out story illustrates.[12] When gay people share their coming-out stories, they usually do so in a narrative arc ending at some epic triumph ("I finally accepted that I am a gay man!") or dramatic consequence (a violent parental response, "my father set a gun on the table and told me I had a choice"). These stories, like most of the narratives we share about ourselves, suggest some conclusion, some wrapping-up of an issue, some cognitive closure, a demeanor of "that was rough, but I got through it, and things are better now," but for gay people coming out is never over. There are always new people to tell. As the literary critic Eve Sedgwick notes in her work on the epistemology of the closet:

> [L]ike Wendy in *Peter Pan*, people find new walls springing up around them even as they drowse: every encounter with a new classfull of students, to say nothing of a new boss, social worker, loan officer, landlord, doctor, erects new closets whose fraught and characteristic law of optics and physics exact from, at least gay people, new surveys, new calculations, new draughts, and requisitions of secrecy or disclosure.[13]

Consequently, clearly delineating how "out" an individual is, is complicated. The language of the closet (out versus in) suggests a binary experience, but in real lived experience, coming out and staying out happens along a continuum. The degree to which the Bible Belt gays expressed their homosexuality ranged across an entire spectrum. For example, I interviewed Bible

Belt gays who were completely out to all their family members, those who were out to some members but not others, those out to just one key person such a sympathetic sibling or grandmother, those who were not officially out but felt their families must "really know," and those actively hiding their sexual orientations from all their relatives. Further, just disclosing that one is gay to one's most important and lasting relationships (parents, siblings, and friends) does not guarantee that one can fully emerge from the closet. To illustrate, when Kimberly's mother (see chap. 3) caught Kimberly kissing her first girlfriend, she told her to leave, and they did not have any contact for some time. After they partially reconciled, Kimberly's mother one, avoided talking about homosexuality, and two, when pressed, would only discuss homosexuality in negative ways. Kimberly explained:

> I got really tired of hearing how wrong it was so I just quit bringing it up. Because I did for a while . . . . I talked to her and I would try to educate her, and try to explain things to her. I sent her pamphlets and all kinds of stuff. I knew it was hard for her. I tried to look at it from her point of view. But, recently I realized that this is who I am and she's just going to have to accept that, and I want her to be a part of my life and I want her to be a part of our lives as we grow together. It's important to me, and I just decided that if she didn't want to know the whole me, then, there really was no point.

Like many other family members of Bible Belt gays, Kimberly's mother has grown more accepting over time. In Kimberly's life though, this period when they just "did not discuss it at all" lasted for years. When Kimberly tried to push herself out of the closet, her mother repeatedly responded by making homosexuality unmentionable. Of those I interviewed who were out to their families, many described a similar "don't ask, don't tell" home environment.

Elena, who is Hispanic, 20, and from El Paso, Texas, came out to her family in stages. At each stage, though, family members tried to manage whom she told and how. Elena is a member of a large Roman Catholic family. The only family role model Elena had to use as a gauge for coming out was her cousin Maurice. Elena said, "he's gay. We think he's gay. He brings his friend to all the family parties. It was always like, okay, but not really talked about because everybody knew that he was gay, but the older generation didn't really want to talk about it." The message Elena learned from her cousin's experience was "We aren't going to talk about it, but everyone knows." Elena's coming-out journey began when her mother found some of Elena's writing exploring same-sex feelings. Elena related:

She calls me freaking out. She is screaming and going crazy and she said she had found this thing that I had written and . . . just losing it. Saying all this stuff about, "how can you say that," and I think she just kept saying, "what the fuck are you talking about? What the fuck are you talking about? Do you even know what the hell you are saying?" A bunch of ugly things about, "Are you really like that? What does this mean?"

Several days and several dramatic scenes later, Elena received what she described as a "creepy" email from her father. He wrote, "What, are you a fucking man hater? So, you want to be a fucking lesbian. You better fix this." Elena interpreted this response to mean, "fix this thing with your mom because her being mad and miserable at home makes it miserable for me." Later, after Elena's mother had come to terms with Elena being a lesbian, she urged her not to tell the rest of the family. They fought about it for some time. Elena explained that her mother's reasoning went from, "you can't tell your aunt because you know how religious she is, to you can't tell them because they will blame me."

As Elena came out to members of her extended family, she was especially cautioned not to tell Felicia, the matriarch of the family, her great aunt, who has played the role of "replacement grandmother" for Elena and mother to her mother. Her aunt and uncle said, "It's not a good idea to tell Felicia because she is older and has got heart problems." Elena never came out to Felicia, but Felicia heard about it and asked Elena's mother if it were true. Elena's mother confirmed that her daughter was gay and Elena learned about Felicia's response later:

So, Aunt Felicia had taken it upon herself to be like, so, "Elena, huh? She's a lesbian?" Mom was cornered in the car, not knowing what to say. Then she was like, "yeah. Yeah she is." "And you knew about this?" She's like, "yeah, I've known for like three years now." So she was upset about it, "What are they going to say about her? How could you let this happen? She is your daughter, why didn't you stop it?" Like, why didn't you like give her that not-gay pill instead of the vitamins, you know.

Felicia did, in fact, blame Elena's mother, and this deeply upset Elena:

I just started crying because I didn't want her to say those things about me, and then she did. I didn't want mom to get blamed, and she did. I didn't want them to say bad things to her, and it was happening and I didn't want them to say things about me and they were. Everything I didn't want to happen happened, and I was like "damn it!" I was mad about it but I was like, well, she knows now, what am I going to do when I have to see her again? Like, I know she knows. I'm sure that she knows I know that she knows. So now what?

So, even though Elena "knows" that her Aunt Felicia "knows" that she is a lesbian, what Elena does *not* know is if she can talk about it, and if so, how? The inarticulation of the toxic closet constrained Elena even while she was struggling to be free of it. To make matter worse, she also suffered the burden of the coming-out paradox. As Tony E. Adams describes:

A gay person always has the potential, in interaction, to be held account-able—by herself or himself and others—for taking a wrong course of action, making the wrong move: there are punishments for a gay person who comes out or does not, for coming out too soon or not soon enough, for trying to complete the coming-out process or finding completion impossible, for coming out most of the time, some of the time, or never at all.[14]

Coming out was a bumpy process of trial and error for Elena, like it is for most Bible Belt gays. While trying to establish a lesbian identity within her extended family, Elena delicately negotiated familial land mines, and was blamed when there was an explosion. Making matters worse, the burden of responsibility concerning her disclosure and secrecy rested on Elena, the oppressed minority. To illustrate, Elena shared that when she came out to her cousins, they responded, "We already know." She explained that, implicit beneath their response was "why are you making such a big deal out of something that's not big news." Hence, even this arguably "positive" response from heterosexual family members carried a buried critique. By responding to her disclosure with a dismissive shrug, her cousins subtly invalidated her struggles. A reasonable question to ask is, if they did "already know," why didn't one of them offer support and help before Elena's official "announce-ment?" The obvious answer to this is because they were raised, like Elena, to maintain the familial culture of silence about homosexuality.

The Preacher's Wife

Gay people contend with the toxic-closet condition of inarticulation throughout their lives. I share a piece of Anna's story here, and one of the relationship tensions she and I experience, to illuminate these dynamics.

Anna is white. A tomboy as a child and a butch teenager, Anna is also visibly gender non-normative. She experienced same-sex attractions from an early age. She grew up in an isolated town in Eastern Kentucky with a population of 6,200 people. In 1985 Anna came out to her family and friends when she was 15. She was even out in high school. Her parents were mostly accepting while her grandparents struggled with it. They regularly attended a Free Will Baptist church that framed homosexuality as sin. Fifteen is very young, and the mid-1980s a less accepting period to come out in such a rural, homophobic region. Few of my interview subjects from rural areas came out as young as my partner Anna did.

On the one hand, Anna resisted the closet at a young age; on the other hand, her adolescent development was still shaped by others' homophobic responses to her difference. Once her homosexuality was an established fact, certain individuals, including extended family members, treated her as if she were a contagious, bad person. What was most puzzling and hurtful to her was the rejection she experienced from people who had previously treated her in a warm and loving manner. It is very confusing, especially for a young person, when someone one respects—in Anna's case, she perceived them as "good people"—suddenly display a completely different demeanor. One of the ways Anna managed this stigma in her small community, a place in which she was forced to repeatedly interact with the same small circle of people, was through controlling her interactions. Anna is masterful at engaging in nondirect pleasant small talk that is simultaneously both nonpersonal— that is, she does not share personal information—and that rebuffs personal kinds of questions from others. Hence, the best deal Anna could cut with her family and community as a young person was to mostly not talk about it and to leave home as soon as she could.

Certain habits linger because of this, one of which I find extremely stressful to manage given my own background and expectations: how to deal with introductions. Anna does not feel comfortable introducing me as her partner to people she fears may be homophobic, especially those connected with her home town. Although this is understandable, the message it sends to me is that there is something surreptitious about our relationship. I would rather experience a homophobic reaction than participate in a "don't ask, don't tell" social interaction that reinforces the assumption that same-sex relationships are inferior to heterosexual relationships. But, sometimes, I don't get to choose how out we are, particularly in matters dealing with Anna's family. I will discuss one such incident in detail to highlight the complex dynamics at play.

Anna's family suffered a painful loss in 2008 when Anna's aunt unexpectedly passed away. This was a devastating event for the entire family. Anna's cousin Kelly asked Anna to write and read the eulogy for the funeral service. I accompanied Anna to the funeral home. Along with family and friends, many members of the Free Will Baptist parish of Anna's childhood were present. The pastor delivered the service and a chorus of members sang. Anna was so nervous she was shaking when she read the eulogy. Later, after the hard task of burying her aunt was finished, Anna chatted with the preacher's wife for a few moments outside in the cold wind. I stood awkwardly beside Anna as the preacher's wife invited us back to the church for a fellowship dinner. Anna did not introduce me to her, and we did not go to the church dinner.

We fought on the way home as I tried to express how uncomfortable it had been for me to stand beside her like an unwelcome appendage, existing in an unarticulated status that literally rendered me mute. Standing next to Anna without being properly introduced to a family friend, and an older woman at that, not only violated my political beliefs but I experienced it as a gross lapse in manners. We were both suffering the consequences of the toxic closet. Anna argued that she did not want to introduce me to someone who might respond negatively. If she explicitly introduced me, Anna feared the preacher's wife might say something homophobic—a very real possibility—and that would both leave her more stressed than she already was, and potentially complicate relations between herself, the church, and her grandparents. It wasn't worth the risk to her. I felt that I had unwittingly colluded in a homophobic script which says same-sex relationships are so shameful they are unmentionable, and that is not an impression I wish ever to convey.

It's easy to examine this small moment (toxic-closet "lite" compared to many of the other stories) and blame an individual: Anna should have introduced me no matter what, or, perhaps I shouldn't have been thinking about myself during such a traumatic time for Anna. Or, we might have faulted the preacher's wife, a seemingly graceful, pleasant enough woman: Why didn't *she* step in and say, "Anna, this must be your partner, Bernadette. How nice to meet you! Anna's grandmother has told me so much about you. You've been together for about 10 years now, is that right? We'd love for you both to join us for our fellowship dinner in remembrance of your aunt." At that moment though, all three of us suffered from varying dimensions of the toxic-closet condition of inarticulation. I knew the right words but did not feel entitled to speak. I was not perceived as a family member. It's even possible that Anna's grandmother had never mentioned me to the preacher's wife. Anna knew what to say but was concerned that doing so would result in a painful interaction. The preacher's wife had not learned to apply the language of relationships with same-sex couples and probably regarded our relationship as sinful. While we each had different individual reasons for our inability, or unwillingness, to speak the words that publicly affirmed mine and Anna's decade-long partnership, this condition of inarticulation was not only personal and individual but also a cultural consequence of the toxic closet.

Same-sex partners may never be treated as well as heterosexual partners in homophobic families. Each and every one of the Bible Belt gays I interviewed experienced this: they either came from a family that did not treat their partner as well as they would a heterosexual partner, and/or they were involved with someone whose family was not as equally welcoming to them as they were heterosexual in-laws. For Anna and me, this small incident of closeting in front of the preacher's wife was painful. We fought about it, we felt bad. We struggled not to blame each other and mostly failed at this. We were reminded of all the ways our partnership is not affirmed and supported by the people around us. But, looking only at the costs of the toxic closet on Anna and me, or on Bible Belt gays overall, obscures the bigger picture. Everyone pays a tax on the toxic closet. In this case, the preacher's wife and the heterosexuals at the Free Will Baptist Church lose all the resources Anna and I have to offer. While it is unlikely either Anna and I would ever officially join the church, we do have a wide range of skills between the two of us that could potentially benefit the parish. Given that she is both technically and mechanically skilled, Anna could perform any number of computer/technology tasks for the parish and in fact does so for other churches as part of her work as a Systems Analyst. I am an accomplished teacher and writer, and could offer assistance in all kinds of writing endeavors from programs to bulletins to grants. This will not happen, though, because as giving as we are, we will not do so under a toxic-closet condition of inarticulation that constructs our relationship as flawed and inferior.

Work and the Toxic Closet

Caroline, who is white, 52, and quoted in the epigraph, works at a Christian college in Kentucky. Caroline described herself as a "Roman Catholic lesbian in a Southern Baptist college." Homosexuality is against the code of conduct at her school. Caroline is closeted, even though she thinks, after thirty years of working there, most of her colleagues suspect she is a lesbian. She was in fact explicitly instructed to lead a closeted life, "I was told my department head knows. I know he does. But I was told many, many years ago, 'just lay low, not bring it to the surface, keep it off campus.'" Caroline explained that she has no friends in her workplace, just acquaintances, "I don't share my life with anybody at the college. There are women I have worked with for thirty years and they do not know who I am."

Heterosexuals expect a certain level of support in their workplaces; most can put their spouses and children on their health insurance plans unlike most gay people in the Bible Belt. It is also common for co-workers to chat about their weekend adventures, discuss their children's accomplishments, and inquire about one another's partners. In many places, workers might even speak openly about relationship issues with spouses and children. Of course, people will only do so in work environments that permit this kind of exchange, and, because of gender norms, it is also likely that women exchange more verbal intimacies in the workplace than men. But, even in the most formal corporate cut-throat environment, a worker may vent about a fight with a spouse, show off an engagement ring, and/or confess that they are dating someone special.[15] Gay people who cannot share both mundane and upsetting life events at work suffer a real injustice as Amy, who is white, 34, and from Central Kentucky, explained:

> It's an injustice to your relationship not being able to talk about that person that makes you so happy, or share with people when your girlfriend does something really sweet for you, or you do something sweet for her. Those kinds of things that would be very normal for you to walk in the office the next day and say, "she came home and had all these flowers for me." It negates your relationship and the importance of it. Because I can't talk about it, it somehow makes it less.

The lesbian who can't chat about the flowers her girlfriend gave her or the gay man who can't discuss the romantic cruise he's planning for his partner to celebrate their 10-year anniversary are excluded from normal exchanges. Further, their inability to engage in office small talk may be read by others as snobbery, shyness, or rudeness. If the office mates suspect the noncommunicative individual is homosexual, they may avoid asking him or her personal questions, and thus collude in a silence that ultimately signals that homosexuality is too shameful to discuss. And for the gay person practiced at hiding his or her sexual identity, it's simply easier not to talk about it. This dynamic creates a self-perpetuating cycle of homophobic silence, which is extremely difficult to change. In fact, this individual may work for an organization that does not have an anti-discriminatory policy for sexual orientation, in one of the many states that also lacks an antidiscrimination law, and thus may face losing her or his livelihood should they come out. In many workplaces in the United States, it is legal to fire someone for simply being gay. Bible Belt states do not have statewide nondiscrimination policies that protect lesbians and gay men like those in other more politically progressive parts of the country.[16] This lack of institutional role-modeling in Bible Belt states reinforces the dynamics of the toxic closet: homophobic people believe that their negative attitudes about sexual minorities are justified and supported, indifferent or well-meaning heterosexuals find it easy to ignore issues of gay rights, gay people struggle with the closet, and everyone feels uncomfortable talking about it.

Not being able to talk about the flowers or the cruise is bad enough, but gay couples face much worse dilemmas at work. Suppose Caroline's partner, Jennifer, is diagnosed with terminal breast cancer. How does Caroline get the time off she needs to care for Jennifer without disclosing her relationship status? Let's compare this to the experience a heterosexual woman enduring the illness and death of her husband of 25 years might have in her place of employment. She would probably be given much emotional and material support from her supervisor and co-workers. Her request for time off would be understood, and hopefully facilitated. People would likely expect less of an overall work output and bring her gifts of food. Unless she was universally disliked, and maybe even then, she would be barraged with genuine offers of help from everyone in her workplace such as, "Oh Lisa, I'm so sorry about Carl, is there anything I can do to be supportive?" Because, of course, everyone recognizes the legitimacy of a heterosexual marriage and feels terrible for a woman who is losing her husband to cancer. But, should Caroline face a similar circumstance, she would most likely receive no comparable support from her co-workers, her supervisor, or the institution. In addition to the stress of losing her beloved partner, Caroline might worry that she could lose her job too. Caroline needs and deserves just as much support as Lisa. This toxic-closet injustice is disturbing to contemplate because it violates our best human qualities of compassion, care, and connection.

Relationship Tensions

When Amy was going through problems with her partner Stacy, she felt as if she had no one she could talk to about it. Amy worried she might make her family, friends, and co-workers uncomfortable if she shared this part of her life. She felt constrained from discussing the issues at work because she was closeted there, but she also felt unable to talk about what was going on with her parents and some friends who did know about her relationship with Stacy. Amy explained that she felt a pressure to be perfect—to prove that same-sex relationships are just as meaningful and valid as heterosexual ones:

When Stacy and I started having problems, I didn't really feel like there was anybody that I could talk to. When we broke up, it was like, "well what the hell happened?" Because no one knew that we were having problems because I didn't feel like they really wanted to hear about it. Whereas I think if I had been in a heterosexual relationship, it would've been like, you know, Bob and I, it would have been very easy to talk about the problem. We couldn't really talk, and that creates a separation and can cause problems.

Amy lacked social support to help process the challenges in her relationship with Stacy. In homophobic communities, families, and regions, when normal relationship tensions emerge, it is very easy for same-sex couples to break up. The lesbian therapist Betty Berzon has written extensively about the unique challenges gay couples face. The take-away message of Berzon's book *Permanent Partners* is for gay couples to "assume permanency" in their relationships: when there is little or no external validation of a partnership, tough times are much tougher. When there's no Mom the gay man can confide in who says, "Oh honey, don't worry, Dad and I love Bill. You two are going to work it out. Every relationship goes through rough patches. Why don't you bring Bill over this Sunday for dinner, so your father and I can make you a nice dinner," the relationship tension grows more suffocating. Even worse, in the Bible Belt, it's more likely Mom does not know about Bill, or, if she does, she refuses to let him in the house, won't acknowledge the partnership, and is hoping that her son and Bill break up.

Flaunting It

Instead of receiving the support they need to weather tough times, same-sex couples who are open about their relationships are frequently censured by heterosexuals as well as other gay people for "flaunting" their homosexuality. In my role as a teacher and public speaker on such issues, I have listened as heterosexuals have explained that they don't have an issue with homosexuality, they just don't understand why so many gay people need to flaunt it because no one goes around announcing their heterosexuality. This is a problematic statement for three reasons. First of all, it's wrong. Heterosexuals constantly flaunt their heterosexuality. Every time a heterosexual wears a wedding ring, discusses his children, and vacations, and all the routine activities he did last weekend with his spouse, he announces heterosexuality. Every time the heterosexual sibling complains to Mom about her distant boyfriend or cheating husband, she announces heterosexuality. Every photo on a desk, engagement party, wedding, anniversary celebration, and baby shower announces heterosexuality. Every obituary lists surviving spouses. We live in a culture in which heterosexuality is proudly on display every minute of every day—and our gay lives are not. In a heterocentric social system, however, we do not perceive these actions by heterosexuals as "flaunting." They are simply part of the everyday texture of our lives, and noticing them may be as difficult as paying attention to the air one breathes.

Second, because of the culture of silence surrounding direct discussions of homosexuality and same-sex relationships, because of this toxic-closet condition of inarticulation, there is no easy language a gay person can use to signal that she or he is gay. In my experience, coming out, is often responded to inappropriately.[17] People look startled. They say peculiar, sometimes homophobic things, and/or act like you have shared something deep and personal. For instance, there is a grocery bagger at the Kroger where I shop who is very friendly and chatty. A 40ish, African American man, he often walks my groceries out to the car. He likes to go outside, and he likes to talk with customers. After about two years of small talk, as we directed my loaded cart through the parked vehicles, he asked me a simple question about my children. I already knew about his three adopted boys and wife, and usually asked about them. I said, "I don't have any children. I am in a lesbian relationship." He was very surprised, did not say much, and quickly left. This individual, like Anna, is also very canny in his communicative exchanges. He will, for example, initiate conversations about politics—i.e., party candidates, and health care reform—without ever betraying a political orientation or saying anything controversial. The next time we saw each other he strayed outside his usual communicative arena and said to me, "I couldn't believe you shared your personal business with me." He did not see his own relationship status as personal, like he did mine.

Any heterosexual can easily discuss their spouse, and no one thinks anything of it. In fact, small talk about spouses and children is usually a good conversation opener among strangers or acquaintances. Consider the last social event you attended: a party, a church gathering, a barbeque. Remember party talk. How often did you hear see someone say, "my husband, my wife, or my kids." I have spoken with women who could not begin a sentence without using the phrase, "my husband." If you are gay and/or in a same-sex relationship, you might be fully in the toxic closet and not reference any partner, even if that person is there, and hence not share this significant dimension of your lived experience. Or you may be out and reference a partner, trying to participate in this routine social exchange. In this case, the person with whom you are chatting will probably look confused. You can clarify, like

I usually do, "that's my partner, Anna, over there, we've been together for 13 years." Now, you've made a big "announcement" and may experience a whole range of bizarre reactions, including an accusation that you are displaying the bad taste of "flaunting" your homosexuality. This is both a double bind,[18] and an illustration of the coming-out paradox.[19] Being closeted constrains normal communication, but coming out is socially awkward and may be perceived negatively.

Third, because we so rarely see representations of gay relationships and gay experiences centered, when they are visible, people notice them more. This is the same dilemma every minority group faces. One Black comedy, one "chick flick," and people perceive ten. We don't see the nine white Supreme Court justices, just the two of color. We don't pay attention to the twelve action films playing, just the one exploring female friendships. We don't notice heterosexuals proudly expressing their heterosexuality in bars, at work, in church; we see the one gay man who is wearing a gay pride shirt, and the one car with a rainbow flag, and people mutter that the gays are taking over. The cars with stickers about "my honor child," or that actually have a whole nuclear family decaled onto the back window, are invisible to us.[20] The language of "flaunting it" when applied to gay relationships and gay expression serves as a "legitimizing ideology,"[21] a set of ideas that maintains the power of the dominant group. In this case, people who say "I just don't like it when gay people flaunt their sexuality" are wielding a discursive tool of oppression that silences gay people and reproduces the toxic closet.

"My Family Knows, We Just Don't Talk about It"

It is not necessary for family, friends, and co-workers to censor one because within the Bible Belt panopticon, the homosexual censors herself. This was evident in the interview and ethnographic data. Among the most troubling and destructive aspects of the toxic closet is that it teaches gay people to participate in their own oppression while protecting the comfort levels of their oppressors. For example Ron, white, 36, and from Eastern Kentucky, is not out to his family. He explained why:

> I still struggle with projecting pain and distress upon my mother. It's not that I fear that she's going to stop loving me or that she's going to toss me out because I can make it on my own, and I do, but I just don't want to cause her any undue pain. She has some medical issues too, that weigh upon my mind. Any extra undue stress causes body reactions. I just think that sometimes, if I told her, what if it caused her to have a seizure?

While it's clear that Ron and his mother love one another, by making the "choice" not to share that he is a gay man for fear it would upset her and potentially cause her health issues, Ron is actively participating in his own oppression and protecting his oppressor. I recognize that identifying Ron's mother, likely a kindly woman, as an "oppressor" is harsh and might make Ron uncomfortable. Nonetheless, Ron's care-taking of his mother, protecting her from the knowledge that he is a gay man, enables his own mistreatment. By settling for less than his siblings receive and still participating in the family unit, Ron accepts a second-class status:

> When I go home for the holidays, and there's my brother and my sister-in-law, there's my stepbrothers and their wives and their children, I think, "here it is Christmas Eve, and my boyfriend is spending the evening with his roommates, why can't I bring him to this function?" So I do get a little bitter and resentful from time to time, but not so much so that I would act on it or say anything about it. But there is that settling for crumbs, but not necessarily crumbs, but something less than what everybody else has.

Of the 59 lesbians and gay men I interviewed, roughly 13, or 22%, concealed their homosexuality from their families. For some of these, a parent or parents died before the individual had a chance to come out, like Donald with his mother. For others, fear of rejection, and concern about how family members might respond inhibited them, like Ron, Jose, and Misty. Most people I interviewed were out to some member or members of their families but not necessarily to the whole family. Jeff, who is 42, white, and from North Carolina, is out to his entire family except his father and stepmother, whom he rarely sees. When I inquired if their families knew they were gay, several responded like Peter, who is white, 30, and from Western Kentucky, does here:

> They know. I've never really said to my family that I am. I've never expressed it to my parents, but they know. They helped me move into a house and saw all the books that say gay relationships and whatnot. They definitely know. It's just not something that's been talked about. At this point I've not seen a huge need to make a point of telling them because to my way of thinking I am gay, but gay is not me. If that makes sense what I am trying to say, my life is not defined by my sexuality. So, I feel like my relationship with them is the same whether I say I'm gay or I don't.

Peter works for a social service center that provides support services to the Hispanic population in the region. He is also a gay activist and the leader of a gay rights group in Kentucky. From a politically conservative family in Western Kentucky, Peter shared that coming out was a challenge. He lives two hours away from his political but not highly religious family—whom he described as "huge George Bush supporters." As co-chair of a local gay rights organization, Peter writes editorials for the city newspaper on gay issues, organizes pride events, and supports the public efforts of other local progressive groups. I am one of many across the state of Kentucky who have received mass emails from him alerting us to homophobic bills proposed in the state assembly. Indeed, Peter advocated visibility in his role as a gay rights organizer during our interview:

> Visibility . . . and I know this kind of contradicts what I was saying about not feeling a certain need to say to my parents that I'm gay, but the visibility in the general populace is very important, and I think one of the big goals is to make us as visible as possible. Because of that visibility people will see that we are not pedophiles and sinners, we're just like them, we get up and go to work in the morning, we pay our taxes, and come home and cook dinner at night.

The contradiction Peter expressed in his interview—"I am gay, but gay is not me. I don't need to talk about it with my parents," yet visibility is important—illustrates one of the more insidious manifestations of the toxic closet. What does it mean that Peter, intelligent, educated, passionate about political change, whose activism involves being out publicly, described his gay identity as secondary in the context of his family? Because, in fact, a significant chunk of Peter's life *is* organized around his gay identity: he is a gay activist. I think, instead, that the reason he had not fully discussed his homosexuality with his parents is not because it didn't matter to his parents, "my relationship is the same whether I say I'm gay or not," but because it mattered deeply, and he was afraid they might react badly.

With this observation, I am not suggesting that Peter is hypocritical and should come out to his parents immediately. Only Peter can decide this, and only he knows best. What I do think this contradiction illustrates is how deeply Peter has internalized his secondary status as a gay man in his family environment. The fact that he does not discuss his relationship status and sexual orientation, the fact that "it does not come up" is a much larger indication of a life defined by his minority sexual orientation. Otherwise, it would emerge casually in conversations about partners, dating, socializing, volunteer work, and friends just as it does when heterosexuals communicate with family members. For example, when my heterosexual brother was single, part of every conversation we had entailed discussing who he was dating and what he thought of her.

To further clarify, what I am critiquing here is not *whether* a Bible Belt gay comes out to a potentially homophobic family member, parishioner, or co-worker, but that she perceives her own silence about herself as fine because "they really know and we just don't discuss it," or "it's nobody's business what I do," and "it doesn't matter because heterosexuals don't announce that they are straight all the time." And the silence, the closet, "don't ask, don't tell" *is* a better deal than abuse, hatred, discrimination, isolation, and ostracism. But, in the privacy of our own heads and communities, it is important to recognize that while this may be a better deal, it is still not a fair deal, and we are being treated poorly. When we can't discuss our gay lives for fear of reprisals, that is a terrible illustration of homophobia.[22] However, when we say it's fine not to talk about being gay because heterosexuals don't discuss their sexuality in public, this demonstrates that we have internalized a sense of ourselves as second-class citizens. This is the most problematic dimension of the toxic closet: in our efforts not to "flaunt it" we cease to recognize our own oppression and reproduce the expectations of those oppressing us.

Peter's Story

In January 2007, Peter and I were wrapping up our interview. I asked him if there was anything else he'd like to share with me that we hadn't covered. This is a standard last question I pose during sociological interviews and typically has the effect of ending the conversation. Peter, however, had something else to share, something that had been eating away at him, something he had shared with only one other person, but that he felt was important to reveal for this project. In a confessional tone, he explained:

> The first real gay experience that I had, it was really bad, it was scary. I wanted to share my story in a format that, if it were to get published, maybe people will take something away from it so that they don't repeat the same kinds of mistakes that I did.

At the age of 21, Peter drove to another state, far from anyone he might know, to go to a gay bar to explore his same-sex attractions:

> I recently turned 21 and I had never had a drink, or done drugs. And at that point, I had never really been exposed to gay people or gay culture

and I was largely ignorant to all this. I went to a gay bar and I didn't have anyone to go with me. It was in Indiana. I didn't know anything. I was so intimidated. It's pretty common with gay bars, the door is really dark, so it's not like a business where you can go up and window shop.

Most gay bars in the Bible Belt have covered windows and low-key or nonexistent signage. They can be difficult to find because of this. Obviously, covered or blackened windows prevent the curious from seeing who is in the gay bar and, hence, who might be gay. The exaggerated privacy surrounding many gay bars by itself conveys a troubling message about homosexuality within Bible Belt communities, to both gay and heterosexual residents. To a questioning youth like Peter though, the covered windows are also a barrier to a foreign world. There is no window-shopping at the gay bar. You have to go in to see what it is like. Peter circled the block three times before mustering the courage to enter:

And I got to the door, and I just peered in, and I didn't really see anything, but I didn't want to look like a suspicious person. Looking back I think, "what on God's green earth was I doing," because I've been to gay bars across the country, who cares? They're just bars like anywhere else, but I was so young and naïve and I didn't know anything.

Peter's anxiety and trepidation were palpable nearly ten years after the incident as he described it.

So I'm sitting up in this bar and this one guy, he approached me and he started talking and he wanted to get out of there. I agreed to go with him because at this time I was also a virgin and I was like, "oh my God, I'm the oldest living virgin on the planet" and I wanted to end that. I was just determined that I was going to get rid of this virginity. But, he was really a prostitute just looking for money, and a drug dealer. I was so naïve. I didn't know what was going on. We went out in a field, and I did get him naked, and we fooled around, but that was it. I gave him 20 dollars and drove him over to this house where he tried to buy weed or whatever, and he tried to put it in my car, and it was just a really miserable experience. I had never done anything like that before, and I have never done anything like that since. I mean, I'm not into prostitutes, and I'm just not into that scene. Not knowing anything, I just walked in to that situation.

He continued:

When it was over I was like, "I'm never going back into a gay bar, I'm never going back into this situation." And, of course, I got over it. I went back and I've been back to many bars and I've made lots of gay friends and come to be something of an advocate and an activist. I don't know if it will get printed, I don't know what you'll do with this story, but I hope that maybe that story will keep other people from doing that or coming to that situation.

Peter concluded, "I guess I'm really sad that my first experience with gay culture was such a failure."

What is saddest to me about this story is not that he had an unsatisfying first sexual experience with someone who didn't care about him at all. This misfortune happens all the time in our oversexualized, abstinence-only raunch culture, and most often to young heterosexual women.[23] The worst part was that a socially conscious and intelligent 30-year-old activist still blamed himself for the painful first time he had a sexual experience with a man, rather than identify this bad experience as a consequence of growing up in a homophobic culture. Peter *internalized* a feeling of personal failure instead of perceiving that, in fact, his culture and family had failed him. Closeted gay children and youth, like Peter, Misty, and Katie, are excluded from the day-to-day courtship rituals their heterosexual peers practice. They do not send Valentine's cards, invite their crush to the prom, or have that special person over for Sunday dinner. They don't get teased about "liking Valerie or Craig in that special way," and when their hearts are broken in both the silly and traumatic ways that happen in middle and high school, their parents aren't able to appropriately console their gay child. Since the relationship, the crush, or the attraction was never openly acknowledged, a subsequent rejection or breakup is not fully understood by the family members of the gay youth. The 14-year-old gay boy deeply distraught by the loss of "his friend" does not get Mom's mini-social-worker analysis of how "sometimes love hurts, relationships are hard, and there are plenty more fish in the sea. Just imagine who you'll meet this summer on vacation at the beach, honey. Dad and I know you'll be over this in no time. What can I fix you for dinner tonight?"

The hypothetical heterosexual 14-year-old girl who *does* receive caring parenting may be mortified that her family knows that her boyfriend dumped her this week for her best friend, and is furious at her little brother for his insensitivity to her pain, but over time she learns that the agony fades, and Mom was right—there are other fish in the sea. In contrast, the just as heartbroken 14-year-old gay boy who does not get any support at all learns from this absence (one that he might observe his heterosexual siblings receiving from their parents) that it is wrong and shameful to experience same-sex attractions. Thus, the heterosexual girl learns to externalize her pain as "part of growing up" while the gay boy learns to internalize his pain as a personal flaw, "something is wrong with me," like Peter did.[24] In matters of burgeoning sexual feelings and expressions of sexual identity, Peter's needs, like those of many Bible Belt gay youth, were neglected. His family and community failed to provide for his basic psychological and emotional well-being. Had they done so, had Peter been able to openly practice teenage romance with boys, it is unlikely he would have had sex for the first time with a prostitute he met in a bar. While this may not be the worse abuse gay youth experience—it is certainly less dramatic than one's mother coming at one with a butcher knife, or throwing herself off a bridge—it has significant psycho-social consequences on childhood and adolescent development nonetheless, and it must be better theorized for the sake of the young people who are needlessly suffering.

This is not to say that Bible Belt parents, or the parents of any gay youth, do not care about their child. Most parents know when their children are hurting and want to ease that pain. However, when the real cause—the same-sex attraction, the rejection by the crush, the breakup, the infidelity—of the hurt is not openly acknowledged within the family unit as a normal, hard, and painful part of growing up that everyone goes through, gay youth receive the message that there is something damaged, tainted, broken, and shameful about their desires, and thus themselves. They do not get the opportunity to learn valuable relationship skills at the same age as their heterosexual peers. As the interviews with Peter, Katie, Misty, and Darlene illustrate, such unresolved tension may cause them to act out in ways that compromise their present and future psychological, material, and spiritual well-being. In these ways, the toxic-closet condition of inarticulation handicaps gay youth.

5

"Going Straight"

The Ex-Gay Movement

The Reverend Dee Dale is pastor of the Metropolitan Community Church in Louisville, Kentucky. She is white, 63, and from Louisville. When I first met her in August 2010 at the Pride Center in Louisville, her arms were folded across her chest and she wore an ominous scowl on her face. The interview got off to a bumpy start. She handed me a photocopy of a sermon she had written and given on the parable of the Good Samaritan, and repeatedly urged me to refrain from judgment, calling the gay people involved in ex-gay ministries, "the walking wounded." "Ex-gay" is a term that describes individuals who once identified as gay and/or experience same-sex attractions but who do not claim a gay identity and are in the process of trying to change their sexual orientation. While some participants in ex-gay programs find the term problematic, preferring instead to be called heterosexual or not labeled at all, ex-gay is widely used by scholars, religious groups, the media, and both leaders and participants in ex-gay programs.

At the Pride Center, I listened, slightly bewildered, as Dee reiterated her message about how we are all God's children and we should not judge. As we continued to talk on parallel tracks, but not exactly to one another, I said, "Well, I'm fully persuaded that God does not want to judge people for being gay, so what I'm interested in is how you help people move from that place where they feel like there is something wrong with them to a journey of self-acceptance." Dee responded that I should come to the church and see for myself. Donald, who is white, 52, and from Indiana originally, now a long-time resident of Kentucky, arrived shortly after this, and his presence cleared the confusion that had clouded my interaction with Dee. As Donald warmly greeted me, and mentioned to Dee what a big fan he was of my work, new understanding registered on her face, her body relaxed, and she was virtually speechless for a full twenty minutes. It emerged that she had not read my introductory email all the way through and had assumed I was supportive of, or at least neutral about, the ex-gay perspective. As pastor of an MCC church for 27 years, Dee has had many run-ins with conservative Christian churches over the years, especially during election periods. She arrived at the Pride Center poised for battle and did not perceive my pro-gay position until Donald joined us. I share the story of the miscommunication with Dee because it partially illustrates the costs—an expectation that strangers are likely hostile to homosexuality—of pastoring a gay-affirming church not only in the Bible Belt but under the shadow of the Southern Baptist Theological Seminary located in Louisville, Kentucky, headed by the openly homophobic Dr. R. Albert Mohler Jr., its ninth president.[1]

Mohler's appointment in 1993 signaled a conservative swing in the history of the venerable institution. Donald and Pastor Dee referenced the "Southern Seminary" frequently during our two-hour interview, listing the names of people they knew who had been expelled, fired, and/or attended sexual-addiction support groups to avoid being expelled or fired from the institution. Dee was officially expelled from Southern Seminary in 1979, and Donald joined an ex-gay group to avoid being expelled from Boyce Bible School, an undergraduate affiliate of Southern Seminary in the 1970s.[2] Still, they said that the seminary has become more conservative and openly homophobic—and anti-female—under Mohler's leadership. For example, the Southern Baptist Seminary once had one of the best and most respected schools of church music in the South. When Mohler assumed leadership of the institution, a great many of the music literature, history, organ, and piano professors and instructors—especially women, gays, and dissenters, meaning those who refused to sign Mohler's "oath of allegiance"—were either fired outright or resigned. They believed that under such restrictive leadership they could not in good conscience teach a wide range of music, including both classical church music and "praise" music. The department is a shadow of what it once was. Mohler also dis-banded the Social Work department altogether because, as Dee explained, "they had to be accepting of all people in order to be social workers and he wouldn't allow it." She also shared that seminary administrators "actu-ally went and sat outside Connections, which is the gay bar, and observed students that were coming out and let them know." As an MCC pastor, Dee has counseled more than 100 gay people who have participated in ex-gay ministries and presided over the funerals of five people who, she believed, "committed suicide as a result of ex-gay ministries." In this chap-ter I explore elements of the contemporary ex-gay movement, including observations at the 2009 Exodus International conference, and insights from Bible Belt gays who have participated in a variety of Christian ex-gay programs. While none of the individuals I interviewed currently identifies as ex-gay, each having decided to accept their same-sex attractions, some spent many years in ex-gay programs trying to change. For example, Don-ald explained that he was "in and out of the ex-gay movement, one group or another, for over fifteen years."

Ex-Gay Ministries

Doubly stigmatized because they acknowledge homosexuality and then try to change what to many seems unchangeable, ex-gay ministries are contro-versial among mainstream Americans, condemned by gay rights groups, and warily tolerated by conservative Christians. Donald explained that many "anti-gay churches are not supportive of ex-gays because they don't want gay people there in the first place." Originating in the early 1970s, ex-gay minis-tries have had 40 years of experience counseling individuals on "conversion" from being homosexual to heterosexual; they acknowledge that the process is not quick or easy but complex and fraught with potential setbacks. The largest Protestant ex-gay organization, Exodus International, has branches in South America, Asia, and Africa, and 240 local ministries in North America. When I asked Donald to estimate how many ex-gay ministries he could name in Ken-tucky, he lost count after eleven and did not include independent Christian counselors. Moreover, most large nondenominational Christian churches, like Vision (see chap. 1), have "Sexual Integrity" or "Celebrate Recovery" sup-port groups for men and women. These groups typically serve those strug-gling with sexual addictions, sexual infidelities, and homosexuality.

The efficacy of ex-gay reparative therapies has been denounced by every major scholarly professional organization, including, for the second time in the summer of 2009, the American Psychological Association. While some ex-gay organizations like NARTH (National Association for Research and Therapy of Homosexuality) draw on scientific studies to support theories of reparative therapy, and engage with the mainstream media to argue for their right to provide therapeutic services to individuals who wish to change their attractions, ex-gay ministries, for the most part, fall under the purview of religious guidance. In these environments, secular psychological, social work, and/or counseling credentials are not necessary to advise individuals. Indeed, conservative Christians, especially fundamentalists, value personal experience of the Lord, which includes testifying about one's own story of sinning, repenting, and reconciliation with God, as equal to and often preferable to secular credentials.[3] Consequently, secular affirmation and support of ex-gay ministries is largely irrelevant to those participating. For a fundamentalist (but not necessarily an evangelical), weighing an official statement from the American Psychological Association against a literal interpretation of the Bible is a no-brainer: God's word wins every time.[4]

Donald and Pastor Dee could not identify a single counselor in local ex-gay groups who is licensed. While formal training is required for any individual who sees patients in a professional capacity, it is not a requirement to provide what Dee called "spiritual guidance" to a fellow Christian seeking support.[5] A lack of licensing and of general oversight can create situations in which the vulnerable may be victimized. For example, Donald shared that he drove 70 miles to visit a Christian ministry in St. Louis, Missouri, only to find that the facility was staffed by two women lacking any kind of credentials and who were also the ex-wives of gay men. The support Donald received in this facility consisted of an hour long conversation in which the two women attempted to convince him that he "wasn't really gay." Donald shared another story in which the leader of a local ex-gay ministry drove him to a known "cruise" area for gay male sex, and they spoke in his truck. This person told Donald that he deliberately infected himself with HIV so, as Donald explained, "he could come out of the gay lifestyle." When I inquired about what happened next, Donald said:

He laughed and chuckled, and said this is kind of a strange place to have a counseling session. And we just sat there and listened to Vineyard church music. Vineyard denomination is a big longtime ex-gay sympathetic denomination. He didn't do anything inappropriate to me sexually, but it was just really weird.

It is easy to find illustrations of dysfunctional, hypocritical, and sometimes bizarre behavior among ex-gay leaders and participants. Mainstream media outlets pick up such stories routinely. One famous example is the story of John Paulk, an ex-gay leader, affiliated with the organization Focus on the Family and the "Love Won Out" conferences, featured on the cover of *Newsweek* (August 1998) with his ex-lesbian wife, Anne. Paulk was spotted in a gay bar in Washington, DC in 2000. Paulk first claimed he did not know he was in a gay bar and that he had stopped to use the restroom. Eventually he confessed that he had knowingly gone into a gay bar to flirt with men and was removed from leadership positions in ex-gay organizations. The incident was widely reported in the news, and spokespeople of gay rights groups, like Wayne Besen with the Human Rights Campaign and Truth Wins Out, used it as further evidence of the futility of conversion therapy. On GayToday.com Besen wrote:

> The ex-gay ad campaign that was supposed to be a knockout punch for gay rights has instead become a punchline. It is a bust of epic proportions and would be laughable if it had not hurt so many innocent victims . . . . These failures are just the tip of the iceberg. Exodus and other ex-gay groups regularly hide the truth about failed leaders. Just recently, the leader of the Exodus ministry in Portland, Oregon stepped down because, according to their newsletter, he was "emotionally entangled" with another man.[6]

Rather than focus exclusively upon such "failures" of the ex-gay movement, this chapter explores the sociological and psychological complexity of individuals involved in ex-gay ministries through participant observation at an Exodus conference and the stories of Bible Belt gays.

Crossover

Among ex-gays, "sexual falls"[7] or experiencing same-sex attractions and sometimes acting on them, like Paulk's going into a gay bar, are commonplace relapses and part of the recovery process. Helen, who is white, 55, from Central Kentucky, participated in ex-gay ministries for seven years and brought up Paulk during our interview:

> When I was there one of the men that was one of the leaders in Exodus, he was married and had a little baby. And they caught him one night in a gay bar. And, of course, his claim was that he was just there and it didn't mean anything. But I knew deep in my heart, I just knew he was miserable in his marriage. He was still gay. He knew he was gay, and that was just a way of getting a moment of peace from the struggle in his own heart.

Helen had been unhappy in her own heterosexual marriage. Her coming-out journey started when she sought help for childhood sexual abuse. Married for twenty-five years, she began having nightmares and flashbacks about the buried abuse. Helen found Crossover, an Exodus-affiliated group that, at the time, provided support for people working through addictions, compulsions, and abuse of all kinds. Now, Crossover primarily serves an ex-gay population. Helen began weekly therapy sessions with a Christian counselor at Crossover for her sexual-abuse issues and, as she began healing, she experienced a re-awakening of her sexuality. At the same time, she felt inhibited from acting upon any emerging sexual feelings:

> I would cry myself to sleep at night. Because of my Christian teaching and understanding, when you're married, you're married and that's it. There's no divorce, you don't divorce. I'm stuck. I can't even begin to describe how miserable I was in every sense of the word. And to feel trapped made it that much worse. Well, after some counseling with the minister, I finally realized that, you know what, I don't have to stay married.

At this point, Helen discovered that she was experiencing attractions to women. Because of her Southern Baptist religious background, her first reaction was fear. Since she was already involved with Crossover, her sexual desires for women became the new focus of her therapy. At this point, Helen began to psychologically unravel. She had panic attacks, suicidal thoughts, and at work one day, she simply fell apart. After the incident at work, she checked herself into a mental health facility. At the completion of in-patient treatment, Helen continued counseling for depression *and* stayed involved with Crossover. This was a dark time for Helen, and her association with Crossover in conjunction with her emerging same-sex desires intensified her experience of mental and emotional disintegration. The final straw for Helen, the incident that triggered her suicide attempt, happened at a Crossover social gathering. At the party, Helen watched two women, one of whom was the director of the group, touching each other in ways that she felt was, if not overtly sexual, certainly flirtatious and romantic. Helen narrated:

> They're touching and playing with their hair and stuff like this, and inside it was just, I don't know, something just (snaps fingers) popped. I went home and I was angry, I was lonely, I was sad, I was mad. The thought that kept going through my mind was: I don't want a man, I can't have a woman, I'm doomed to be miserable for the rest of my life. To be lonely and sad, and that was what kept playing in my mind. And then I kept

seeing those two. I went and laid down. It was the next morning actually. I just couldn't get out of bed. I was just so depressed that I couldn't get out of bed. And then it was like another person just came out of me, I don't know how to describe this, but it was like another person that wasn't even me, I just sat up in bed and said, "I'm not afraid to do this." And I put my clothes on, and I went down to the drugstore right down the road from me and I got a bottle of sleeping pills and I took those and my antidepressant together. And the second I did it, I thought "oh, alright, what have I done?" I called a friend, and she called 911, and of course I don't remember what happened because by the time I got to the hospital I was out of it, but they pumped my stomach, and thank God for that. That was a terrible thing for me to do for my kid's sake. And I regret that terribly, but it was just where I was, it was the spot where I was.

While Helen directly attributed her suicide attempt to her repressed same-sex attractions and her participation in Crossover, she did not hold Crossover responsible for her self-destructive behavior. In fact, she met her life partner, Leslie, through Crossover. Further, Helen appreciated the support Crossover offered her in the beginning of her time with them. She also believes that the people working in ex-gay ministries are sincere and truly wish to be helpful. Helen concluded that she had "mixed feelings" about ex-gay programs "because, on the one hand, there are probably those people out there who cannot reconcile and need support, but for the most part, I think that it does more harm than good." Shaking her head thoughtfully, Helen noted that Crossover had only been damaging for her partner, Leslie, who repeatedly turned to alcohol as a refuge from her same-sex attractions while she was involved in Crossover.

Unlike Helen and Donald, Derek, who is white and 39, did not regret his time spent with Crossover Ministries in Central Kentucky. A self-described "right-wing homophobe" before he came out, Derek avoided all romantic relationships until he was 25 because of his repressed same-sex attractions. He too tried to "pray the gay away." During Thanksgiving break in his sophomore year of college, Derek confessed his attractions to a youth minister in his hometown. This minister responded that "it's a phase" and that "I had some same-sex attractions too once upon a time." In his senior year of college, Derek met a young professor struggling with homosexuality and together they did a "Homosexuals Anonymous" course. Derek explained, "We met on a weekly basis and one of our straight friends would come with us to chaperone." Derek felt that it had been helpful to have someone with whom he could share his struggle. After college, Derek still believed that

God would change him, felt a calling to be a United Methodist Minister, and entered a conservative seminary program in Central Kentucky. After a few months, he found Crossover Ministry and attended weekly meetings for two years. Derek shared:

> I maintain that Crossover was an integral part of my coming-out process because I would have had a really hard time just getting to know non-Christian gay people because they were so far outside of my social circle, outside of the people that I would have found it acceptable to be friends with on a general basis. Because, at that time, I felt that my friends should be Christian. I was part of that mind-set that your grocer should be Christian and your exterminator should be Christian. So, random non-Christian gay people were more sinful than the average sinful person. So it was hard to find people that I could relate to on the level of struggling with being gay. It was a very helpful step in coming out that I could talk about being gay, and I could relate to other gay people, without immediately abandoning or changing my faith drastically.

Derek finally came to the conclusion that, after years of praying to God to change him, perhaps God did not want him to change after all.

Brandy, who is white, 50, and from Louisville, also participated in Crossover for six years while she struggled to come to terms with her same-sex attractions. Brandy did not experience any same-sex desires until she was in her mid-twenties and then, because of her conservative Christian religious background, framed the desires as a "choice" and turned to Crossover for support. She said that "in the beginning I really enjoyed it and liked hanging out with people and doing stuff." When she first started at Crossover she was still worshipping at the "crazy church" and maintaining an on-again, off-again relationship with a woman, Tracy. Brandy stopped attending Crossover meetings only after the director temporarily suspended her because she kept having sex with Tracy. Like many ex-gays, Brandy was in a pattern of committing "sexual falls," confessing and repenting, and then "falling" all over again. Brandy, however, is the only person I interviewed suspended from an ex-gay program for having too much gay sex. Crossover was not hateful about the suspension. Brandy recalled that the director, exasperated, said, "Brandy, try to be serious about this. I just want you to think about if you really want to be involved with this process. I've got to suspend you for a while."

Brandy did not feel damaged by her time in Crossover. She had already had an unusually invasive Christian accountability experience with the church she called the "crazy church" that participated in the shepherding movement (see chap. 3). For Brandy, compared to the "crazy church," those involved in Crossover were tolerant and accepting. The accountability expected of those in Crossover was much less intrusive than that of her previous church, the environment was more supportive and forgiving, and finally, through her association with Crossover, she had the opportunity to travel around the country attending Exodus International conferences in Seattle, Chicago, and San Diego with her way partially funded by Christian groups.[8] Brandy, Helen, and Donald had each attended Exodus International conferences as part of their conversion work.

"I Don't See a Bunch of Broken People"

In July 2009, I drove to Wheaton, Illinois, to observe firsthand the programs, speakers, attendees, and worship at the biggest ex-gay event of the year. Although I was eager to see the ex-gay ideology and behavior up close and personal, I also struggled with anxiety about voluntarily immersing myself in an environment governed by a worldview so counter to my own. Just planning to attend the conference induced some trepidation in me, so I invited a friend, Lisa, who is white, 40, in seminary studying to become an Episcopal priest, and also a Bible Belt gay from Tennessee and a longtime resident of Central Kentucky, to join me.

After a 7-hour drive to Wheaton, Lisa and I checked in at the conference hotel, changed clothes, and headed to the opening keynote speech by Alan Chambers, president of Exodus International. While waiting in line to register, we spotted two women who looked so visibly queer, Lisa, also a trained psychologist, worried about their mental health. It turned out that those particular women were at the college with a group of protesters and had ended up in the wrong registration line. Gay rights groups from the Chicago area had organized a protest of the Exodus conference and were outside the auditorium holding colorful signs, giving speeches, and chanting. Lisa and I spent a few minutes watching the protest, briefly visited with the protesters, and then entered the college auditorium. A Christian rock band was playing praise music to open the ceremonies. The auditorium was three-quarters full when Lisa and I entered, and most of the audience stood while the band performed, many with their arms outreached to God, eyes half-closed in worship. No one was exactly dancing because dancing was against the rules at Wheaton College, but there was a lot of lyrical swaying and rhythmic body movements during the music.

Lisa, mild-mannered and tolerant most of the time, was practically spitting with irritation as the praise music dragged on for 45 minutes. Tired after the long drive, the music lulled me into a trancelike state. I woke suddenly from my stupor when the band leader spoke to the crowd, guitar in hand, sweat glowing on his brow, aroused by his own performance, "When I look at you, I don't see a bunch of broken people. I see sons and daughters of Christ!" This was before I understood how central the theme of "brokenness" is in the ex-gay literature, and within conservative Christianity more generally.[9] As Joshua explained earlier, "brokenness" is a Christian "code word," used in reference to a variety of sins, weaknesses, woundings, and problems (see chap. 3). The generously applied "brokenness" covers a range of destructive behaviors—alcoholism, abusive behavior, distant parenting, pornography addiction, homosexuality, even selfishness—potentially engaged in by heterosexuals and homosexuals alike.

The people present ranged in age from what looked to be their late teens to those in their 60s and 70s. Most were white. Exodus conferences serve not only individuals struggling with homosexuality but also parents of homosexual children and women married to homosexual men, and members of each of these groups were present. Some parents attended with their children and some did not. I considered approximately 40% of the people I encountered during the conference to be gender-nonconforming, that is, their gender presentations did not conform to heterosexist standards of butch men and feminine women, including leaders of the organization, Christine Sneeringer and Alan Chambers.

Christine Sneeringer and Alan Chambers—Quintessentially Queer

Christine Sneeringer, a woman Janet Parshall, host of the American Family Association program "Speechless: Silencing the Christians" called "living proof that there is no homosexual gene" served as emcee throughout the conference. Sneeringer introduced speakers, made announcements, and was available to participants at the Women's Oasis, an evening support group. I was intrigued with Sneeringer. In the "Speechless" documentary she is featured with before-and-after pictures of her gender transformation. Her before-pictures show a cute, happy, confident, butch girl and teenager, and her after-photos depict a butch-looking woman wearing femme drag. Ex-gay theories argue that incomplete gender socialization, among other factors, causes homosexuality in both women and men; they encourage participants to engage in traditional masculine and feminine behavior as part of the treatment.[10] Ex-gay literature promotes rugged "manly" activities like sports and camping for men. For example, Donald shared the title of a recent local "Love Won Out" conference: "Ex-Gays and Sports: Why Try?" He said, "We all sat around and had a good laugh about it. Because none of us were jocks, but they were going to have an ex-gay conference on how to cultivate your inner athlete." For women, feminine re-socialization includes focusing on the external qualities of femininity—how to apply makeup, dress, and walk in heels. Helen, who also worked in the Crossover office for a period of time, disliked this component of conversion therapy:

> I'm not butch, but I'm not feminine either. I'm kind of in the middle I guess. But I don't wear makeup. I never have. Don't like it. Don't wear dresses. Well, they wanted me to wear dresses, or pant suits at least, and eventually they started working me into trying to wear makeup. I remember one time they had a slumber party for the women, and we were doing each other's nails, and we were supposed to practice makeup and I thought, "this is the most miserable thing, this is so stupid." I didn't participate in all of it because I thought this is the stupidest thing ever. I hate this. And I remember the first time I agreed to go ahead and put the makeup on, and go to work. I got to the Crossover office and I felt like a freaking clown. And I thought, "give me that little red ball to put on my nose and I'm all set to go." So I washed it off and I didn't do it again.

However ill-fitting they appeared to me, Sneeringer willingly adopted such feminine markers of makeup, pearls, and clothing, and was a confident, charismatic, and self-deprecating emcee. She welcomed the participants, congratulating them on making it, in the face of what she knew was often "a lot of drama" getting here. She, like some of the other speakers, tried to lighten the mood by joking about her gender presentation:

> I was pretty excited when I got on campus, finally made it. I started asking where I needed to go. I was asking a passerby for one particular hall and he goes, "Are you here for the Athletics Convention." And I thought, "Now I can't even tell you what I'm here for." And there's a Cheerleader's Convention going on at the same time. Why couldn't he have asked me if I was here for that? So I don't know what that's about.[11]

In addition to announcements about changes in the schedule and special events for the under-25 crowd, Sneeringer gave us specific instructions on prayer:

> We're going to have fun this week, as much fun as healing can be when you are getting your guts ripped out. So, in the spirit of that, let's talk about

the Prayer Team first. Because when your guts are getting ripped out, you want to know who to go to for prayer. You want to make sure you are going to the right people. The Prayer Team can be identified by an orange dot on their name tags, so those are the people you want to ask for prayer from. If they don't have an orange dot and they still want to pray for you, just tell them to pray from a distance.

Several of my interview subjects discussed attendees meeting partners, flirting with, having sex with, and developing crushes on people they met in ex-gay ministries, particularly at Exodus conferences. Helen went to three separate Exodus conferences, the last one with Leslie. At this point in their relationship both Helen and Leslie were feeling very attracted to one another, but they were committed to the ministry and trying to stay away from each other. Helen recalled that they carried out a secret romance during the Exodus conference, sneaking away to hide and kiss. I asked her if she noticed others engaged in similar behavior and she responded:

Oh gosh, yes. I didn't actually see anything, because they're too smart. Because you'd get kicked out and whatever. So I didn't actually witness anything, but it was like I knew. I remember our director saying later, toward the end of the conference, "Exodus really has to get a handle on this." But I hadn't come clean at this point, she didn't know that Leslie and I were hiding and getting together during the conference. She was just talking about how she saw that that was a problem and that Exodus needs to find a way to be able to have these conferences and keep a handle on that.

Brandy, who went to five Exodus International conferences during her time participating in ex-gay ministries, observed the same phenomenon:

At the ex-gay conferences a lot of people become close friends, but some people become lovers from there. Which is really crazy. In fact, one guy I know has decided he's going to live openly gay. But every conference he went to, he slept with his roommate every night. And you sign an agreement that you will not have sexual contact. And I'm sure if the opportunity had arisen, I would have slept with somebody there. And that's terrible because you sign this agreement that I'm going to be on the straight and narrow. But I think a lot of people are just lonely. They just want somebody to love them.

To curtail such forbidden connections, Exodus leaders attempt to micromanage the participants' contact with one another by deciding who is allowed to room together and designating with whom it is appropriate to pray. After Sneeringer's instructions about to whom to go for prayer, with visions of prayer circles transforming into gay orgies should the unsuspecting struggling homosexual pray with someone *not on the Prayer Team* dancing in my brain, she introduced Alan Chambers.

Alan Chambers, white, middle-aged, a dynamic public speaker and frequent guest and commentator in media outlets, and president of Exodus International since 2001, does not like labels. At the opening keynote, Chambers said, "Don't define me by what I used to do. Don't define me in a way God would never choose to define me. I am not a former homosexual or an ex-gay. I'm not a sissy, not a fag, not a queer, not a Mama's boy. I am not a gay man. I am a son of the Most High. I am the Righteousness of Christ." Chambers is a contentious figure. He leads an organization that makes most conservative Christians at the very least, uncomfortable, and LGBT folks incensed. Further, Chambers, like Sneeringer, visibly embodies and promotes the concept of an identity in flux, and in these ways both are excellent illustrations of queer theory, as are ex-gay ministries overall.[12] The queer theorist Davis Halperin writes, "Queer is by definition whatever is at odds with the normal, the legitimate, the dominant. There is nothing in particular to which it necessarily refers. It is an identity without an essence. 'Queer' then, demarcates not a positivity but a positionality vis-à-vis the normative."[13] The sociologist Adam Isaiah Green observes that queer theory resists the naturalization of any identity, "exposing 'queer' cracks in the heteronormative façade."[14] An English professor and queer scholar, Annamarie Jagose writes that queer is a category that is in the process of formation. Jagose explains, "Its definitional indeterminacy, its elasticity, is one of its constituent characteristics."[15]

In her book *Straight to Jesus: Sexual and Christian Conversions in the Ex-Gay Movement*, Tanya Erzen notes, "Although the political goals of the ex-gay movement and queer activists are radically distinct, by accepting that a person's behavior and desire will not necessarily correspond with their new ex-gay identity or religious identity, ex-gay men and women enact a queer concept of sexuality when they undergo queer conversion."[16] Lynne Gerber concurs in her article, "The Opposite of Gay: Nature, Creation, and Queerish Ex-Gay Experiments." Gerber writes, "In carving out this space between rejection and acceptance of homosexuality, they utilize discursive and cultural strategies that resemble the gender indeterminacy and gender play celebrated by queer theorists—who have very different socio-political aims."[17] In his physical presentation, Chambers, like Sneeringer, "queered" the atmosphere, but Chambers also drew on language that explicitly destabilized the idea of any fixed identity. He repeatedly asked the audience to reflect upon the following two questions: "Who *are* you and why are you here?" The visible queerness of Christine Sneeringer and Alan Chambers opening the Exodus International Conference set a certain seductive tone for the proceedings that, I speculated, might invite hope in the participants, *maybe this will work for me, maybe it won't be so bad, maybe I can change and be happy too.* And the motivating and uplifting message of Chambers's keynote—"God loves you"—seemed designed to allay fears and welcome participants into the loving arms of Christ, not punish them for "unnatural" feelings.

"Jesus Is All That You Need"

Upon taking the stage, Chambers quickly addressed the actions of the protesters outside, whose chants were barely audible inside the auditorium. Chambers assured us that "there is never going to be a person on the face of the earth who can do for you what Jesus can." He continued:

> Listen to what's going on outside. They don't know that. And it doesn't cause me to hate them. It causes me to beg God to intervene in their lives. Those people aren't the enemy. They aren't the enemy to Exodus. They aren't the enemy of the church. They are not the enemy of God. They are missing from who God created them to be. And I don't mean heterosexuality and Exodus. They're missing from the community of believers where they belong.

In this way, Chambers framed the protesters and gay activists as people to pity:

> As I think of them, the image that comes to my mind is of those hungry, starving, balloon-bellied babies in Africa, and your eyes well up in tears seeing them living in a dust bowl and you think, "Sure, I'll give 18 cents a day."

Chambers's analogy comparing the demonstrators to starving babies in Africa disturbed me as it framed LGBT activists not only as severely lacking spiritual nourishment but also drew on racist and colonialist imagery. He explained that these "hardened gay activists" are starving for the only thing that can save them: the love of Jesus Christ. Within Exodus, the label "activist" can be applied to anyone living an openly gay lifestyle not trying to free themselves from homosexuality.[18] In this way, it can equally describe lesbian moms too busy to even attend a Gay Pride parade to the executive director of a gay rights organization to a gay rights protest group at an Exodus conference.

Then Chambers softened his message. He explained that the activists were angry, and they had a reason to be because "the church hasn't gotten it right." By excluding gay men and lesbians from the body of Christ, the church has lost valuable skills and resources. He urged the crowd to speak with the protesters and tell them that God loves them. Chambers then spoke about the intent of the conference:

> The purpose of this conference, the purpose of Exodus isn't to make gay people straight. You won't get a stamp on your forehead with the word "heterosexual" for coming. God wants to do something much bigger. The opposite of homosexuality isn't heterosexuality, it's holiness.

Chambers explained that his work with Exodus is to help people become closer to God, not to change them—that's something only the Holy Spirit can do. He continued:

> When I embarked on my journey out of homosexuality I thought, mistakenly, probably like many of you, that my goal was heterosexuality. And God got a hold of me along my journey and said, "That's not My plan for your life. That's not My biggest goal for you—to be straight—because straight people go to hell too," right?

With the comment that "straight people go to hell too," Chambers attempted to level the playing field for the attendees: God does not love heterosexuals any more than He does those experiencing same-sex attractions. Underlying this is the Christian theological sin/fall narrative that all of humankind struggles with sin, risks hell, and would benefit from more holiness. Exodus recasts the sin of homosexuality from the "worst sin imaginable" like many of the Bible Belt gays I interviewed heard in their churches growing up, to one of many minor sins, like gossiping or lying, of which everyone is guilty from time to time.[19] In her study on ex-gay Christian men, the sociologist Michelle Wolkomir quoted an ex-gay group leader, "The first step in healing is to normalize homosexuality, to make the men realize it is no worse a sin than a white lie. I always tell them [the group] that men have distorted the biblical significance of sexuality. It gives them hope and lets them start to rethink their lives."[20]

The audience seemed to calm during Chambers's talk, the anxiety decreased. People seemed to sit back more comfortably in their seats. The

esbianism is more complex than gay
this was because men were made
ing (a biblical reference from Gen-
e forms than men do. Women are
able, and tender. Our sexuality is
e to connect emotionally. And in all
sometimes women confuse platonic
cially the case if our fathers are dis-
d gave men a power and authority
animals after all," D'Ann said, "so
live out the words that their fathers
t they are beautiful because women
ncluded that women's driving force
."

and seeks to heal homosexual-
. Reparative therapy draws upon a
-sex attraction as a consequence of
d. Specifically, a child fails to ade-
parent.[26] Using this psychological
del and briefly referencing attach-
one needs their mother during the
e quality parenting at this stage are
ically, she continued, lesbians flat
"normal" child bonds with a same-
when one has a best girl friend and
oes not achieve a strong same-sex
ut it. It will be a mystery she seeks
ips with other women. "God cre-
't know, and drawn to people who
esbian is therefore simply trying to
e means.

dels—classic and contemporary—
nd with her same-sex during the
a girl, like Christine Sneeringer for
busive father and a passive mother
er mother's femininity with weak-
ayed in her father's toxic masculin-
fathers are working out their own
n conceded, "times have changed."
ssic model. With changing gender

conference organizers had acknowledged their potentially heroic efforts to make it to the conference. Now they could relax and let God do his part. They could even try to have fun, while their "guts were getting ripped out." And there was something fun and giddy about the event. At Exodus, they did not need to hide that they were gay, or maybe gay, or trying not to be gay. Nobody—not their conservative Christian family members or gay friends— was allowed to give them a hard time. The men could sport ethnic scarves and wear androgynous shoes (which I observed) and no one would criticize them.[21] Because their presence simultaneously signaled that they struggled with same-sex attractions but that they knew it was wrong and they were working on it, they did not need to hide any "gayness." At this particular moment, the toxic closet was irrelevant, and there was something freeing about that.[22] Everyone was in the same boat, trying to do the same thing. For the next four days, they did not need to control their uncontrollable desires, being there was enough, God would do the rest.

"God Wants to Do Some Impossible Things This Week"

An effective speaker, unafraid to take pregnant pauses between sentences, Chambers then directly addressed the stigma and oppression much of the audience likely had suffered and offered the emotionally satisfying message that their stigmatized homosexuality did not define them:

> Sissy, queer, Mama's boy, fag. Those words are not you. Whatever it is that you've been labeled, whether it's been by somebody else or by yourself— damaged goods, used, abused, worthless—and I'm just thinking of the names that have been attached to me, God would never call you any of those names, ever. Your identity will never be found anywhere else but in Christ . . . I am a New Creation. I am a Holy Vessel. How about you? What does God call you? He calls some of you "Beautiful Daughter."

Chambers validated the suffering endured by participants and framed the abuse they might have experienced as a consequence of human weakness, not a reflection of God's feelings. Finally, Chambers turned to the heart of the conundrum with which each attendee struggled—temptations. He effectively used his own story as a model:

> On those days when I'm having trouble and 19 years into it, I still have trouble, I go to the Lord and say, "Tell me who I am. Because these people say I'm something else. My feelings today are telling me I'm something

else. Remind me who I am." He says every time, gladly, "You're My
and I love you, and I'm so proud of you. I'm so glad I chose you. Y
my favorite." That's what He says about you too . . . . We serve an ama
God. He's not out to condemn you. He's out to love you. Change will
pen if you trust Him. I can't tell you what that change will look like in
life. I can't tell you if you'll have a wife or kids like I do. That may n
your miracle. Your miracle may be living the most amazing life of celi
under a new identity. It's healing you. I just really believe God wants
some impossible things this week.

The warm and loving tone that Chambers, and many other Exod
ers adopted, in contrast with their exacting if understated message, v
nitively disorienting for me. Listening to the DVD recording of Ch
transcribing it for this chapter, I felt emotionally manipulated, and
not one religious belief in common with the speaker. For the perso
conservative Christian identity is important to him or her, the
would likely have a stronger impact, as Donald's 15 year on-again–c
participation in ex-gay ministries illustrates.

Chambers's simple and evocative message that "God loves you
you need to worry about is pleasing God" was psychologically and e
ally persuasive. A spiritual seeker myself, I felt its sway: the idea th
Great Being has a Perfect Plan for me if I just let Him take cont
sticking point though, and one which I found surprisingly easy to
the sea of lyrical language, was that there's no room in God's Perf
for same-sex love. Entry into heaven, membership among the f
of Christ is dependent upon, if not ridding oneself of all same-se
tions—so difficult even Chambers frames it as "the impossible"–
never acting upon them. Thus, underneath the warm and helpful
of Exodus leaders is the uncompromising expectation that people v
not free themselves from homosexual desires should not have sex
bers closed his keynote by dramatically raising a large leather-bou
and said the following:

We don't have all the answers at Exodus. We only have one answe
world that promises truth around every corner, enlightenment is
everywhere you turn, there is only one place you can find it. It is rigl
in the Word of God, and there is nothing else that I know to be tr
this. Therapy might be beneficial for you. Support groups might he
trusting the Savior, trusting that His Word is true is the only thing y
count on. You will never be disappointed by this.

D'Ann opened by saying plainly that
male homosexuality. She explained tha
from dirt but women from a human b
esis). Accordingly, women come in mo
nurturing, responsive, sensitive, vulne
more fluid. Women are emotional and li
this emotional bonding and connecting,
affection for sexual affection. This is esp
tant or abusive. D'Ann explained that G
not given to women. "Adam named th
men's words have special meaning. Girls
speak to them. Dads need to tell girls tha
have an innate desire to hear this." She c
is for "affirmation, attention, and affectio

Psychologically, Exodus understand
ity with reparative or conversion therap
psychoanalytic model that explains sam
arrested gender development in childho
quately identify with her or his same-se
childhood and adolescence reparative m
ment theory, D'Ann explained that ever
0–3 age range.[27] Those who do not recei
suffering their mother's brokenness. Ty
line between the ages of 4–10 when the
sex peer. In the case of girls, it is the time
thinks boys are "yucky." The girl who
connection at this age will be curious ab
to untangle through romantic relations
ated us to be curious about things we do
are mysterious," D'Ann explained, and a
meet legitimate needs through illegitima

D'Ann cited two reparative family m
to explain why the young girl fails to b
4–10-year age range. In the classic model
example, grows up with an overbearing
from whom she detaches. She associates
ness and identifies with the strength disp
ity to avoid being a victim. These abusiv
brokenness with this behavior. "But," D'A
Not long ago, most lesbians fit in this cl

roles, a new model of the roots of lesbianism—the overbearing mom and the passive dad—may also inhibit a young girl from appropriate gender identification. Additionally, divorced and single-parent homes fail to provide adequate parent-child relationships. In all these cases, the young girl does not experience proper modeling of femininity by her mother and instead learns that femininity is something to be feared and/or despised. Neither does she receive the necessary affirmation from her father. She hits puberty and fails to become attracted to the opposite sex. Having covered most family forms (with the exception of same-sex parents) in the workshop by this point, I began to wonder how Exodus explains any child surviving her own childhood and adolescence heterosexually identified.

Exodus operates with the assumption that homosexuality is not innate. Using the Kinsey scale, D'Ann illustrated this. She said that most women are bisexual, and that all women are vulnerable to lesbianism.[28] She herself had had an intense friendship that might have turned into something more were it not for the grace of God. Thus, ex-gay reasoning digs a deep hole: better to take the position that homosexuality is a sin of which everyone is equally in danger of committing than affirm same-sex relationships as part of God's beautiful design. I had been particularly struck by D'Ann's claim that only God's grace saved her from falling into the easy trap of lesbianism. I wondered if she considered how unwelcoming that might potentially sound to the participants earnestly attending: that God had not seen fit to grace them. Who could fail to interpret this as "you are better than I am," or "I am not good enough for God to grace" I thought? During the Q&A, I raised my hand and, when she called on me, I asked, "In the close friendship you described to us, why do you think it did not become more, why did God grace you?" I left unspoken "and not the rest of us" because I did not want to come across as confrontational. She responded, "I really don't know because I certainly did not do anything to deserve it." D'Ann drew on the well-worn and convenient conservative Christian response to difficult questions: God's ways are mysterious and beyond our simple human understanding. This exchange drew the attention of the woman seated next to me who whispered that I had asked a good question and she would like to answer it after the workshop if I was interested. I was, of course, very interested in her answer. Meanwhile, the two of us bonded with much eye-rolling over the long-winded, pompous remarks of an older man (a heterosexual father of a lesbian) about his Christian journey. There were only two men in the room and this one took up half the Q&A time. My companion whispered to me while he was droning on that "that was just the sort of Christian thing I would have said five years ago." Then she apologized for being uncharitable.

After the workshop, we lingered in our seats and "Jeannie" answered my question. First, she explained that she had been out of the lesbian lifestyle for 17 years. Her story included alcoholism and a terrible car wreck in which someone died and she felt responsible. Jeannie perceived the car wreck, alcoholism, and homosexuality as all part of her personal brokenness. To her, freedom from homosexuality was freedom from all of it. By submitting to God, she was able to live a clean lifestyle. When I brought up my question and said that it sounded like the workshop leader was implying that God did not love the rest of us, Jeannie looked surprised. She said, "No, God loves us more. God tests his favorites." The participants' struggles were proof of God's special favor, not evidence against it. Hence, like the phrase "brokenness," "God's grace" was also promiscuously applied to every scenario. No matter what the situation one can find evidence within it of God's special love. If this is hard to wrap one's head around, that's to be expected because godly ways are beyond human understanding.

The theme that God tests God's favorites came up repeatedly at the conference. After my conversation with Jeannie and reviewing my notes, I realized it had been central to Robert Gagnon's morning talk on "The Bible and Homosexual Practice." Gagnon, one of the general session speakers, is an associate professor at Pittsburgh Theological Seminary. He is well known in the ex-gay world for his theological work against homosexuality. Gagnon, like most of the speakers, began with a prayer. He prayed that the people listening would receive his words.[29] Most of Gagnon's opening comments romanticized and valorized the suffering endured by the crowd. He said, "We all have crosses to bear," and "You are all my heroes." Gagnon explained that the greatest manifestation of God's power is not to be delivered from desires but to have the desires remain and receive the tools to endure. God will not remove the thorn in your flesh. Instead, God's grace enables you to endure the thorn. Thus, God's grace does not equal deliverance; God's grace means that God is enough. God creates moments of difficulty in our lives in order to feel the presence of Jesus. Gagnon cautioned the crowd that we need to live for God and not ourselves. Our suffering makes us die to ourselves so we can be a more perfect vessel for Christ. Hence, the more God loves us, the more suffering God places on our path. Gagnon grandiosely stated, "God is not a great cosmic sadist, but a great cosmic surgeon." God will change us to make us look more like Jesus, no matter what the cost. Gagnon then proceeded to rush through a detailed textual analysis of biblical scripture that I thought would require at least four hours to fully explain, yet he managed it in thirty minutes. He concluded his talk with the bleak message, "Take up your cross, deny yourself and lose yourself. Give up everything for Jesus."

conference organizers had acknowledged their potentially heroic efforts to make it to the conference. Now they could relax and let God do his part. They could even try to have fun, while their "guts were getting ripped out." And there was something fun and giddy about the event. At Exodus, they did not need to hide that they were gay, or maybe gay, or trying not to be gay. Nobody—not their conservative Christian family members or gay friends— was allowed to give them a hard time. The men could sport ethnic scarves and wear androgynous shoes (which I observed) and no one would criticize them.[21] Because their presence simultaneously signaled that they struggled with same-sex attractions but that they knew it was wrong and they were working on it, they did not need to hide any "gayness." At this particular moment, the toxic closet was irrelevant, and there was something freeing about that.[22] Everyone was in the same boat, trying to do the same thing. For the next four days, they did not need to control their uncontrollable desires, being there was enough, God would do the rest.

"God Wants to Do Some Impossible Things This Week"

An effective speaker, unafraid to take pregnant pauses between sentences, Chambers then directly addressed the stigma and oppression much of the audience likely had suffered and offered the emotionally satisfying message that their stigmatized homosexuality did not define them:

> Sissy, queer, Mama's boy, fag. Those words are not you. Whatever it is that you've been labeled, whether it's been by somebody else or by yourself— damaged goods, used, abused, worthless—and I'm just thinking of the names that have been attached to me, God would never call you any of those names, ever. Your identity will never be found anywhere else but in Christ . . . I am a New Creation. I am a Holy Vessel. How about you? What does God call you? He calls some of you "Beautiful Daughter."

Chambers validated the suffering endured by participants and framed the abuse they might have experienced as a consequence of human weakness, not a reflection of God's feelings. Finally, Chambers turned to the heart of the conundrum with which each attendee struggled—temptations. He effectively used his own story as a model:

> On those days when I'm having trouble and 19 years into it, I still have trouble, I go to the Lord and say, "Tell me who I am. Because these people say I'm something else. My feelings today are telling me I'm something

else. Remind me who I am." He says every time, gladly, "You're My son, and I love you, and I'm so proud of you. I'm so glad I chose you. You're my favorite." That's what He says about you too . . . . We serve an amazing God. He's not out to condemn you. He's out to love you. Change will happen if you trust Him. I can't tell you what that change will look like in your life. I can't tell you if you'll have a wife or kids like I do. That may not be your miracle. Your miracle may be living the most amazing life of celibacy under a new identity. It's healing you. I just really believe God wants to do some impossible things this week.

The warm and loving tone that Chambers, and many other Exodus leaders adopted, in contrast with their exacting if understated message, was cognitively disorienting for me. Listening to the DVD recording of Chambers, transcribing it for this chapter, I felt emotionally manipulated, and I shared not one religious belief in common with the speaker. For the person whose conservative Christian identity is important to him or her, the message would likely have a stronger impact, as Donald's 15 year on-again–off-again participation in ex-gay ministries illustrates.

Chambers's simple and evocative message that "God loves you and all you need to worry about is pleasing God" was psychologically and emotionally persuasive. A spiritual seeker myself, I felt its sway: the idea that some Great Being has a Perfect Plan for me if I just let Him take control. The sticking point though, and one which I found surprisingly easy to forget in the sea of lyrical language, was that there's no room in God's Perfect Plan for same-sex love. Entry into heaven, membership among the followers of Christ is dependent upon, if not ridding oneself of all same-sex attractions—so difficult even Chambers frames it as "the impossible"—at least never acting upon them. Thus, underneath the warm and helpful attitudes of Exodus leaders is the uncompromising expectation that people who cannot free themselves from homosexual desires should not have sex. Chambers closed his keynote by dramatically raising a large leather-bound Bible and said the following:

We don't have all the answers at Exodus. We only have one answer. In a world that promises truth around every corner, enlightenment is found everywhere you turn, there is only one place you can find it. It is right here in the Word of God, and there is nothing else that I know to be true but this. Therapy might be beneficial for you. Support groups might help, but trusting the Savior, trusting that His Word is true is the only thing you can count on. You will never be disappointed by this.

In a chaotic, fragmented, postmodern world, conservative Christians use the Bible as bedrock, tool, map, and rule book.[23] As Helen's narrative of suicidal thoughts, panic attacks, and depression illustrates, the conservative Christian experiencing same-sex attractions may negotiate an extremely fragmented reality. In this battle with temptation and confusion, Exodus advocates biblical inerrancy and faith in God.

Understanding the Roots and Causes of Lesbianism

An in-depth look at gender identity development in women and
what happens in the heart of a woman that leads her down the path
of lesbianism.
—Workshop description, Exodus Conference Guide

The Exodus conference was structured so that the specific needs of participants were attended to in different tracks. Opening (9–10:30 a.m.) and closing (7–9:30 p.m.) general sessions, featuring a big-name speaker like Robert Gagnon, were held in the auditorium with no other conflicting events. In between were morning and afternoon workshop offerings geared toward members of particular groups. There were general workshop offerings as well as those for women, men, parents, leaders, and couples. No one prevented a man from attending a workshop developed for women, or a woman from attending one for men, but participants sex-segregated in the workshops at which I was present.

Men outnumbered women at the Exodus conference by two and often three to one at every workshop and general session I attended except the lesbian workshop.[24] Further, the ex-gay movement generally is male-dominated. Dee believes this is because ex-gay groups serve conservative Christians who are socialized to see women as "less than men." She continued, "They don't really care if the women change, and don't seek out women like they're out seeking men." I counted approximately 40 people in the lesbian workshop, two of whom were men.[25] D'Ann Davis, a staff member with Living Hope Ministries in the Dallas–Fort Worth area led the "Understanding Lesbianism" workshop. An attractive, wholesome-looking white woman, who appeared to be in her early thirties, D'Ann passed out a worksheet to the participants titled "Understanding Gender Development." The Kinsey scale that depicts sexual orientation on a continuum from 0 to 6, with 0 being heterosexual and 6 homosexual, boldly followed the title of the handout.

D'Ann opened by saying plainly that lesbianism is more complex than gay male homosexuality. She explained that this was because men were made from dirt but women from a human being (a biblical reference from Genesis). Accordingly, women come in more forms than men do. Women are nurturing, responsive, sensitive, vulnerable, and tender. Our sexuality is more fluid. Women are emotional and like to connect emotionally. And in all this emotional bonding and connecting, sometimes women confuse platonic affection for sexual affection. This is especially the case if our fathers are distant or abusive. D'Ann explained that God gave men a power and authority not given to women. "Adam named the animals after all," D'Ann said, "so men's words have special meaning. Girls live out the words that their fathers speak to them. Dads need to tell girls that they are beautiful because women have an innate desire to hear this." She concluded that women's driving force is for "affirmation, attention, and affection."

Psychologically, Exodus understands and seeks to heal homosexuality with reparative or conversion therapy. Reparative therapy draws upon a psychoanalytic model that explains same-sex attraction as a consequence of arrested gender development in childhood. Specifically, a child fails to adequately identify with her or his same-sex parent.[26] Using this psychological childhood and adolescence reparative model and briefly referencing attachment theory, D'Ann explained that everyone needs their mother during the 0–3 age range.[27] Those who do not receive quality parenting at this stage are suffering their mother's brokenness. Typically, she continued, lesbians flat line between the ages of 4–10 when the "normal" child bonds with a same-sex peer. In the case of girls, it is the time when one has a best girl friend and thinks boys are "yucky." The girl who does not achieve a strong same-sex connection at this age will be curious about it. It will be a mystery she seeks to untangle through romantic relationships with other women. "God created us to be curious about things we don't know, and drawn to people who are mysterious," D'Ann explained, and a lesbian is therefore simply trying to meet legitimate needs through illegitimate means.

D'Ann cited two reparative family models—classic and contemporary—to explain why the young girl fails to bond with her same-sex during the 4–10-year age range. In the classic model, a girl, like Christine Sneeringer for example, grows up with an overbearing abusive father and a passive mother from whom she detaches. She associates her mother's femininity with weakness and identifies with the strength displayed in her father's toxic masculinity to avoid being a victim. These abusive fathers are working out their own brokenness with this behavior. "But," D'Ann conceded, "times have changed." Not long ago, most lesbians fit in this classic model. With changing gender roles, a new model of the roots of lesbianism—the overbearing mom and the passive dad—may also inhibit a young girl from appropriate gender identification. Additionally, divorced and single-parent homes fail to provide adequate parent-child relationships. In all these cases, the young girl does not experience proper modeling of femininity by her mother and instead learns that femininity is something to be feared and/or despised. Neither does she receive the necessary affirmation from her father. She hits puberty and fails to become attracted to the opposite sex. Having covered most family forms (with the exception of same-sex parents) in the workshop by this point, I began to wonder how Exodus explains any child surviving her own childhood and adolescence heterosexually identified.

Exodus operates with the assumption that homosexuality is not innate. Using the Kinsey scale, D'Ann illustrated this. She said that most women are bisexual, and that all women are vulnerable to lesbianism.[28] She herself had had an intense friendship that might have turned into something more were it not for the grace of God. Thus, ex-gay reasoning digs a deep hole: better to take the position that homosexuality is a sin of which everyone is equally in danger of committing than affirm same-sex relationships as part of God's beautiful design. I had been particularly struck by D'Ann's claim that only God's grace saved her from falling into the easy trap of lesbianism. I wondered if she considered how unwelcoming that might potentially sound to the participants earnestly attending: that God had not seen fit to grace them. Who could fail to interpret this as "you are better than I am," or "I am not good enough for God to grace" I thought? During the Q&A, I raised my hand and, when she called on me, I asked, "In the close friendship you described to us, why do you think it did not become more, why did God grace you?" I left unspoken "and not the rest of us" because I did not want to come across as confrontational. She responded, "I really don't know because I certainly did not do anything to deserve it." D'Ann drew on the well-worn and convenient conservative Christian response to difficult questions: God's ways are mysterious and beyond our simple human understanding. This exchange drew the attention of the woman seated next to me who whispered that I had asked a good question and she would like to answer it after the workshop if I was interested. I was, of course, very interested in her answer. Meanwhile, the two of us bonded with much eye-rolling over the long-winded, pompous remarks of an older man (a heterosexual father of a lesbian) about his Christian journey. There were only two men in the room and this one took up half the Q&A time. My companion whispered to me while he was droning on that "that was just the sort of Christian thing I would have said five years ago." Then she apologized for being uncharitable.

After the workshop, we lingered in our seats and "Jeannie" answered my question. First, she explained that she had been out of the lesbian lifestyle for 17 years. Her story included alcoholism and a terrible car wreck in which someone died and she felt responsible. Jeannie perceived the car wreck, alcoholism, and homosexuality as all part of her personal brokenness. To her, freedom from homosexuality was freedom from all of it. By submitting to God, she was able to live a clean lifestyle. When I brought up my question and said that it sounded like the workshop leader was implying that God did not love the rest of us, Jeannie looked surprised. She said, "No, God loves us more. God tests his favorites." The participants' struggles were proof of God's special favor, not evidence against it. Hence, like the phrase "brokenness," "God's grace" was also promiscuously applied to every scenario. No matter what the situation one can find evidence within it of God's special love. If this is hard to wrap one's head around, that's to be expected because godly ways are beyond human understanding.

The theme that God tests God's favorites came up repeatedly at the conference. After my conversation with Jeannie and reviewing my notes, I realized it had been central to Robert Gagnon's morning talk on "The Bible and Homosexual Practice." Gagnon, one of the general session speakers, is an associate professor at Pittsburgh Theological Seminary. He is well known in the ex-gay world for his theological work against homosexuality. Gagnon, like most of the speakers, began with a prayer. He prayed that the people listening would receive his words.[29] Most of Gagnon's opening comments romanticized and valorized the suffering endured by the crowd. He said, "We all have crosses to bear," and "You are all my heroes." Gagnon explained that the greatest manifestation of God's power is not to be delivered from desires but to have the desires remain and receive the tools to endure. God will not remove the thorn in your flesh. Instead, God's grace enables you to endure the thorn. Thus, God's grace does not equal deliverance; God's grace means that God is enough. God creates moments of difficulty in our lives in order to feel the presence of Jesus. Gagnon cautioned the crowd that we need to live for God and not ourselves. Our suffering makes us die to ourselves so we can be a more perfect vessel for Christ. Hence, the more God loves us, the more suffering God places on our path. Gagnon grandiosely stated, "God is not a great cosmic sadist, but a great cosmic surgeon." God will change us to make us look more like Jesus, no matter what the cost. Gagnon then proceeded to rush through a detailed textual analysis of biblical scripture that I thought would require at least four hours to fully explain, yet he managed it in thirty minutes. He concluded his talk with the bleak message, "Take up your cross, deny yourself and lose yourself. Give up everything for Jesus."

Basic Training: "Learning to Use Your Armor and Weapons"

Exodus participants had been told that God loves us, and they urged us to embrace our suffering as evidence of God's special favor. The "Understanding Lesbianism" workshop had emphasized the biblical mandate of femininity—highlighting our emotional, nurturing natures. Not surprisingly, the men's workshop, "Basic Training: Resisting Temptations," also drew on gender-essentializing language, that of the warrior battling with Christ. I counted 75 people at the "Basic Training for Men" workshop and only three women, two of whom were me and my friend Lisa. Jayson Graves, white, who appeared to be in his mid-30s, a Christian psychotherapist, director of international counseling ministries Healing for the Soul and the Soul Healer Foundation, facilitated the proceedings. Jayson had also served as the youth track leader for Focus on the Family's "Love Won Out" conferences. Jayson hailed from Colorado and exuded, for me, an unexpected outdoorsy, West Coast, earthy-crunchiness. He was also buff, and very handsome. As soon as we saw Jayson, Lisa nudged me and muttered, "I bet he'll be on the minds of a lot of men this evening." Jayson distributed a handout titled, "Basic Training: Learning to use your Armor and Weapons." The handout began by stating, "God has given us many resources for recovery—now it's up to us to use them all and use them well."

A confident and comfortable public speaker, Jayson organized the workshop with the following biblical quote from Ephesians:

> Therefore, take up the full armor of God, so that you will be able to resist in the evil day, and having done everything, to stand firm. Stand firm therefore having girded your loins with truth, and having put on the breastplate of righteousness, and having shod your feet with the preparation of the gospel of peace; in addition to all, taking up the shield of faith with which you will be able to extinguish all the flaming arrows of the evil one. And take the helmet of salvation, and the sword of the spirit, which is the word of God.—Ephesians 6:13–18, People's New Testament Commentary.

Jayson sought to connect with and validate the participants by sharing that everyone struggles with temptations, even him, and said, "anyone who has ever masturbated has had a same gender experience." He explained that "God is a realist" and "God gets glory from doing things in partnership. Do not ask God to save you," he instructed, "ask God to partner with you." Jayson used a warrior metaphor to motivate the participants: the "full armor of

God" is a spiritual mantle one can don against worldly evils. In this endeavor, participants were urged to imagine the historical armor of a Roman soldier complete with girdle, breastplate, shoes with iron nails, a helmet, and a great shield with a sword as one's weapon. Jayson explained that healing required effort and attention, and suggested a number of practical tools to keep one's mind free of unhealthy desires, "unwanted thoughts should be washed with the word of God." Most useful to participants was regular, twice daily Bible study. This, in concert with rigorous, cardiovascular exercise—"moving around does not count," Jayson clarified—checking in daily with an accountability partner, attending a weekly support group, reading Exodus-approved self-help literature, and simply making time for healthy fun were all godly actions to foster sexual integrity. Jayson also cautioned the participants to carefully screen the people with whom they associated. He said, "We're all affected by the people around us. We need to be selective." Part of the ex-gay journey involves ending or distancing oneself from relationships that support homosexuality, in other words, gay friends and partners.

Jayson's laid-back speaking style, his facility in dealing with questions from the crowd, and crunchy manner of dress and demeanor contrasted sharply with his message. In the discussion on boundaries, Jayson said flatly that "a boundary everyone needs is a filter on the Internet." He also cautioned the participants against even masturbating, as that could lead to unwholesome thoughts. Hence the "Basic Training" for men was essentially training in suppression of all sexual feelings for those whom God blesses with extra tests and to whom God does not grant the gift of heterosexuality.

Afternoon Fellowship with the Parents

The afternoon fellowship group for parents had a more informal feel than the other workshops. This group met at the campus grill rather than one of the many conference rooms, and offered participants a free buffet of fruit, cheese and cookies. At the grill, after some opening remarks by a longtime member of Exodus who compared learning that her daughter was a lesbian to her near-death experience from a violent appendicitis, we broke into small groups to offer one another support. I joined the mothers of gay sons in a wooden booth. Before the mothers shared their stories, I revealed to the group that I did not have a gay son. I said, "I am a researcher working on a project exploring homosexuality and religion, and will leave if this makes any of you uncomfortable." They all politely reassured me that it was fine for me to be there, and I stayed, distracted by the guilt I was experiencing about my lack of full disclosure.[30]

I imagined that I would have nothing in common with those at an ex-gay event, especially the heterosexuals whom I perceived as bigots. As the sociologist Kathleen Blee wrote while researching women in the Ku Klux Klan:

I was prepared to hate and fear my informants. My own commitment to progressive politics prepared me to find these people strange, even repellent. I expected no rapport, no shared assumptions, no commonality of thought or experience. What I found was more disturbing. Many of the people I interviewed were interesting, intelligent and well-informed.[31]

Like Blee, I expected no rapport so was surprised by how connected I felt to the mothers of gay sons while listening to their painful stories. Most made comments that illustrated they loved their sons and wanted to support them. For example, one mother shared a long narrative about her last visit to her gay son. Her son was busy with work so she spent most of the visit with his partner. She explained that she prayed about the visit ahead of time, and God had told her to be open and be ready. She then related with quiet triumph that her son's partner had questioned her about her religious beliefs, and she had had the opportunity to speak with him about God's love. From her account, it sounded as though she had been a pleasant guest who never said anything openly homophobic, even when she shared God's word. Compared to some of the stories of the Bible Belt gays I had interviewed, whose parents refused even to let partners into their homes, this mother, who traveled to Baltimore to visit her son and willingly spent time with his partner, seemed to me just one step away from a PFLAG (Parents and Friends of Lesbians and Gays) mom. And she was not the only one. After listening to several similar accounts, I carefully ventured a question of the group. I asked, "Since it seems like you recognized that your sons were different from an early age, have you ever considered that perhaps God made your sons like this? Are you sure homosexuality is a sin?" This query was met with a uniform shaking of heads "no," as every mom in the circle firmly said, "No, I'm sure it's a sin." The mothers were not rude, but they were clear: they had never considered homosexuality anything but a sin, and certainly not part of God's miraculous creation.[32]

Three of the seven mothers cried during our hour-long support group meeting. They worried that their sons would end up in hell, and wondered what they as parents had done wrong. While she cried, one mother discussed listening to her co-workers at her Christian school make hateful, homophobic remarks. Her son had just come out to her and was suffering both bullying and inner pain. This mother said that she felt closeted and silenced around these co-workers and in her church. Another mother responded supportively, "we understand our sons' struggles. We've seen that they have always been different. We can be our son's link to God and the church. We all have a personal brokenness." As our discussion wound down, it became clear that these mothers were not two-dimensional homophobic caricatures; among their church communities, they perceived themselves as the progressive arm of the various institutions within which they interacted. In this way, they are closer allies of gay rights advocates than I had imagined because they, too, experience the "sticky stigma" of homosexuality and negotiate painful homophobic attitudes.[33]

According to Exodus materials, the root cause of homosexuality is failed parent-child relationships. In essence, Exodus faults the parents. In their report on "Love Won Out," professors Cynthia Burack and Jyl J. Josephson noted that this is a "contradiction and tension" in the organization. They wrote:

> Presenters acknowledged the tension between the developmental model of the origins of homosexuality and the importance of not blaming parents, some of whom are the consumers and audience for ex-gay ministries. We observed a number of people attending the conference together who appeared to be parents with their teenaged children. In spite of careful rhetoric about not blaming parents, their developmental model does blame parents who bring their children to ex-gay ministries for children's same-sex attractions.[34]

I also observed a number of parents attending with their children, most of whom appeared to be in their late teens and early 20s. No parent present during the afternoon meeting took issue with the reparative model that held failed parent-child relationships responsible for homosexual attractions. Perhaps this is because some experience psychological relief with *any* answer that explains why their child is homosexual, even an answer that makes the parent responsible, which can be better than no answer at all. It offers the "myth of control," the idea that one can control the circumstances of one's life. The feminist philosopher Susan Wendell theorizes that the myth of control grants people relief when they do not fit cultural standards of bodily ability or beauty.[35] Believing one can actually control some bodily aspect, even when that means accepting responsibility for the lack (i.e., "I must be heavy because I eat too much"), allows one to feel that change is possible, and further, something one can control. For the Exodus mother who accepts that her own brokenness somehow created the homosexual brokenness in her child, the myth of control provides a path of action: If she works on her personal brokenness and improves her relationship with God, maybe her child will change as well. There was much discussion at the conference, by both leaders and participants, about the importance of attending to one's own personal brokenness however it manifested.

The mothers of gay sons closed their discussion with a prayer. We joined hands and bowed our heads as each woman shared her own personal thoughts with God and the group. I did not pray, but I did experience a moment of extreme disorientation when one of the mothers, the "leader" of our little group, the one who had visited her son in Baltimore and seemed like a PFLAG mom to me, prayed for my project, this book you are reading, *Pray the Gay Away*. She said, "Lord, help guide Bernadette in her research. Give her strength and clarity and insight. With all your abundant goodness, support Bernadette in this important work. In Jesus' name, we pray." During this, I bit my lips hard to keep a nervous smile off my face. The tension I experienced from my own deception grew so intense that I left the conference. I stayed only two days out of the five. I left early not because I was worn out with the people or the event, but because I was uncomfortable with my own misrepresentation. My private little toxic closet was eating me alive. I worried that I was taking advantage of the participants by engaging in conversations in which I invited others to share intimacies while revealing nothing of myself or my true intent. If I had stayed any longer at the Exodus conference, I feared internal pressure would cause me to come out as a lesbian and a political progressive, and I was not clear that that would be the best choice for anyone.[36]

By the afternoon fellowship meeting with the parents, I found myself, to my surprise, empathizing with many of the Exodus participants. In spite of our real or imagined political and social differences, I found I could at least chat over coffee, giggle about a pompous speaker, and hold hands in a wooden booth with people I used to perceive, as the anthropologist Susan Harding deconstructed, as the "repugnant cultural other."[37] With the exception of a few famous headlining speakers, notably Joseph Nicolosi and Robert Gagnon, the majority of the people participating in and leading workshops were pleasant, caring, welcoming, and supportive. What mostly separated us were the ways they were trying to resolve "the contradiction" of homosexuality and Christianity. This organization wanted to change it. I obviously believe that this is unnecessary, a waste of time and energy, and that living one's whole life without sexual intimacy is not "God's miracle of celibacy" but rather unsustainable and unhealthy. For the participants at the conference hall, surrounded by other struggling homosexuals and supportive heterosexuals, emotionally charged by Exodus's message of God's love, this might seem possible. Back at home, in their day-to-day lives, celibacy is not a long-term option, as Helen clarified. She explained that attending Exodus conferences left her with lingering feelings of anomie upon her return home. She stated that "All three of the conferences I attended left me confused, frustrated, angry, hurt, and I would be depressed for days after. Because I was taking in what they said, thinking they must be right. It disturbs me to the core how they twist and mangle scripture." For me, while participating in the Exodus International conference had been a rich, ethnographic experience, I too felt disturbed during my experience, and I was relieved to leave.[38]

Conversion Rates

How effective are ex-gay ministries at effecting conversion among participants? The answer to this question depends upon who you ask. The Exodus website directly addresses it under "Frequently Asked Questions" with the heading, "What's your 'success rate' in changing gays into straights?" The answer opens with a quote from Corinthians about being washed and sanctified by the love of Jesus Christ. The website continues:

> No one is saying that change is easy. It requires strong motivation, hard work, and perseverance. But we find hundreds of former homosexuals who have found a large degree of change—attaining abstinence from homosexual behaviors, lessening of homosexual temptations, strengthening their sense of masculine or feminine identity, correcting distorted styles of relating with members of the same and opposite gender. Some former homosexuals marry and some don't, but marriage is not the measuring stick; spiritual growth and obedience are.[39]

Statistically, Exodus cites a longitudinal study conducted by George A. Rekers, emeritus professor of neuropsychiatry and behavioral science at the University of South Carolina School of Medicine, suggesting the vaguely worded "change rates in the range of 30–50% are not unusual." Rekers, a Southern Baptist minister, was an advisor and officer with NARTH (National Association for Research and Therapy of Homosexuality), an organization devoted to developing therapeutic strategies for, and promoting research on, conversion from homosexual to heterosexual. A news story broke in May 2010 that Rekers had hired a gay male prostitute to help him with his luggage during a European vacation, and Rekers resigned his leadership position with NARTH.[40] The work of researchers, like Rekers and Paul Cameron, a psychologist affiliated with the Family Research Institute, a conservative Christian organization, provide data that Dr. Gregory M. Herek calls "bad science in the service of stigma." In his edited volume *Stigma and Sexual Orientation*, Herek details the methodological errors, including errors in sampling, response rate, questionnaire validity, interviewers, and publication venue, in Cameron's data-driven claims that homosexuals threaten "public health, social order, and the well-being of children."[41] Further, since Cameron's work has appeared in low-ranking journals such as the *Journal of Psychology and Theology, Psychological Reports, Journal of Psychology, Adolescence,* and *Omega: Journal of Death and Dying,* it has been largely ignored by the scientific community. Nonetheless, the anti-gay findings of Cameron and Rekers are accepted as "fact" by those who are unfamiliar with the peer-review system of social science publications, and those for whom the work serves to support a particular political and religious agenda.[42]

In her book *Be Not Deceived,* Michelle Wolkomir attempts to estimate the change rate of Exodus even while she qualifies this estimate, writing, "At present, the only conclusion possible is that some people can achieve some level of change sometimes."[43] Wolkomir, a sociologist, cites a study conducted by Robert Spitzer, retired professor of psychiatry from Columbia University, who found "11 percent of the men and 37 percent of the women had achieved 'complete change.'" In May 2012, Spitzer publicly apologized for this study saying that the research had methodological flaws. Wolkomir also quotes Bob Davies, the North American executive director of Exodus, who anecdotally explained that "a long-time counselor with Exodus estimated that a third of his clients had significant changes in their sexuality, another third had little change, and a third gave up and/or returned to active homosexuality."[44] Among the Bible Belt gays I interviewed who had participated in ex-gay programs, Brandy speculated that perhaps 20% of the people she knew from ex-gay ministries were in heterosexual relationships. Helen, mentioned earlier, felt the change rate was zero. She said, "I think there are some who are just choosing to be celibate, but a true conversion doesn't exist. I've never seen it and I don't believe that it's possible personally." Donald could only think of one person he knew in a heterosexual relationship, and believed less than 1% of those in ex-gay programs had changed.

There is a thriving community of individuals who have participated at one point in their lives in ex-gay ministries, but who have come to believe change is impossible. Organizations such as Truth Wins Out, founded by the former Human Rights Campaign spokesperson Wayne Besen, and the website Beyond Ex-Gay an "online community for those who have survived ex-gay experiences"[45] provide resources for "survivors" of ex-gay programs, and information about the ex-gay movement. Since 2007 Beyond Ex-Gay and the activist group Soulforce, founded by Mel White, have sponsored a yearly conference for people formerly involved in ex-gay ministries. On their website, Beyond Ex-Gay described the value of such a venue, *"The ex-gay experience is unique in many ways. No one understands it better than those of us who have been through it. Creating a communal space for ex-gay survivors to tell their stories allows us to share what led us into an ex-gay lifestyle and the ways we have been able to recover from it."*[46] At the 2007 ex-gay survivors conference held in Irvine, California, former ex-gay leaders Michael Bussee, cofounder of Exodus; Darlene Bogle, former Exodus ministry leader; and Jeremy Marks, former Exodus International leader each publicly apologized for the role he or she had played in ex-gay ministries. All three also clearly stated that they felt they had never seen evidence that *any* participant changed her or his sexual orientation in Exodus. However, Bussee, like Derek and Brandy, does credit Exodus for having some positive impact on his life and the lives of others:[47]

> I need to say at this point that some of us had positive, life-changing experiences attending our Bible Studies and support groups. Many experienced God's love and the welcoming fellowship of others who knew the struggle. There were some real changes but not one of the hundreds of people we counseled ever became straight. Instead, many of our clients began to fall apart, sinking deeper into patterns of guilt, anxiety and self-loathing. Why weren't they changing? The answers from church leaders made the pain even deeper. "Well, you might not be a real Christian. You don't have enough faith. You're not praying and reading the Bible enough. Maybe you have a demon." The message always seemed to be, "you're not enough."[48]

Bussee continued, "No one was really becoming ex-gay. Who were we fooling anyway?" Jeremy Marks came to the same conclusion as Bussee:

> During the time I became president of Exodus International Europe however, I felt increasingly unhappy at what I saw as being the dishonesty of my fellow Exodus ministries. No one seemed willing to look at the issue of our failure to fulfill the promise of Eden that we claimed to believe was possible. Nor was anyone willing to consider that there might be an alternative view.

Bogle explained that when Dez, her partner, was dying of breast cancer, she urged Bogle to come forward and "become a voice once again for the gay and lesbian community":[49]

Before I met Dez, I considered myself ex-gay because I had ceased sexual activity. I spent my time promoting change in others. When these changes did not occur, the people in my care frequently asked how long it would take for their desires to change. I lied and encouraged them to just keep praying and reading their Bible. When they asked how long it took me, I avoided the question. My heart was in the right place, but my message was not.

Bogle began to cry as she apologized for "teaching a lie":

I apologize to those individuals and families who believed that my message of change was necessary to be acceptable to God. In recent years I have seen the resulting damage from rejection, shame and conditional love. I apologize for my part in presenting a God of conditional love, and ask forgiveness for the message of broken truth that I spoke on behalf of Exodus.

I am, unsurprisingly, more inclined to trust the estimates of "change" from former and current ex-gay leaders since these are the people who have had the most contact with participants, but for the purposes of this analysis I also consider the data from Exodus. Exodus data finds that 50–66% (and I am inclined to believe it is much higher) of ex-gay participants fail to achieve the psychological and spiritual relief of "change" that they believe is necessary to render them worthy to God. What are the consequences for those who repeatedly try and are still unable to change their sexual orientations?

The Consequences of Ex-Gay Ministries: "We Were Hurting People"

Former ex-gay leaders Bussee, Marks, and Bogle each came to the conclusion that the Exodus project of change was ineffective and damaging to participants. At the ex-gay survivors' conference, they used strong language to describe the negative consequences of Exodus in the lives of the people to whom they had ministered including words such as "guilt," "anxiety," "shame," and "self-loathing." Marks called Exodus a "spiritually and emotionally corrosive ministry style." Bussee explained that the cycle of failure and repentance caused some Exodus participants to "become very self-destructive":

One young man in our program got very drunk and deliberately drove his car into a tree. Another fellow leader of the ex-gay movement told me that he had left Exodus and was now going to straight bars looking for guys to beat him up. He explained that the beatings made him feel less guilty. He was atoning for his sin. One of my most dedicated clients, Mark, took a razor blade to his genitals, slashed himself repeatedly and then poured drain cleaner on the wounds because after months of celibacy, he had a fall. In the midst of all this, my own faith in the Exodus movement was crumbling.

Jeremy Marks addressed not only the negative consequences of ex-gay ministries on individuals but also his "collusion" with an oppressive system:

I'd like to take this opportunity first to make a personal apology, to say how sorry I am and ask forgiveness of all gay, lesbian, bisexual and transgendered people who might be listening to this for my part in colluding with the religious Right of the Western world. Though at the time we did not see it this way, our collusion involved setting up and maintaining an oppressive anti-gay, and I must also say, equally anti-Christian view of homosexuality, one that profoundly dishonors Jesus Christ and betrays the gospel.

The Bible Belt gays I interviewed had mixed feelings about their time spent in ex-gay programs. Derek, for example, felt that Crossover had been beneficial to his coming-out process, and Brandy enjoyed the travel and socializing that Exodus and Crossover facilitated. In contrast, Tonya, who is white, 30, and from Southern Kentucky, joined a nondenominational Christian organization as a first-year student at a large university and later regretted her time spent trying to change her sexual orientation while involved in the organization. This Intervarsity group was not officially an ex-gay group, but it drew upon ex-gay literature and ideology to peer-mentor student Christians on their relationships with God. Tonya explained:

I remember that summer thinking to myself, "I could go two different ways." I could go with the religious crowd, or I could come out. I was really excited about the coming-out process, but when I got to school, there weren't any advertisements. I was sort of lost. It's a huge school, especially for someone who is from a little small town and not knowing a whole lot of people, and not knowing anybody there. There are a whole lot more religious groups than there are gay groups on campus. So I get up there, and of course, who gets to me first, the religious groups. They seemed really nice, they seemed really gracious and I clicked with them. I liked them and stuff. The part of me that wanted to come out of the closet sort of got suppressed for about 3 or 4 years.

After two years of Intervarsity meetings, Tonya told one of the staff members that she was "struggling with homosexuality." This woman responded, surprisingly, that everyone, even she herself, has same-sex fantasies, and they developed an accountability plan:

> So, anyhow, I was accountable to her. Basically, if I had times when I was really struggling with my thought process, and I couldn't get the fantasies out, I was supposed to call her and we'd pray and yada, yada yada. Well, it never worked because you can't pray it away. You can't wish it away. You can't do anything. You can't reprogram yourself. You are who you are, you know, and that took a long time for me to realize that but it did eventually happen.

They met once every couple of weeks to explore how Tonya was doing in her walk with Jesus:

> I'd usually fib, because if I called her every time I thought someone was hot, or I was struggling with fantasies, well, I'd be calling her 24/7. So, that's just me, and I'm sorry. It's kind of like a kid, under the age of 21, seeing everyone else being able to drink and not being allowed to. Well, if you think you're not allowed to, what are you going to do? You're going to want to do it even more. So, it didn't help me at all.

Tonya felt that her involvement with Intervarsity had had a negative impact on her personality. She said, "all I did for that time was feel shame and guilt, and cried myself to sleep. It did me no good at all." Talking with Tonya about the mechanics of accountability, specifically that she and other group members were taken to task by untrained peers, it sounded as if there were something psychologically disturbing and inappropriate, something *Lord of the Flies*-esque about the process, in addition to the homophobic messages gay students received. Tonya elaborated:

> It's cultish in a way. I remember realizing that after I came out. I feel completely brainwashed by the time that I was in there. I still feel that I am having to clean my head out and get out all those negative thoughts, all of the junk that my brain sort of got filled with. Some of the things that I was taught, the way that they make you think, or have you think about things really damages your psyche. It preys on people with low self-esteem, which I had. It drags you down.

Tonya explained that they did not publicly criticize anyone. She distinguished between the public meetings that she enjoyed, and the private sessions in which she felt pressured to confess. "The ugly part of it was when you met one-on-one with someone, or in your Bible study, which I also led. You would have these relationships with people where you felt comfortable and then you basically felt like you had to confess all this stuff to all these people and then you felt like crap." Tonya regrets the time she spent with Intervarsity:

> I realize now how absolutely stupid and foolish I was. I really wish I had gone ahead and came out. I would be much, much farther along now, as far as healing and things. Part of the problem is, I was all into the Christian stuff. Then I came out, and the two can't possibly go together. We've always been taught that, right? Religion and homosexuality. The two can't possibly go together.

Tonya concluded, "it caused a whole lot more stress that I didn't need in my life." Jennifer, who is white, 39, and also from Southern Kentucky, said of her involvement with ex-gay ministries, "The Exodus thing, I was just trying to find some way to feel better inside. I think it goes back to where I always thought I would never be good enough to go to heaven."

"Look at How I Failed God"

Conservative Christians who participate in ex-gay programs highly value their Christian identity, so much so that they seek others' support to help pray the gay away. For these people, and for many people in the Bible Belt, Christian is a "master status," an identity so important that it overshadows others.[50] Adopting this master status involves participating in the following "definition of reality":[51] there is only one truth that can be found in a literal, commonsense reading of the Bible that condemns homosexuality. Such a belief not only justifies unequal treatment of gay people, as the sociologist Michael Schwalbe argues, it arrests the imagination in such a way that "makes inequality appear natural and inevitable."[52] To illustrate, conservative Christians are discouraged from imagining healthy same-sex relationships as a rewarding and functional dimension of one's daily lived experiences, and they certainly do not support any institutional recognition (i.e., domestic partner benefits) for same-sex couples. This religious-based political opposition to same-sex relationships hurts all the same-sex couples in the region.

Bible Belt gays live in areas with a high concentration of conservative Christians. Most of the women and men I interviewed either grew up in families that openly espoused a conservative Christian perspective on homosexuality, and/or heard this perspective aired in churches, workplaces, and schools. Exodus largely serves the needs of Christian conservatives as Burack and Josephson observed:

> There is a tacit, and sometimes explicit, understanding in the ex-gay movement that the movement primarily serves those reared in conservative Christian families. Hence the theme of compassion is primarily turned inward toward members of the Christian community, both same-sex-attracted people and their families and congregations.[53]

For the heterosexual conservative Christian who believes homosexual behavior is a sin, but wants to understand and support loved ones who say they are gay, ex-gay materials provide much information. Many local pastors can provide the titles, and sometimes books, featuring ex-gay arguments to concerned parishioners. Nondenominational mega churches, like Vision, have support groups devoted to conversion. Ex-gay books, DVDs, research, and pamphlets are easily available for online purchase. Much of the literature is even given away for free. Although I did not ask this of the women and men I interviewed, three people gave me ex-gay literature that they had received from their parents.

Further, on a personal level, the ex-gay message that homosexual relationships offend God and inevitably cause pain is particularly persuasive to those raised in conservative Christian churches, like Donald and Joshua. Joshua (see chap. 3) explained that his mother read a great deal of ex-gay literature after Joshua came out. He believes the arguments made in ex-gay materials strengthened her resolve that she must not accept Joshua's homosexuality because he was choosing it and thus deliberately offending God. Joshua charged ex-gay resources with deepening his familial estrangement. Donald explained that he returned to ex-gay ministries for support when a homosexual relationship ended, and considered the failure of a homosexual relationship proof of the ex-gay position—that such relationships are unsanctified. Donald shared that he felt the most damaging part of his time spent in ex-gay ministries was that "it triggered periods of depression." He continued:

> Because I'm feeling all this conflict, and I feel all this anger and the anger will be turned inward and produce depression. Also I think I could have been on the verge of suicide a few times because of feeling so frustrated that I didn't have enough faith or I wasn't really a Christian because . . . you know, fifteen years and I'm still gay. Look at how I failed God.

Thus, if Exodus primarily serves conservative Christians, Bible Belt residents are potentially disproportionately represented among those influenced by the ex-gay message that "change is possible."

Like Burack and Josephson, I observed that ex-gay ministries employed "a combination of theological conviction, emotional appeal, and evidence-based arguments" to persuade participants that the ex-gay path was the best way to partner with God.[54] The one message I never heard, not at any Exodus event or in the literature, was that the individual struggling to rid herself of homosexuality was "bad," "abominable," or "damned." Such language was reserved for those who chose to live an openly gay lifestyle. Compassion was extended to those struggling to free themselves from homosexuality. This is likely the primary reason Exodus continues to exist at all. The recent merger of Focus on the Family's "Love Won Out" conferences with Exodus International (due to "financial challenges") suggests that ex-gay ministries, particularly large conference-style events, do not break even on the costs.[55] Coupling financial issues with the stigma of homosexuality, it's possible to imagine conservative Christian organizations cutting ex-gay ministries. As Michael Bussee said, "Perhaps one day groups like Exodus will go out of business and people will no longer feel that they must deny who they really are to attempt to become what they are really not."

6

"Prepare to Believe"

The Creation Museum

Be prepared to experience history in a completely unprecedented way. The state-of-the-art 70,000 square foot museum brings the pages of the Bible to life, casting its characters and animals in dynamic form and placing them in familiar settings. Adam and Eve live in the Garden of Eden. Children play and dinosaurs roam near Eden's Rivers. The serpent coils cunningly in the Tree of the Knowledge of Good and Evil. Majestic murals, great masterpieces brimming with pulsating colors and details, provide a backdrop for many of the settings.
—Creation Museum website description[1]

In 2007 with much media fanfare, the Creation Museum, a $27 million facility founded by the group Answers in Genesis, opened in Petersburg, Kentucky, about 100 miles from Thomasville. The primary purpose of the Creation Museum is to educate visitors in "young earth creationism," a branch of intelligent design theory that argues that the universe is less than 10,000 years old. Since its opening, the Creation Museum has had over one million visitors, and there are plans underway to build an Ark theme park in a neighboring county. Answers in Genesis describes itself as "a nondenominational parachurch ministry,"[2] and the Creation Museum markets itself to attract visitors from a variety of faith backgrounds. Those who espouse creationism adhere to a literal interpretation of biblical events in the book of Genesis. While Answers in Genesis has no official position on premillenialism (one of the doctrinal elements that distinguish fundamentalists from charismatics), the "Statement of Faith"[3] (available on the group's website that employees of the Creation Museum are required to read and support), as well as the museum displays and materials, reflect the fundamentalist perspective that

in the Bible God revealed everything necessary to live a good, pure, sanctified life.

Seeking to better understand the religious climate of the Bible Belt, the
experiences the people I interviewed described, and in particular, the thought
processes undergirding the actions of some conservative Christians, I visited
the facility three times in an 18-month period: June 2008, November 2009,
and December 2009. In June 2008, during the annual National Women's
Studies Association Meetings held in Cincinnati, Ohio, I toured the facility
with three sociology colleagues. In November 2009, I took 14 students from
an undergraduate upper-level class on a field trip to the museum. And in
December 2009, I brought my oldest friend, Charles, also a Bible Belt gay, to
the museum. During these visits, I collected materials (i.e., pamphlets, programs, tickets, and flyers), made notes, took photographs, examined the displays, attended lectures and video presentations, and discussed the museum
experience with all of the individuals who joined me in this ethnographic
research.[4] A slice of Bible Belt culture, the Creation Museum has invited and
received much media attention. In this way, it has had not only regional but
a national and international impact as well. A conservative Christian belief
in creationism is compatible with homophobia, and the Bible Belt panopticon is especially pronounced in the Creation Museum. This chapter explores
fundamentalist ideology through the lens of the Creation Museum. Approximately one-third of the Bible Belt gays I interviewed, like Misty and Joshua,
came from fundamentalist families and, overall, about three-quarters of
interview subjects grew up in conservative Christian families. Unpacking
fundamentalist thought sheds light on their experiences.[5]

A Walk through the Creation Museum

Petersburg, Kentucky is a few miles west of the Cincinnati-Northern Kentucky International Airport, located across the Ohio River in Florence,
Kentucky. In those few miles, the landscape changes abruptly from urban
sprawl and airport hotels to rural Kentucky. Answers in Genesis deliberately chose this location to be close to a major airport and within a day's
drive of two-thirds of Americans, defined as about 650 miles. The Creation Museum is well marked with billboards and easy-to-read highway
signs which remind drivers when they should exit and where they should
turn. Arriving, the visitor enters a roomy parking lot and is directed by
a uniformed official to a specific area of the lot. Church buses and vans
announce their affiliations and, when I was there, close to 30% of the vehicles sported some kind of Christian signage—license plate holders, bumper

stickers, even entire Bible verses.[6] On the front door, the museum guest reads a warning that visitors engaging in disruptive behavior may be dismissed from the museum. There is a $21.95 entry fee, with an additional $7 to see the Stargazer's Planetarium Created Cosmos show. The motto "Prepare to Believe" is plastered throughout the grounds. The ticket price includes access to the museum displays, multimedia presentations, a petting zoo, and rotating live lectures.

The main exhibit, a labyrinth panorama of Genesis stories (the Creation, Adam and Eve, the Fall, Noah's Ark, the Tower of Babel) winds through two floors. As a first-time visitor, I was a little overwhelmed by the amount of information offered on placards and video presentations sprinkled throughout, and I was struck by how lifelike the human and animal figures seemed. For example, an animatronic representation of Methuselah moves and speaks, sounding uncannily like Yoda from the *Star Wars* movies. In a sea of information, the facility repeats several key points: the universe is only 10,000 years old; Adam's sin caused the Fall; God judged Adam's race to be so wicked that God flooded the earth; the flood caused the dinosaur extinction; fossil records and natural selection is supported biblically and scientifically; and finally, Jesus came to save us from our sin. The visitor is instructed to simultaneously question secular scientific findings—for example, the phrase "millions and millions of years" is repeatedly discounted in multiple displays—and to accept without question God's word. In fact, the message is clear that questioning God's word is a sin, one for which there is much evidence of God's wrath. This point of view is consistent with the conservative Christian perspective that homosexuality is a sin, and the godliness of heterosexuality unquestioned. If one "chooses" homosexuality, that person is a sinner and there will be a price to pay.

At the multimedia presentation, "Men in White," two hip 30-something white male angels dressed in white T-shirts, pants, and wings, mock biology teachers while using scientific language to argue for young earth creationism. Teachers are shown to be stupid, foolish, inept, and out of touch; school itself is described as a close-minded place which forbids discussion of God's role in the universe. Outside, the grounds include a petting zoo. Promotional materials encourage guests to visit the zonkey and zorse—a cross between a zebra and donkey and a zebra and a horse. Answers in Genesis argue that the zonkey and zorse are evidence of the rapid speciation that occurred after the flood. A secular scientist would call such animals zebra hybrids, or zebroids, the offspring of a zebra with another equine species. After touring the exhibits, I bought a sandwich and a cup of soup from Noah's Café, and perused the souvenirs available at the Dragon Hall Bookstore.[7]

The Importance of Genesis

The account of origins presented in Genesis is a simple but factual presentation of actual events and therefore provides a reliable
framework for scientific research into the question of the origin
and history of life, mankind, the earth and the universe.
—Answers in Genesis "Statement of Faith," sec. 2, no. 3

The religion scholar Nancy Tatom Ammerman observed that the "Fundamentalist spirit is . . . a crusading one. They battle against their own imper-
fections, and they engage in verbal campaigns against evil wherever it may
be found,"[8] and that "compromise and accommodation are among the most
dreaded words in the Fundamentalist vocabulary."[9] Ken Ham, founder of
the Creation Museum and primary spokesperson for Answers in Genesis,
is such an uncompromising crusader. In his DVD recording "The Collapse
of Christian America," Ham explained that he perceives his life work is to
support Christian beliefs in a literal interpretation of the first book of the
Bible: Genesis. Ham, a builder and leader of creationist organizations for
more than 30 years, warned his audience that those Christian denominations
which are vague on or omit teaching the Old Testament Bible, especially the
book of Genesis, cause young people to leave the faith. Ham explained that
young people have questions about the stories of Genesis—about how God
made the universe, how Noah survived the flood, how to account for the
dinosaurs—and when Christian leaders either cannot or do not answer these
questions, the seeds of doubt are sown. For Ham, the subject of creation/
evolution is foundational to biblical authority and the most important issue
facing Christians. Creationists, like Ham, perceive biological evolution as the
root cause of secular immorality and, consequently, responsible for a host of
social problems such as abortion, sexual promiscuity, socialism, terrorism,
crime, pornography, relativism, drug use, divorce, and homosexuality.[10] Ham
passionately argues that to "give up" Genesis weakens the "sword of righteousness," the Bible itself, and ultimately threatens the Christian worldview.
      Fundamentalists want and expect order, including knowing what is right
and what is wrong so that they can best follow God's plan. They need clear-
cut answers to questions of faith, of conduct, and of God's will. Ham specifically and repeatedly states that the goal of Answers in Genesis is to answer
every scriptural question a person has applying a literal interpretation to
history and the natural world, including questions such as: How did all the
animals fit on the Ark? Where did Cain get his wife? Where did the "races"

come from? How did the animals repopulate the earth after the flood? The Creation Museum attempts to answer these questions. In this way, it supports the fundamentalist imperative that Ammerman observed in her study of "Bible believers," who found that "a believer must 'be always ready to give an answer.'"[11] Concerning questions about homosexuality, fundamentalists might quote from Leviticus 18:22: "You shall not lie with a male as those who lie with a female; it is an abomination." Contemplating the historical context of this scripture or possible errors in its translation are irrelevant and blasphemous to a fundamentalist because the Bible is to be read ahistorically as absolutely and eternally infallible.[12]

Unfamiliar with the museum and its mission, my good friend Charles spontaneously commented when walking through the reproduction of the Ark, "This was where it all fell apart for me as a child." Raised in a conservative Christian church in southern Ohio, he explained that he started questioning the plausibility of the Genesis stories as a young child. After we finished our walk-through, Charles noted, "This place is trying to answer all the questions I had as a child." He wondered how it might have affected him as a small child had the facility existed 30 years ago and his parents had taken him. The Creation Museum is family-friendly and invites children and young adults. On each of the three times I visited, I estimate 30–40% of the guests were under 18, and most of those were young children. During our class field trip Hank, who is African American and heterosexual, shared that he had overheard a young boy ask his mother a question about one of the displays. Hank explained that the mother then sharply drew the child's attention to a placard right in front of them, which equated questioning with sin. The mother said to the child, "Look, this is what happens when you question, you go to hell."

Where Did Cain Get His Wife?

Why should the Bible be factual? For fundamentalists, the belief that the events of the Bible actually took place is essential to their worldview. To question the veracity of these events is to question God's existence. They also fear nuanced readings of the Bible that allow multiple meanings. For example, during a public talk in Lexington, Kentucky, Bishop Gene Robinson quoted the following scripture from John 16:13, "But when he, the Spirit of truth, comes, he will guide you into all truth. He will not speak on his own; he will speak only what he hears, and he will tell you what is yet to come."[13] Robinson views this verse as supportive of homosexuality because among the truths the Holy Spirit has yet to reveal may include new insights about human sexuality. To any fundamentalist, in addition to being suspicious of the source of the interpretation, Bishop Robinson's reading of this passage contains too much gray area. It does not clearly distinguish right from wrong and thus allows too much wiggle room for an innately flawed human to sin. A fundamentalist might even concede that Bishop Robinson means well and pray for his salvation, while characterizing his interpretation of scripture as dangerous and seductive. Answers in Genesis oppose such nuanced readings of the Bible and argue that events recorded in Genesis are historically and scientifically factual. Yet, given the amount of scientific information now available about the planet, animals, and human bodies, actually making these claims becomes tricky.

One question that the Creation Museum devotes much time to is where Cain found a wife, i.e., how did the entire human race emerge from two people: Adam and Eve? If Genesis is factual, the children of Adam and Eve must have reproduced with one another, hence Cain married his sister. The explanation that Cain married his sister naturally causes most to wonder about the genetic consequences of incest so Answers in Genesis addresses this question directly. According to a pamphlet I bought at the museum gift shop describing this, Cain and his family escaped genetic deformities related to incestuous reproduction because:

> Cain was in the first generation of children ever born. He (as well as his brothers and sisters) would have received virtually no imperfect genes from Adam and Eve, since the effects of sin and the Curse would have been minimal to start with. In that situation, brother and sister could have married (provided it was one man for one woman, which is what marriage is all about—Matt. 19:4–6) without any potential to produce deformed offspring.

The pamphlet continues:

> By the time of Moses (about 2,500 years later), degenerative mistakes would have accumulated to such an extent in the human race that it would have been necessary for God to bring in the laws forbidding brother-sister (and close relative) marriage (Lev. 18–20).

Note how Answers in Genesis uses scientific knowledge and language like "imperfect genes" and "degenerative mistakes" to explain how Cain married his sister, who is unnamed. From a creationist standpoint, the logic follows that the closer the relationship to Adam and Eve, the closer to God were the descendants, and thus, the more "perfect" they were. The Creation Museum is at pains to provide such answers and thus avoid blatant inconsistencies in their presentation of readily available "facts."

Answers in Genesis's scientific rendering of events in Genesis, like their argument for Cain marrying his sister, is not plausible to outsiders but is acceptable to some conservative Christians. For those new to fundamentalist theology, adopting a young-earth creationist framework of the universe is challenging. However, as Ammerman notes, when "converts devote more and more time and energy to religious activities and adopt Fundamentalists as their primary reference group, even ideas that are difficult to apprehend become plausible."[14] Ammerman found that the more time and energy a new convert invests in a fundamentalist community, the more likely that person is to take the leaps of faith necessary to embrace previously far-fetched explanations of the physical and social world. Interestingly, this finding does not hold true for fundamentalists struggling with same-sex attractions, as chapter 5 illustrates. The majority of participants in ex-gay ministries do not find that their same-sex desires diminish through intense involvement in conservative Christian communities nor through the elimination of their relationships with gay people.

Our Class Field Trip

The information that you provided to us regarding your group, purpose of your visit, and all other information is considered to be factual. In the event that this information is not true and correct, we reserve the right to cancel the visit at any time or to request that you leave the property.
—Confirmation notice, the Creation Museum

In the fall of 2009 I proposed the idea of a class field trip to the Creation Museum in an upper-level course on religion and inequality; the enrolled students responded enthusiastically. I secured funding from my department to cover costs. All of the students participated even though it was not a required class event. In addition to my class of 12 students, two members of our gay-straight alliance, Terry and her partner, Kelly, a lesbian couple, joined us. The group included ten women—five of whom identified as lesbian—and five men. Fourteen of the group were white and one was African American. Six of the group were raised in conservative Christian homes, two did not grow up with any religion, and the remainder came from a mix of

mainstream religious backgrounds. None of the students identified as fundamentalist, and all are politically progressive. The Creation Museum appears
to attract two kinds of visitors: (1) Bible believers who can go to a place that
both affirms their faith and entertains in a Disneylike fashion, and (2) skep-
tics and curiosity seekers. Our group fell into the latter category.

The students had strong, mostly negative reactions to the facility, which
surprised me. While my previous visit to the Creation Museum had been
taxing, I did not assume such would be the case for the students. Indeed, I
had an unexamined expectation that for a number of reasons—age, sexual
orientation, scholarly intent—that they would be less drained by it than I
had been. After all, this was a class field trip for them and, by definition, at
least a little fun, not a five-year research project. Instead, all of the students
were more distressed and uncomfortable than I had expected. For example,
Melinda, who is white, heterosexual, and was raised Pentecostal, stated:

> I was very angry from the moment I got there. I didn't understand why
> I had such a strong response until I got home and realized that, while at
> the museum, I felt just like I did as a little girl and a young women when
> my parents forced me to attend church where they could shove what they
> believed down my throat. I guess I still have some suppressed issues with
> all of this, since I STILL can't talk to my parents or anyone in my family for
> that matter about what I truly believe. Friday I felt like a closeted whatever
> I am more strongly than I have in years, and that was hard to deal with.

Student reactions to the museum included feeling paranoid, angry, glared
at, unwelcomed, and generally tense.

The mood in the van on the two-hour ride to the facility was sleepy,
yet festive. The students were excited to take a trip and interested in the
museum. Although we had spent much of the semester analyzing manifestations of Christian fundamentalist and conservative Christian thought, for
some students these ideas remained an academic abstraction and not a real
experience. For example, one student, Karen, who is heterosexual and white,
had a disturbing encounter at the facility; she wrote: "I went in there with
an open mind. I had thought maybe I will see something or learn something I agree with or believe. Wow was I mistaken." Walking up to collect
our tickets, everyone was upbeat and a little nervous. I was hoping that no
one would get us kicked out, and was completely preoccupied by how I was
going to pay the balance on our tickets. My credit card had a Human Rights
Campaign (a gay rights organization) symbol on it so I was afraid to use it
and perhaps "out" us to the museum staff as a gay group of nonbelievers

(which we were not), and I had an irrational fear that my debit card could potentially be overcharged. One of the students had brought her mother and sister and, with everyone milling about, I counted, and re-counted the group, each time coming up with a different number. Finally, I settled on a number, handed over my card, and we were herded in to get a group photo against a green screen.

The photo was optional, and we could have declined. The students all looked to me for direction, and since I am generally a fan of group photos and did not want to stand out as uncooperative, I suggested that those who wanted to could participate in a group picture. All the students complied. Museum personnel instructed us to stand on footprints staggered in two lines. Several students later commented that they felt the museum staff had been rude during the photo, swiftly shoving us into place. One student in particular, Joanna, who is a white lesbian and is usually sweet natured, was visibly flustered by the staff instructing us where to stand. She exchanged tense words with the employee closest to her. I observed that the staff was rushed and a bit brusque during our photo. At the time, I attributed this to an institutional pressure to move groups through quickly so as to maximize the number of visitors purchasing photos. Later, I reflected that these brusque attitudes heightened our feelings of disorientation: we perceived our own response time as slower than it actually was based on the impression we received from the museum employees (all older white women and men) that we were moving too slowly and did not know what we were doing. While no one was forced into being photographed, I think some students did so because it was easier to conform than not, a fact that suggests we were all already feeling the effects of the Bible Belt panopticon. Later, I bought two copies of our photo, one with a Noah's Ark background and the other a dinosaur panorama. In the photo, most students are smiling with expressions of cheerful trepidation.

Compulsory Christianity in the Bible Belt Panopticon

I suppose overall the biggest thing that I took away from the
museum is that regardless of how much I disagree with someone, I
would NEVER want anyone to feel around me the way I felt there.
—Terry, white, lesbian

As Michel Foucault theorized, when individuals imagine they are constantly under surveillance, they learn to regulate their own behavior to conform to the expectations of a higher authority.[15] In chapter 1 I extended Foucaults's analysis within Bible Belt Christianity by demonstrating how visible markers of Christianity in the region's physical landscape along with social norms that one comply with and defer to prevailing Christian attitudes, or what I call compulsory Christianity, function as a Bible Belt panopticon. In the Creation Museum, these effects were not only present but exaggeratedly so. This is not surprising. Although most Bible Belt residents feel a pressure to conform to customary Christian attitudes, there is some range within which an individual might situate herself. This is not the case in the Creation Museum. The facility makes it extremely clear that there is only *one* proper belief system, and anyone who does not ascribe to it is an outsider destined for hell.

After the photo we all split up to experience the facility at our own pace, in small groups or as individuals. Carl, who is white and heterosexual, described his observations of the exhibits:

> Everything about the museum screamed the opposite of what it should. Rather than free to roam about looking at the exhibits, and free to come up with your own opinion, you are forced through narrow and disturbing hallways full of signs of the coming end-times. You are told what message to take and what to believe. It's hardly a museum at all, and more like a shock lesson in young-earth creationism.

I had just sat down on a bench outside of Noah's Café for a moment to rest and collect my thoughts when Karen approached me, visibly agitated. She had just had an upsetting encounter. Karen shoved her bag at me saying, "Dr. Barton, I took everything out of my bag before I came in here, even ibuprofen." She explained that she had been targeted by security and someone had made a rude comment to her. Karen later explained:

> Hank and I started our walk through together, but not even five minutes into it we noticed that we were being glared at by everyone because I am a small blond white girl and Hank is a good looking black man, and for whatever reason it seemed as though the two of us couldn't believe the same thing everyone else in the building did. So Hank and I parted ways and decided to finish the walk through alone. While I was coming up on the Noah's Ark part of the story the rent-a-cop and his pet decided to walk around me twice, making it a point for me to know that I looked out of place which made me uncomfortable even more.[16] As soon as the pair walked away from me, a man with his two kids walked up to me and said, "The reason he did that is because of the way you're

dressed. We know you're not religious, you just don't fit in." I was wearing a pair of leggings and a tan long sleeve shirt that came down well past my behind. I saw nothing about the way I dressed to be out of the ordinary but I guess it was. After that honestly I couldn't have got out of there fast enough.

Karen was one of two students raised without any religious education and, perhaps partially because of this, approached the Creation Museum with the fewest preconceived notions of any student in the class. Several times during the semester Karen had expressed concern with our critical analysis of Christian fundamentalism, worried we weren't giving them a fair hearing. This changed after her visit to the Creation Museum. She concluded, "I am glad I got to go on this trip and see what such a large number of people believe, but it has done nothing but confuse me and honestly scare me a bit. The museum has really pushed me away from religion." The response Karen had to her visit to the Creation Museum—the security guard's physical intimidation coupled with verbal sanctioning from a museum visitor, "we know you're not religious, you just don't fit it"—mirrors the responses of Bible Belt gays to repeated denunciations of homosexuality in Bible Belt Christianity.

After calming Karen down, I hunted for the rest of the class. Most of the students had finished looking at the exhibits and were getting some lunch in Noah's Cafe before the planetarium show. Everyone seemed a little tense, but it wasn't until later that I learned specifics of the students' impressions and encounters. For example, Kelly, who is a white lesbian, felt out of place immediately and, later, very angry. She explained:

This museum and the people in it treated us differently from the time of our arrival, in my opinion. Maybe I was being hypersensitive for fear that I would be the one to get our whole group kicked out of the place, but I was honestly afraid for my safety at times just being in that place. Before we even set foot inside the museum, I noticed the signs on the door [loosely from memory]: "We reserve the right to refuse service or to ask someone to leave if they have inappropriate behavior, use inappropriate language, wear attire containing inappropriate messages, while also maintaining the right to decide at any other time if someone should be forced to leave the premises." Such bullshit—they should just write out what exactly they mean by all that: If you don't agree with what we have to say here, and it is expressed in a way that we or other patrons hear, see, or even think they see . . . we can kick your evil ass out of here.

Museum signage alerts guests that improper actions and/or statements are grounds for dismissal from the facility. In other words, dissenting thoughts and action are evidence of sin that might have otherworldly (that is, keeping one out of heaven) and material (that is, barring entrance to the museum) consequences. None of those who accompanied me to the Creation Museum believed that young-earth creationism was credible. At the same time, no one felt comfortable discussing their concerns or confusion about creationism with any museum staff. The environment did not encourage a free exchange of ideas among people with differing perspectives. Instead, the students felt silenced, intimidated, and paranoid that they would be "found out." James describes:

> I actually felt like a character in a futuristic police state, where you feel as if you are constantly being watched, followed, and listened to. I felt that if not careful, I was going to be called out for not being "one of them." The security and dogs didn't help this feeling either.[17]

Caroline, who is white, heterosexual, and raised Old Regular Baptist, explained, "I did feel like we got a lot of glares, especially by the security guards. Even when I smiled they looked at me like I was something horrible. I was uncomfortable." Alexandra, also white and heterosexual, shared that her paranoia increased after an exchange with a museum employee in the basement coffee shop:

> We went to the basement to get some coffee when the weirdest thing happened to us. Now, me, Joanna, Beth, and Katherine do not have any sort of heavy Eastern Kentucky accent, but the man making our coffee asked, "Are you all with the Morehead State group?" I asked him how he knew this and all he said was, "I was speaking with a girl from your group earlier today." None of us had Morehead gear on. Weren't there a few different schools there that day and other visitors? I was so creeped out that I wanted to leave.

It emerged that Melinda had been directly queried about why she was at the museum by a staff member, probably the one who asked Alexandra if she was with the Morehead group. Melinda wrote:

> Well, I have to say that I actually got to use our response to the question "why are you here?" When I was getting lunch in Noah's Cafe, the cashier asked me what group I was with and why I was there. When I told him I

was with Morehead State University, where I was taking a class on religion, and we were curious about the Creation Museum, he said, "Well just remember that science and religion can go together, don't forget that that's very important." However, he seemed less upset that I was a college student studying the Creation Museum and more upset with the fact that James wasn't paying for my lunch!

Although most of the class experienced this panoptic effect, the lesbian couples (Beth and Joanna, and Terry and Kelly) by far expressed the most discomfort with feeling "visible." Beth responded:

For most of the individuals in our group, our class's visit to Ken Ham's fundamentalist empire, the Creation Museum, was an odd experience to say the least. Collectively, we felt a general sense of discomfort while on the museum grounds. Some of us reported feeling constantly ridiculed or stared at. Those of us who are gay, myself included, felt especially uncomfortable in the environment. We sensed eyes bearing holes into our skulls the entire duration of our visit. Joanna and I released simultaneous sighs of relief—after being painfully aware of our homosexuality for hours in a way we are usually not. Terry and Kelly expressed a similar experience of alertness—and shared in our paranoia about touching one another at all, much less inappropriately.

Joanna concurred:

We left, among other reasons, because I couldn't handle any more glares, stares, my own paranoia filling me up and lies in general. I was surprised that Ken Ham was there too, but was not eager to see him since I have heard that he broke lots of environmental laws just erecting this museum. I don't know if I could have kept my mouth closed, big surprise . . . . I was surprised that the guy at the coffee shop knew that the few of us who were together were from the Morehead group. This made us all even more paranoid. How did he know? He never gave us a straight answer when we queried him. All and all, this was not a pleasant experience. It was prettier than I had imagined though. There were times I felt woozy and dizzy. I felt like we had been there forever and I had no concept of time, like I was lost in a maze.

Both couples were careful not to touch one another while they were in the facility. Kelly said:

The entire time we were there, I kept pushing Terry away from me. No matter how near or far she was from me, it always felt like she was too close for comfort. I know I was just being paranoid, but I couldn't shake the feeling that people could look at us and somehow automatically see that we were more than just two girls who were friends.

Terry noted this as well:

I'm not used to feeling deceptive, or not myself. Kelly and I were both very aware that people were possibly looking at us—which certainly fueled some paranoia. She didn't even want to really be seen standing closer than an arm's length apart (which I kept forgetting) until we entered the "State of the Nation" address which included several disappointing remarks re: gay marriage and homosexuality. To be a lesbian sitting in the middle of a group of people who scoffed, agreed and were very passionate about their anti-gay beliefs . . . it REALLY impacted me to the negative. In fact, I ended up being angry and scared to even be there.

I was with Terry and Kelly much of the time and observed this personally. Kelly looked tense and avoided sitting close to Terry. At the same time, Kelly did sit next to and touch me. Meanwhile, although Joanna and Beth kept a distance from one another, they touched and hugged other heterosexual female class members.

Each member of the lesbian couples disciplined herself according to an imagined conservative Christian authority even though they knew, intellectually, their fears of being found out as gay couples were illogical: Who would know they were together? Also, since they were experiencing such a strong sensation of homophobic surveillance, it would then have made sense not to engage in displays of affection with any other woman, not just their partners. Kelly, in fact, felt comfortable being close to me, and I am a lesbian. The Bible Belt panopticon engendered *precisely* the expected response: the eradication of visible homosexual intimacy. It also forced us all to participate in our own oppression. This is one of the most psychologically destructive aspects of the toxic closet, and it exacts a heavy toll on same-sex relationships.

All but two of the students reported a panoptic effect. The first Katherine, white, heterosexual, and a foreign exchange student from East Germany, wrote, "Personally, I had only felt angry and frustrated with the 'museum,' but I did not feel nervous, entrapped, watched, or even scared, as most other classmates had." The second, Hank, our only student of color, listened closely to his classmates process their feelings about visiting the museum during our class discussion following the field trip. After 30 minutes of this conversation, Hank looked at everyone then chimed in with amazement, "What you are all describing is how I feel all the time here. It's even worse in the Morehead Wal-Mart."

Religion and Science

By definition, no apparent, perceived or claimed evidence in any field, including history and chronology, can be valid if it contradicts the scriptural record. Of primary importance is the fact that evidence is always subject to interpretation by fallible people who do not possess all information.
—Answers in Genesis "Statement of Faith," sec. 4, no. 6

The museum is set up so that the visitor is first introduced to the difference between a biblical worldview and a secular worldview. Museum displays and literature argue that "scientists reach different views about the past, not because of what they see, but because of their different starting points: autonomous human reasoning or God's Word."[18] The Creation Museum presents the message of young-earth creationism in a sophisticated package, one that the visitor is encouraged to read as official, legitimate, and empirically supported, in other words, "scientific." This mixing of scientific empiricism and religious fundamentalism was disorienting for me and those whom I brought to the facility, though likely not for the conservative Christian visitor already accustomed to deferring to the authority of biblical scripture and comfortable with the belief that fallible humans may not understand elements of God's creations. During my second visit to the Creation Museum, I arrived just in time for Dr. Georgia Purdom's live lecture on the "Wonder of the Cell." With a doctorate in Molecular Genetics from Ohio State University, Purdom is well trained in the rules of empiricism and skilled in the language of science. Her lecture consisted of an extremely technical description of the elements of the cell in discipline-specific language including, for example, explanations of "alleles" (a form of gene) and a "chromatid" (one-half of a replicated chromosome).

I personally felt mentally taxed trying to follow the talk. Noticing how confused I was, I wondered how the rest of the audience was doing digesting the material. I observed that the auditorium was about half full, almost everyone was over 50 and white. Everyone was also quiet and polite. There were about 20 individuals in Mennonite or Amish clothing and headdress at the museum that day, and several were attending the lecture.[19] Such a couple sat directly behind me during the cell lecture. The man nodded off early and snored softly throughout. His wife poked him every time Purdom made a scriptural rather than scientific comment, which was not very often. In my struggle to cognitively manage unfamiliar scientific terms, I forgot that I was even in the Creation Museum. Purdom concluded her lecture with the following statement, "Evidence is not the best argument for God. The Bible is the best evidence we have. All knowledge and truth come from the Word of God." This format—information overload coupled with crisp theological statements—was present throughout the museum.

Creationists posit evolution and creationism as equally valid scientific theories. It is the task of the visitor to weigh these "differing perspectives" and choose which makes the best argument. In the Creation Museum, "creationists are connected to God, the Bible, and the Christian way, encouraging visitors to trust in their morality as well as their scientific expertise" while evolutionists are connected with racism, genocide, communism, crime, abortion, and homosexuality.[20] Evolutionists are of Satan; creationists are of God. It is clear then, which one the visitor should decide is most valid. To secular scientists, the very act of framing evolution and creationism as empirically equivalent is ridiculous and, even worse, some argue, dangerously distorts the meaning of science and adds to a general public confusion about what science is. In their article "Antievolutionism: Changes and Continuities," the anthropologist Eugenie Scott and the deputy director of the National Center for Science Education Glenn Branch argue that "The scientific community must keep its collective eye on antievolutionism as it evolves, for science suffers if the public understanding of science suffers."[21] Scott and Branch explained that "The audience for YEC [young-earth creationism] is the approximately 30% of Americans who accept a conservative, more or less literalist theology."[22] For this 30%, the rules of secular reason and empiricism are already subordinate to biblical literalism.

"The Room of Shame"

The museum exhibits are laid out to illustrate the history of creation and the subsequent journey of humankind under an umbrella framework, which Answers in Genesis describes as the "Seven C's of History": creation, corruption, catastrophe, confusion, Christ, cross, and consummation. About 95% of the museum exhibits explores the first four C's. For example, the origin of the universe, the creation of Adam and Eve, and Adam naming the animals all fall under "creation." When Adam eats from the Tree of Knowledge, sin enters the world. Like several other students, Alexandra, who is white and heterosexual, began to feel uncomfortable as she explored the area of the museum covering "corruption":

> I was fine upon arrival and was excited to see that museum. The first hour I was interested in the reading that went with the museum and enjoyed looking at the detailed statues. Right about the time I started to get antsy was when we entered the part of the museum that stated all the things in the world that are bad happen because we don't have God. One of the televisions in the room stated that marriages fall apart because they don't study the scripture. My parents' marriage did not end because we did not attend church at the time. Teenage girls get pregnant even if they do study scripture and believe in God.

The room Alexandra describes here includes streaming video images of a boy looking at pornography on the computer, a distraught pregnant teenage girl, and an angry couple divorcing. Also within the exhibit on corruption is what my students dubbed "the room of shame." The "room of shame," officially called Graffiti Alley in museum materials, is a narrow, crooked space with an urban, gritty feel. It is cramped, dirty, chaotic, and noisy. This effect is especially pronounced since the visitor enters it after leaving "Creation," a beautiful, open, green space filled with animals and plants, and soothing sounds of the natural world. At the entry to Graffiti Alley the visitor reads, "Modern World abandons the Bible" in a graffiti-gang tag script. Once inside, the guest hears urban noises of sirens and machinery. Most of the area is composed of scuffed-up brick walls. Papier-mâchéd articles from newspapers and magazines like *Time* and *Newsweek* cover the brick. Some of the titles of the stories read, "Lessons of the Schiavo Battle," "Is Gay Marriage Next?" "The Battle over Gay Teens," "In Sorrow and Disbelief," "No Lord's Prayer in School," "Just a Routine School Shooting," "The Battle over Stem Cells," "No Heaven, No Hell, Just Science," and "The Pill Arrives." Museum literature describes this part of the facility as the "Cave of Sorrows and Corruption Valley" in which guests are invited to "reflect on the consequences of disobedience toward the Creator."[23] Exiting Graffiti Alley the visitor reads TODAY MAN DECIDES TRUTH. The word "TRUTH" is crossed out with red spray paint, with "WHATEVER" painted below this message also in gang tag script.

Graffiti Alley is both physically and metaphorically dark. Most of the students expressed that they felt disturbed in it. For example, Melinda related:

Mostly, I HATED the room of shame (or at least that's what I called it), I took a look at a few of the pictures on what I have dubbed the hate wall and walked straight through the rest of the room, and really that was my reaction to the whole place, I couldn't get away from it quick enough and was more than ready to go home. It is an extremely hate-filled place!

The Creation Museum presents abortion, divorce, gay marriage, pornography, school violence, and the legalization of medical marijuana next to images of war, genocide, and famine as the terrible consequences of a secular society that has "abandoned the Bible" and lost its way. The facility links confusion, chaos, and violence with urban gang imagery and news stories on social issues about which conservative Christians hold strong opinions. One might argue that Graffiti Alley serves as a kind of "sin porn," a visible representation of shameful sins. The sociologist Arlene Stein theorized about the role shame plays among conservative Christians in her article, "Revenge of the Shamed: The Christian Right's Emotional Culture War."[24] Stein found that when parishioners failed at the "law of God" preached in their churches week after week, they felt ashamed. Manipulating these feelings of shame is one way leaders in the Christian Right control the actions of participants. Tonya, raised Southern Baptist, talked extensively about feeling ashamed during our interview. As a first-year student Tonya joined her university Intervarsity Christian group to try and pray away her homosexuality (see chap. 5). Week after week she met with her prayer buddy and attended Bible study groups. Within this circle, members were encouraged to confess their sins, and private feelings were made very public. Tonya explained:

> At our Bible studies a typical question was, "So, how are you doing with the Lord?" What that was supposed to mean was, are you getting up and reading the Bible? Are you praying? Are you staying out of trouble? It really made a lot of private things very public and not private anymore. Certain people would feel a lot more guilt and shame, and it would sort of shame them out, and they would have to talk about it while other poor people sat back and listened. At that moment in time you're taught that God is ashamed of you, so you're ashamed of yourself, and you feel like everyone else is ashamed of you as well, and that you're never going to live up to all the stuff that you're supposed to do as far as being a Christian.

Stein argues that conservative Christian leaders manufacture the kind of shame Tonya describes here and then, when people are feeling insecure, encourage them to channel those feelings into fear and disgust toward a despised "Other"—often, homosexuals. Stein explains that, under these conditions, anti-gay activism is psychologically reparative. It enables conservative Christians to mediate their own feelings of inadequacy by projecting them onto gay people. Stein writes, "Because desire is so powerful and prohibitions against non-normative sexuality are so central to Christian orthodoxy, is it any wonder that people would seek to project one's unacceptable sexual feelings upon others and seek to punish those who openly flaunt these desires?"[25] Stein's work focused on anti-gay activism among residents of a rural Oregon town; the Creation Museum has a broader mission. It democratically places homosexuality among a range of sins to arguably engender the effect Stein noted: it allows guests to project potential personal shame about their ungodly desires and/or actions onto despised others while framing all sin as the consequence of a corrupt culture that has forsaken God.

As a class, we had planned to stay for at least four hours. Museum literature urges guests to plan 4–6 hours to fully explore all the exhibits. We arrived around 11:30 a.m. Our planetarium show was at 1:30 p.m. I learned later that four students who had driven separately left after this show. Of the remainder, everyone except Terry and Kelly spent the rest of their visit outside at the petting zoo. When I exited the last lecture of the day at 4 p.m., I was surprised to find that some students had already fled while the rest were waiting for me outside. They were completely done with the place.

Christians "Under Siege"

The Creation Museum's combination of spectacle and religiosity garners much media attention. International (*Sydney Morning Herald, Guardian* (UK), national (*New York Times, USA Today, ABC News, Vanity Fair*), and regional (*Cincinnati Enquirer, Charlotte Observer, Kentucky Humanities Council*) newspapers and magazine articles have featured stories about the facility.[26] The tone of most secular stories ranges from strained incredulity to outright mockery while conservative Christian media outlets and blogs praise the facility. Answers in Genesis and the Creation Museum continue to be a controversial cultural hot spot. In 2011, Kentucky's governor, Steven Beshear (D), offered $37.5 million in tax breaks to Answers in Genesis to build an Ark Theme Park near the Creation Museum. Depending upon one's religious and political orientation, the facility is either "a target of ridicule"[27] as a 2010 *New York Times* article described, or, as many fundamentalist Christians believe, a monument to God. For my part, the opening of the Creation Museum practically in my backyard was an opportunity to collect interesting data that might shed light on the contours of conservative Christian thought.

In addition to the data I collected at the facility, and the many hours I spent digesting the material with sociologists—both students and faculty—*and* scientists, family, friends, and acquaintances, I have some personal knowledge of the workings of Answers in Genesis, particularly how insistently media-savy the organization is. I presented an earlier draft of this chapter at the 2010 American Sociological Meetings in Atlanta, Georgia. A reporter from LiveScience.com spotted the title of my presentation in the conference brochure, contacted me, and featured this work in an article.[28] The LiveScience story focused on how "unwelcoming" the Creation Museum felt to my students.[29] The story was reprinted in the *Christian Science Monitor*, picked up by a number of blogs and other media outlets, and was personally responded to by Answers in Genesis and Ken Ham himself on his blog. In fact, Answers in Genesis responded to the charge of being "unwelcoming" on three separate occasions, finally going through the article line by line to dispute the claims made by the reporter.[30] The rebuttal began with the following two paragraphs:

> On Wednesday, the popular LiveScience.com site posted a commentary that slammed the Creation Museum with blatant untruths, misinformation, and anti-Christian bigotry. The LiveScience commentary has also been picked up by such highly visited news websites like MSNBC, Yahoo News, etc. As such, it became necessary for the Creation Museum and Answers in Genesis to respond to the hit piece . . . . On Thursday, we posted a brief yet thorough rebuttal of the commentary's major errors (see Live(ly) Science Debate). Our article today is a point-by-point exposé of all the errors and misrepresentations made by both the senior writer of LiveScience and the college instructor, whose research about the museum formed the basis of the LiveScience commentary.[31]

This was the first I learned that my research had been featured in a "hit piece." Indeed, it is possible that Answers in Genesis purposely framed it as such to draw more media attention. Answers in Genesis welcomes media attention, even negative attention. It gives the organization an opportunity to highlight "anti-Christian bigotry" and fight back against "misinformation" (perceived or real) by the secular media as well as continue to keep the Creation Museum in the news.[32] Nancy Tatom Ammerman notes, "Outsiders often miss the profound sense of threat felt by Fundamentalists to their freedom of religion. On all sides they see themselves as under siege."[33] Communicating this threat to followers is an effective means of mobilizing financial and social resources as scholars of social movements have long noted, and Answers in Genesis is particularly persistent and skilled at doing so.[34]

The Creation Museum and Bible Belt Gays

The only legitimate marriage is the joining of one man and one woman. Any forms of homosexuality, lesbianism, bisexuality, incest, fornication, adultery, pornography, etc., are sinful perversions of God's gift of sex.
—Answers in Genesis "Statement of Faith," sec. 3, no. 12

Homosexuality itself is not central to Answers in Genesis or the Creation Museum, although affirming heterosexual marriage is included in the Answers in Genesis "Statement of Faith." Rather, homosexuality is one of many sexual "perversions" contrary to biblical scripture. In light of this book, what does the presence of the Creation Museum in the Bible Belt mean for Bible Belt gays? One thing it suggests is that the region is a hospitable place for conservative Christians. Further, its presence illustrates the lengths to which some will go to testify their faith to others. For fundamentalists, part of being a good Christian entails witnessing to others about the truth of the Bible, including salvation through Jesus Christ, with the goal of saving souls for God. Fundamentalists separate people in the world into the "saved" and "unsaved." Those who are saved, those who adhere to a literal interpretation of the Bible, believe they are superior over those who do not; in other words, "they automatically outrank anyone who is unsaved."[35]

Fundamentalists appreciate their orderly black-and-white world with its clearly laid-out guidelines. They need to believe that following God's rules, as delineated in the Bible, guarantees their eternal salvation; those who do not follow God's law will burn in hell. They believe there is a reason for everything, that they can know these reasons, and furthermore, that the Bible provides believers with the *right* reasons. For the Bible-believing fundamentalist, the need to be right about God's law emerges from a fear of hell. To illustrate, item eleven in section three of the Answers in Genesis "Statement of Faith" reads: "Those who do not believe in Christ are subject to everlasting conscious punishment, but believers enjoy eternal life with God." Under this threat of everlasting punishment, after one has accepted the incestuous reproduction of the human race, ascribing to a fundamentalist doctrine that homosexuals are an "abomination" is easy, and partly illustrates how homophobic attitudes persist so stubbornly in the Bible Belt.

What differentiates the Bible Belt from other parts of the United States is the concentrated institutional presence and influence of what the scholar and political strategist Suzanne Pharr calls the "theocratic Right," also commonly referred to as the "religious Right" or "Christian Right."[36] These are designations that identify organizations, like the Creation Museum and Answers in Genesis, that seek to promote and legislate morality.[37] Pharr explains that "The broad goal of the theocratic Right is to replace democracy with theocracy, merging church and state so that authoritarian (and male) leaders enforce a fundamentalist vision in this country's public and private life."[38] Opponents to creationism contend that adhering to a fundamentalist interpretation of the Bible is a form of intellectual and psychological violence, which has subsequent material consequences. One group that suffers such violence and ostracism is Bible Belt gays. There is no room for gay people in a fundamentalist community, although "struggling" homosexuals undergoing reparative therapy may be tolerated and even supported, as excerpts from chapter 5 demonstrate. The Creation Museum is an exaggerated microcosm of a fundamentalist subculture present in the Bible Belt. It is, thus, part of the terrain that some Bible Belt gays negotiate, but not one within which they will likely ever feel welcome as full participants.

7

"The Opposite of Faith Is Fear"

Destruction and Transformation

I once dressed up as Jerry Falwell for Halloween. It was the scariest
thing I could think of."
—Misty, white, 24, from Eastern Kentucky

In 2004, the FRC published a 13-page brochure titled "The Slippery Slope of
Same-Sex Marriage." It opens with a photo of a horse and the heading, "A
Man and His Horse," and the following metaphor:

> In what some call a denial of a basic civil right, a Missouri man has been
> told he may not marry his long-term companion. Although his situation is
> unique, the logic of his argument is remarkably similar to that employed
> by advocates of homosexual marriage. The man claims that the essential
> elements of marriage—love and commitment—are indeed present: "She's
> gorgeous. She's sweet. She's loving. I'm very proud of her . . . . Deep down,
> way down, I'd love to have children with her." . . . It seems the state of Mis-
> souri is not prepared to indulge a man who waxes eloquent about his love
> for a 22-year-old mare named Pixel.

Neither, the FRC contends, should Americans tolerate same-sex marriage.
Conservative religious groups like the FRC, AFA, Eagle Forum, Traditional

Values Coalition, Creation Museum, and National Organization for Marriage frame same-sex marriage as a "threat to marriage" and "oppose the homosexual movement's efforts to convince our society that their behavior is normal because we fear the judgment of God on our nation."[1] The AFA lists ten principles on their website that "guide AFA's opposition to the homosexual agenda." These include framing gay rights as an outgrowth of the sexual revolution of the past 40 years that will "lead to the normalization of even more deviant behavior," stating that homosexuality is unnatural and that "the root of homosexuality is a sinful heart," and opposing "the efforts of the homosexual movement to force its agenda on our sentiments in schools, government, business and workplaces through law, public policy and media."[2]

Although much is said about homosexuals and homosexuality by those attempting to restrict gay rights, like the AFA, Bible Belt gays have had few opportunities to weigh in on what we think about the individuals and institutions advocating discrimination. Frequently the "other" of scientific inquiry and, even more pronouncedly, public stereotyping, lesbians and gay men are rarely centered as the leading characters in our own lives in the eyes of the heterosexual United States.[3] Indeed, heterosexuals largely control public conversations about homosexuality (in newspapers, radio, and television), whether they are politically conservative or progressive. Gay people are talked *about* but seldom *listened* to. When asked for their thoughts, as I did in audiotaped interviews, they had much to say.

Among the Bible Belt gays I interviewed, Misty, quoted in the epigraph, imputed conservative Christians with the most serious charge. She explained, "For me, or someone gay who has not had good experiences, living in the Bible Belt's culture is technically experiencing the church embodying or using ethnocide against you." Ethnocide, also called cultural genocide, involves the systematic destruction of a group's culture.[4] It is commonly used in reference to an ethnic group such as Latino/as. Since being gay is not an ethnicity, and gay people have not yet been able to create and establish a unique culture, one cannot destroy something that does not exist. Nonetheless, Misty applied the elements of ethnocide to her own experience using Raphael Lemkin's linguistic definition of cultural genocide. This includes forced transfer of children to another group, forced exile of individuals representing the group, prohibition of a national language, and systematic destruction of books and religious works.[5] Misty wrote:

Religion in the Bible Belt (and some similarly in wider culture) promotes the prevention of equal rights among same-sex parents. Forced and systematic exile is children kicked out of their homes and communities because they are gay. Prohibition of speaking about being gay openly, or saying "my girlfriend" in public eradicates language. Not to mention the religious language of "purging" evil. I think this idea of a gay cultural genocide in America is very important.

Throughout *Pray the Gay Away*, I have illustrated discrimination, oppression, exile, and silencing in the real lived experiences of Bible Belt gays negotiating religious-based homophobia in their daily lives. In this chapter I explore what Bible Belt gays think about public expressions of homophobic rhetoric, like "The Slippery Slope" pamphlet, as well as what it means to grow up in an environment that prohibits and demonizes expression of one's gay identity; in short, the ways that Bible Belt gays respond to institutional and individual manifestations of suppression and oppression.

Publicly Vilified

The majority of those I interviewed observed changes in the ways that homosexuality has been discussed in public forums since 2000. Fifty percent of the older (over 40) Bible Belt gays I interviewed explained that when they were younger (in the 1970s and 1980s) homosexuality was simply not talked about. Brother Damien, in the religious order of the Orthodox Catholic Church of America, who is 44, Native American, from Central Kentucky, and raised Pentecostal, explained:

> The churches didn't do that back then. Interestingly enough, at that point in time, most churches, even the conservative churches, and the fundamentalist churches weren't that obsessed about homosexuals. I think that was something that was developed by the moral majority and the religious Right movement. Back then, there really wasn't a lot of the hate speech in churches, except racism. I don't think they really thought a lot about homosexuals. I mean certainly it was sin, there's no question. Most of the conservatives in the fundamentalist churches across the United States had the attitude, "of course it's a sin." It was so obvious you don't even discuss that. The Bible said it was a sin. So they didn't need to preach about it, they didn't feel like they needed to talk about it. It was an embarrassing subject too.

When homosexuality is largely unmentionable, it is possible to live in denial about exactly how supportive (or not) one's neighbor or grandfather or co-worker is, and, in the short run, this ignorance and denial can be less disruptive to a gay person's daily emotional well-being. Although public displays of rampant homophobia can be an illustration of how vital a social movement is (otherwise the majority group would not be so threatened), for those individual lesbians and gay men encountering homophobic political ads, bumper stickers reading "one man + one woman = marriage," and yard signs that might simply read "Vote Yes on Amendment 13 to Save Marriage" are very stressful.[6] When specific gay political issues —antidiscrimination legislation, gay marriage laws, initiatives prohibiting gay men and lesbians from adopting or fostering children, and domestic partnership benefits— enter the public discussion every two years during election cycles, the lesbians and gay men I interviewed described how taxing it was to negotiate loud homophobic displays.

Several of my interview subjects, like Amy, who is white and 34, Cathy, who is African American and 35, and Jeff, who is white and 42, all of whom live in Lexington, Kentucky, shared how they felt seeing anti-gay bumper stickers and political ads during political campaigns. Amy explained that she wanted to rip off and deface the stickers, and slam her car into the vehicles:

> It made me mad that I could let a bumper sticker piss me off that bad and make me that upset. You know that feeling where your stomach is in knots and your heart's beating? It would just piss me off, and I wanted to peel stickers off their cars, draw skirts on the man. It makes you think to do all these things that you wouldn't actually do.

When I asked Cathy how often she felt angry when she heard negative messages about homosexuality during the 2004 political season, she responded:

> Every time I look at a W [George W. Bush] sticker on the back of somebody's car. Every time I hear the president on TV. Every time I hear a Republican speak. Every time I hear someone talk about traditional family values, any time I hear family values in my head that means get rid of all the gay people.

Jeff explained that his interpretation of homophobic hate speech differed depending upon his mood. Sometimes he understood it as a manifestation of ignorance, at other times as an expression of cruelty. Among the most troubling impact the media bombardment of hate speech had on Jeff was that it changed the way he perceived heterosexuals. He said, "It makes me wary of straight people. It makes me see them as straight people whereas before I would have just seen them as individuals." Jeff elaborated:

Since the Bush administration, the anti-gay marriage amendments to the Constitution and the anti gay rhetoric, I feel post-traumatic stress, anxiety, not safe, angry, and hurt. I don't want to let people out in the traffic, like, "You didn't vote no on that amendment, why should I let you by me?" Maybe I should start treating straight people that way, not go to weddings, not validate their relationships.

Researchers at the University of Kentucky gathered data on the minority stress gay people experienced in those states that included an anti-gay marriage amendment on an election ballot. An American Psychological Association press release quotes Sharon Scales Rostosky, one of the lead researchers, on their findings. "The results of this study demonstrate that living in a state that has just passed a marriage amendment is associated with higher levels of psychological stress for lesbian, gay and bisexual citizens," Rostosky said. "And this stress is not due to other pre-existing conditions or factors; it is a direct result of the negative images and messages associated with the ballot campaign and the passage of the amendment."[7]

Dimensions of Homophobic Hate Speech

Bible Belt gays experience homophobic hate speech and attitudes in a variety of intersecting institutional, generalized, and personal forms. *Institutional homophobic hate speech* is voiced by religious (Rick Warren, James Dobson), political (Rick Perry, Sarah Palin), military (General James Amos) leaders, and/or organizations advocating an institutional perspective opposing homosexuality. *Generalized homophobic hate speech* is said in the company of others but is not directed at any particular individual; *personally directed homophobic speech* consists of both open and veiled threats and insults. While gay people must process all forms of homophobic hate speech personally, little of it is personally directed, especially in the Bible Belt, a region with strong social norms to be polite, mannerly, friendly, and present an appearance of agreeability (i.e., personalism) with others. At the same time, rampant expressions of institutional and generalized homophobic hate speech in the region bolster individually held homophobic attitudes and encourage those who have dissenting opinions to remain silent about their support for gay people.

The following excerpt from the 2010 Texas GOP platform is an example of *institutional homophobic hate speech* that merges politics and religion. Under a heading simply titled "Homosexuality," the Texas State Republican Party asserts:

We believe that the practice of homosexuality tears at the fabric of society, contributes to the breakdown of the family unit, and leads to the spread of dangerous, communicable diseases. Homosexual behavior is contrary to the fundamental, unchanging truths that have been ordained by God, recognized by our country's founders, and shared by the majority of Texans. Homosexuality must not be presented as an acceptable "alternative" lifestyle in our public education and policy, nor should "family" be redefined to include homosexual "couples." We are opposed to any granting of special legal entitlements, refuse to recognize, or grant special privileges including, but not limited to: marriage between persons of the same sex (regardless of state of origin), custody of children by homosexuals, homosexual partner insurance or retirement benefits. We oppose any criminal or civil penalties against those who oppose homosexuality out of faith, conviction, or belief in traditional values.[8]

Kathleen Blee, a sociologist who has studied members of the Ku Klux Klan and Aryan Nation, describes the "negative labels" and "myth-making" that members of dominant groups impose upon minorities as "accomplished hate."[9] Negative labels reduce a group of people to a stereotype while myth-making involves sharing stories about a group that demonizes them. When the Texas GOP says, "We believe that the practice of homosexuality tears at the fabric of society," they are activating a false, yet taken-for-granted story of homosexuality: fags are disease-ridden destroyers of families. Institutional, generalized, and personally directed dimensions of homophobic hate speech are illustrations of accomplished hate. Institutionally expressed homophobia creates a climate in which generalized homophobia goes unchallenged and where personally directed homophobia is tacitly sanctioned. Accomplished hate is a form of "accomplished inequality," which constrains the options of members of a minority group.[10] Blee observes that, "The group to which negative qualities have been attached are treated with caution, secrecy, cruelty or violence. If they react in kind, their negative qualities are confirmed. If they do not react, they are seen as weak or cowardly."[11] This is a "double-bind" and part of the toll of being a member of a minority group.[12] On an individual level, cognitively managing the understanding that remote powerful groups are actively attempting to construct oneself as inferior and unworthy is stressful, and requires psychological and emotional resources.

Most gay people try to avoid those that are homophobic—they do not listen to Focus on the Family broadcasts, they do not attend churches preaching against homosexuality, and some may turn off the news when gay

The fact of the matter is that the religious Right does us real, true genuine harm. And so it is a danger to us. Those people are dangerous to us. Those people have kept me from being equally compensated with my straight colleagues for twenty years. These people are out to make sure that we fare less well in this society than we would if we were full members of this society, and that's very serious business. So it's not a mere matter of religious belief. These people are trying to manipulate the law to make sure that their biases are captured in coercive law. And it's wrong, and it does us genuine harm. People suffer on account of it, and ultimately people die on account of it, because it contributes to a culture where people think it's just alright to do harm; to sexual and gender minorities, so it contributes to the harmfulness of the culture itself.

Thus, in deconstructing institutional homophobic hate speech, Bible Belt gays typically go through stages of ridicule, logical rebuttal, and concern.

Such hate speech is also "dangerous" and "harmful" because it supports and validates personally directed homophobia and generalized homophobic speech. Generalized homophobic speech is made by someone close to a Bible Belt gay in a personal setting, but is not personally directed. To clarify, consider the difference between someone calling a known or suspected gay man, "you ugly fag!" and the teenager who comments, "that's so gay" to describe someone or something as bad or stupid. The first is a direct attack, the second a frequently repeated homophobic expression that creates a hostile climate for sexual minorities. Illustrations of generalized homophobia are numerous. For the Bible Belt gay, the most painful homophobic speech is made by someone—a teacher, parent, friend, neighbor, relative, preacher—for whom one respects and cares. This hate speech may be personally directed but is more often generalized, and keeps Bible Belt gays, like Ron, in the toxic closet. Ron, who is not out to his parents, shared a time when his mother made a homophobic comment about his college roommate. After a weekend visit, Ron's mother said, "That boy is queer, I can smell him all the way." In addition to being a form of generalized homophobia, this comment also serves as a warning to Ron that he better not be gay and, obviously, that being gay is disgusting and terrible. Every time a gay person hears a homophobic comment, every time a preacher denounces homosexuality, every grunt and sniff of disapproval expressed about homosexuality in the company of a gay person is an example of generalized homophobia. While listening to Ken Ham's DVD recording "The State of the Nation" at the Creation Museum in a half-full auditorium of others during our class field trip, Terry, quoted in chapter 7, felt very disturbed by the reactions of audience members to Ham's

rights issues arise. When confronted with an institutional homophobic mission statement, like the Texas GOP 2010 platform or an anti-gay political advertisement, the Bible Belt gays I interviewed processed the hate speech sequentially.

First, they tended to try to dismiss leaders of the Christian Right, such as Pat Robertson and Jerry Falwell, as "nutcases" and the Texas GOP as far-right theocrats out of touch with mainstream America. To illustrate, Peter, who is white, 29, and from Western Kentucky, said that the things that conservative Christian spokespeople like Pat Robertson say "are intensely absurd to me, but we validate him by giving him attention." Among the controversial comments that Robertson, host of the television program the 700 Club, has made include discussing Hurricane Katrina as God's punishment for the sin of abortion, and framing the earthquake that struck Haiti in 2010 as "what happens when people make a deal with the devil." And, famously, Robertson "totally concurred" with Jerry Falwell[13] who, just after the terrorist attacks on 9/11, said the following:

The abortionists have got to bear some burden for this because God will not be mocked. And when we destroy 40 million little innocent babies, we make God mad. I really believe that the pagans, and the abortionists, and the feminists, and the gays and the lesbians who are actively trying to make that an alternative lifestyle, the ACLU, People For the American Way—all of them who have tried to secularize America—I point the finger in their face and say "you helped this happen."

Peter explained that he felt frustrated by the attention the media pays to religious leaders making homophobic remarks because he believes that such attention has the direct and indirect effect of validating homophobic attitudes:

I'm really disappointed sometimes in the press, that they give them so much attention. When Pat Robertson, when he makes statements like, so and so had a stroke because he's friendly to gay people . . . publishing that in the paper, putting that on CNN, that gives him a sort of validity. Because even if people like you and me say that he needs to be on some kind of medication, there are plenty of other people that say, "wow, he makes some sense, I've got to write a check out to him."

Similarly, Laura, 37, Native American, Melungeon and white, and from Southeastern Kentucky reported:

After some of the rude comments—the Tinky Winky stuff was just ridiculous, and Dobson came out saying that Sponge Bob was gay. It's just ridiculous. If that's what those people are focusing on, they are not helping one damn person out there and they must not be worth anything other than just have a show and spout off their mouth, so I really don't pay a whole lot of attention to them.[14]

Amy, quoted earlier, also discussed the following conservative political advertisement as "ridiculous" and "stupid":

It was for somebody in Tennessee, and his main push was for the illegals. It was horrible, because he was going off about all these illegal aliens and how they're getting free education, free food stamps, free blah, blah, blah, blah. So, he's rattling off on a rampage about that, and then, all of a sudden, there's a two-second musical interlude and then there's the homosexual. He goes on about how the illegals are bringing their homosexual lovers over. It ended with something about the homosexual fiesta or something stupid at the end. It was the most ridiculous thing I've ever heard. But I was like, "yeah, this is ridiculous, but still . . ."

Second, when pressed to think more deeply about the substance of such homophobic statements, many Bible Belt gays moved quickly from dismissing institutional homophobic hate speech as ridiculous to observing the lack of logic inherent in the ideas, as Peter does here:

Think about what he's [Falwell on 9/11] saying logically. He's saying that God sends punishment to people who are friendly to gay people. First of all, Christianity is supposed to be about people being friendly, so why would God punish that? Does God not have other things to worry about?

Both Amy and Peter then speculated on how disturbing it was that a political or religious authority (in the case of Amy's ad, someone running for Congress) would publicly express false information in the service of maintaining discrimination and oppression. What did it mean, they pondered, that some people actually believed these stereotypes? Amy continued:

I mean it was horrible, it was a horrible ad, and we laughed at it, but it was horrible. The things he was saying were horrible. They were just untruths, but oh my God, people really believe this, people really think this.

Peter warned:

That's very dangerous that people will believe those things. There are a lot of awfully lonely people out there who are looking to latch on to things, and they see Pat Robertson, he's a man of God, he's educated, you know, he has something going on for him. So, let me fill the void in my life by latching on to what Pat Robertson has to say. And that's very dangerous, because it just promotes these cycles of ignorance and hatred and obviously this man is using the platform of hatred to get attention, to get money.

Finally, some interview subjects, like Will, held religious leaders such a Jerry Falwell and Pat Robertson "culpable in everything bad that happen to gay people" because their public comments fuel and support homopho bic attitudes in others. Will, who is white, 46, and from Northern Kentuck commented:

Based on everything I hear and everything I read, and everything I think I know, I like the bumper sticker that says the "Christian Right is Neither." It is so un-Christian. They advance religious bigotry and every time someone is discriminated against, or fired or evicted from an apartment, or gay bashed, I think the religious Right has some culpability in everything bad that happens to gay people.

Ron, who is white, 36, and from Eastern Kentucky, expressed this as well:

I think they are perpetuating harm. I think they are preying upon people who don't have the ability to intellectualize and they're inciting fear and hatred and aggression. I hold them responsible for a lot of the harm that's been done to gay people in this country, such as Matthew Shepard's death, such as things that I've experienced where I live. It's not because I came out, but it's because someone saw me with a person who was known to be gay and they superimposed that on there.

Institutional homophobic hate speech is most dangerous when it is codified in laws that frame gay people as second-class citizens, not entitled to the same rights as heterosexuals. Mary, who is white, 61, and from Central Kentucky, believes that conservative Christians "are out to harm us in substantial, material ways." She said:

framing of gay marriage as part of the "collapse of our Christian nation." After Ham denounced homosexuality, those around us sniffed and muttered their approval of Ham's condemnation. Like Terry, I also felt unsettled and vaguely threatened after this audience response.

In contrast to institutional and generalized homophobic hate speech, personally directed homophobia is targeted at a specific individual. In my case, illustrations of personally directed homophobic hate speech include my neighbor calling homosexuality an abomination after I told him I was a lesbian, a student turning in a homophobic essay to me after I come out in the classroom, a stranger shouting "dyke" at Anna and me while we are walking, and an audience member comparing homosexuality to pedophilia in the Q&A after I give a public talk on being gay in the Bible Belt. These all feel like attacks, usually require me to respond to the perpetrator, arouse strong feelings of fear and anger, and take a heavy toll on my psychological well-being. Sometimes violence accompanies hate speech. In fact, hate speech in the form of epithets (slurs) or literature (pamphlets) is generally part of the evidence that constitutes a "hate crime."[15]

For young people experiencing same-sex attractions, institutional, generalized, and personally directed homophobic hate speech arrest the expression of a gay identity while it is forming. Misty believes that conservative Christian ideology, attitudes, and practices, especially when they are legally enforced, seek to suppress and eradicate gay culture, and dubbed this a form of ethnocide.

"Their Agenda Is One of Prejudice and Greed and War Mongering"

Growing up in the Bible Belt afforded the women and men I interviewed much contact with conservative Christianity. When I asked interview subjects what they thought about people like Pat Robertson and organizations like the 700 Club and the American Family Association, they typically expressed frustration, confusion, hurt, fear, and anger. They critiqued conservative Christian opposition to homosexuality using historical, political, philosophical, practical, economic, moral, and theological arguments. To begin with, unsurprisingly, most interview subjects had extremely negative opinions of conservative Christians, especially the figureheads of such groups. Kimberly, who is white, 32, and from Texas, succinctly said, "I don't like any of those people actually." Misty said:

I think they are bigoted, and I think they are closed minded, I feel like there is no hope for them. I feel like they are so conservative, so right minded, that they have that power of denial, to deny common sense. It is my experience with the religious Right that things that make perfect damn sense can be denied and can be swept away because that does not go with their belief systems.

Cathy, quoted earlier, believes that conservative Christians are hypocrites:

People like that I find tend to be the biggest hypocrites. When I said I think they are all closet homosexuals, I'm kind of joking and I'm kind of not, because I think people, people like that who have such strong and really rigid, rigid, rigid, religious based beliefs about everything else in the world, and they can justify their crazy thoughts about illegal aliens with a Bible verse, those people are hiding something. That's why you see pastors who get caught in relationships with male prostitutes while they are using crystal meth.

Susan, who is white, 41, and from Southern Kentucky, was raised in a Holiness church. Holiness is a charismatic denomination in which parishioners worship with much "hand clapping, shouting, and speaking in tongues." Her grandfather was a Holiness preacher, and Susan was an active participant in church activities throughout her childhood and adolescence. Like Misty, she regularly heard homosexuality condemned from the pulpit and in the pews. Susan still identifies as Christian but does not attend a church because, she said, "I never have really found a church that I felt was affirming and comfortable enough to really consider myself a part of it." She continued:

I have a lot of negative feelings toward them. I totally disagree with what they say and preach. I think that the whole God Christianity thing is supposed to be based on love, and I think that the religious Right in general is just all about hate, and it's all negative. There's nothing positive about it.

Sarah, white, 43, and from Eastern Kentucky, said that she prefers not to think about members of the Christian Right. When she does, she feels sorry for them because "they have a perspective that is so narrow and they are missing out on so much."

Brother Damien expressed a great deal of pent up righteous fury about conservative Christians during our interview. He spoke for 20 minutes on the sins and crimes they commit and argued that by doing so in the name of Jesus, they perform Satan's work. He said:

I believe that the religious Right movement is from the devil, is from Satan. It is being orchestrated by the devil. Because what does the devil do? What does the devil delight in doing? The one thing that Satan delights in more than anything else is to take people who consider themselves to be Christians and to make them, to manipulate them into believing that evil is good, and to embrace hatred and prejudice, which in fact they've done. Basically their agenda is one of prejudice and greed and war mongering, and they justify this by taking Jesus and using him as a figurehead, because their Jesus is not the Jesus of the Gospels.

Damien likened such spokesmen as James Dobson and Pat Robertson to the Pharisees that Jesus condemned in the New Testament. Linda, who is white, 29, and the preacher's kid from Texas, also believes that conservative Christians are poor representatives of Jesus Christ. She said, "I think people like that *like* having someone to hate, to be perfectly honest with you." Linda explained that she has stopped listening to anything conservative Christian leaders have to say:

I don't listen to them at all. I think that they don't have any right to speak for God. I don't think they have any right because if they're half as good at what they do, at being "men of God," then they know damn well, they're fully aware, of what they're putting out there as false. They know damn well it's not true. But they'll still spout it because it's what people are used to hearing. It's what people almost want to hear, because they want to have it confirmed for them that everything they've been told their whole lives isn't based on a lie. I feel like anybody who is so ready to judge another person, so ready to condemn them to the pits of hell, to me, is not a good representative of Jesus Christ, sorry but they're not.

Keith, who is white, 47, and from Northern Kentucky, and his partner, Henry, who is white, 51, and from Illinois, also critiqued conservative Christian attitudes about homosexuality on theological grounds. Keith, a former Catholic priest who was defrocked and excommunicated (following an arrest for having sex in a local park with a man) related:

What we experience in this country are these very fundamentalist, very ridiculous churches that are absolute, and have this power over the media, have money and spend it and try to blackmail people. Try to entice them into fear and all this kind of stuff. Their effect is scary. It's very frightening to me. I do not believe that they are really of God in a sense of . . . they're going to such extremes in trying to separate people and make absolute statements about who's right, who's wrong, and who's okay and who's not okay and who's legitimate in the church and who's not legitimate, how you do this and how you do that. All they're doing is tearing people apart instead of helping people. I think they're there for power and just trying to influence and confuse people. I think they're foolish. I do not think that technically they should call themselves a church. Not in a strict sense of what the scriptures tell us church is about.

Henry, like Keith, and many Bible Belt gays, observed that leaders of the Christian Right use fear to manipulate people:

It's their way or the highway and they try to put that fear in that only their way is the right way, and their reading of the scriptures. They pick and choose what they want out of the scriptures to justify their hatred, especially [the book of] Leviticus. They always want to quote that when they talk about gay and lesbians. But they don't really want to go into the whole book of it. They quote so much in the Old Testament and not what Jesus says. They manipulate it, and I think it's very political.

Derek, who is white, 39, originally from Ohio but a longtime resident of Kentucky, felt especially frustrated with the ways that conservative Christians have, in his words, "hijacked" Christianity and the identity of Christian in order to exclude gay people. He believes that the media perpetuates this perception by not presenting gay Christian and conservative Christian beliefs with equivalent institutional weight. For example, when publishing perspectives on Christianity and homosexuality, the media will interview the pastor of a local well-known megachurch and balance this with the thoughts of an individual gay Christian. Derek explained:

The media really feeds this by just going to any random person that will talk to them about the issue, but then going to the anti-gay people who are Christian to get their official response. And then you try to say, "well, if you're going to talk to them, why didn't you talk to our official advocacy spokesperson in the Kentucky Fairness Alliance?" They just talked to some random gay person on the street and that's very frustrating.

This kind of media construction stacks the deck against perceiving gay Christians as valid because any single gay Christian stopped on the street is likely not as verbally polished as an institutional leader, nor do such individuals offer a consistent institutional message. The anti-gay Christian rights issues arise. When confronted with an institutional homophobic mission statement, like the Texas GOP 2010 platform or an anti-gay political advertisement, the Bible Belt gays I interviewed processed the hate speech sequentially.

First, they tended to try to dismiss leaders of the Christian Right, such as Pat Robertson and Jerry Falwell, as "nutcases" and the Texas GOP as far-right theocrats out of touch with mainstream America. To illustrate, Peter, who is white, 29, and from Western Kentucky, said that the things that conservative Christian spokespeople like Pat Robertson say "are intensely absurd to me, but we validate him by giving him attention." Among the controversial comments that Robertson, host of the television program the 700 Club, has made include discussing Hurricane Katrina as God's punishment for the sin of abortion, and framing the earthquake that struck Haiti in 2010 as "what happens when people make a deal with the devil." And, famously, Robertson "totally concurred" with Jerry Falwell[13] who, just after the terrorist attacks on 9/11, said the following:

> The abortionists have got to bear some burden for this because God will not be mocked. And when we destroy 40 million little innocent babies, we make God mad. I really believe that the pagans, and the abortionists, and the feminists, and the gays and the lesbians who are actively trying to make that an alternative lifestyle, the ACLU, People For the American Way—all of them who have tried to secularize America—I point the finger in their face and say "you helped this happen."

Peter explained that he felt frustrated by the attention the media pays to religious leaders making homophobic remarks because he believes that such attention has the direct and indirect effect of validating homophobic attitudes:

> I'm really disappointed sometimes in the press, that they give them so much attention. When Pat Robertson, when he makes statements like, so and so had a stroke because he's friendly to gay people . . . publishing that in the paper, putting that on CNN, that gives him a sort of validity. Because even if people like you and me say that he needs to be on some kind of medication, there are plenty of other people that say, "wow, he makes some sense, I've got to write a check out to him."

Similarly, Laura, 37, Native American, Melungeon and white, and from Southeastern Kentucky reported:

After some of the rude comments—the Tinky Winky stuff was just ridicu-lous, and Dobson came out saying that Sponge Bob was gay. It's just ridicu-lous. If that's what those people are focusing on, they are not helping one damn person out there and they must not be worth anything other than just have a show and spout off their mouth, so I really don't pay a whole lot of attention to them.[14]

Amy, quoted earlier, also discussed the following conservative political advertisement as "ridiculous" and "stupid":

It was for somebody in Tennessee, and his main push was for the illegals. It was horrible, because he was going off about all these illegal aliens and how they're getting free education, free food stamps, free blah, blah, blah, blah. So, he's rattling off on a rampage about that, and then, all of a sudden, there's a two-second musical interlude and then there's the homosexual. He goes on about how the illegals are bringing their homosexual lovers over. It ended with something about the homosexual fiesta or something stupid at the end. It was the most ridiculous thing I've ever heard. But I was like, "yeah, this is ridiculous, but still . . ."

Second, when pressed to think more deeply about the substance of such homophobic statements, many Bible Belt gays moved quickly from dismiss-ing institutional homophobic hate speech as ridiculous to observing the lack of logic inherent in the ideas, as Peter does here:

Think about what he's [Falwell on 9/11] saying logically. He's saying that God sends punishment to people who are friendly to gay people. First of all, Christianity is supposed to be about people being friendly, so why would God punish that? Does God not have other things to worry about?

Both Amy and Peter then speculated on how disturbing it was that a political or religious authority (in the case of Amy's ad, someone running for Congress) would publicly express false information in the service of main-taining discrimination and oppression. What did it mean, they pondered, that some people actually believed these stereotypes? Amy continued:

I mean it was horrible, it was a horrible ad, and we laughed at it, but it was horrible. The things he was saying were horrible. They were just untruths, but oh my God, people really believe this, people really think this.

Peter warned:

> That's very dangerous that people will believe those things. There are a lot
> of awfully lonely people out there who are looking to latch on to things,
> and they see Pat Robertson, he's a man of God, he's educated, you know,
> he has something going on for him. So, let me fill the void in my life by
> latching on to what Pat Robertson has to say. And that's very dangerous,
> because it just promotes these cycles of ignorance and hatred and obvi-
> ously this man is using the platform of hatred to get attention, to get
> money.

Finally, some interview subjects, like Will, held religious leaders such as
Jerry Falwell and Pat Robertson "culpable in everything bad that happens
to gay people" because their public comments fuel and support homophobic attitudes in others. Will, who is white, 46, and from Northern Kentucky,
commented:

> Based on everything I hear and everything I read, and everything I think
> I know, I like the bumper sticker that says the "Christian Right is Neither."
> It is so un-Christian. They advance religious bigotry and every time some-
> one is discriminated against, or fired or evicted from an apartment, or gay
> bashed, I think the religious Right has some culpability in everything bad
> that happens to gay people.

Ron, who is white, 36, and from Eastern Kentucky, expressed this as well:

> I think they are perpetuating harm. I think they are preying upon people
> who don't have the ability to intellectualize and they're inciting fear and
> hatred and aggression. I hold them responsible for a lot of the harm that's
> been done to gay people in this country, such as Matthew Shepard's death,
> such as things that I've experienced where I live. It's not because I came
> out, but it's because someone saw me with a person who was known to be
> gay and they superimposed that on there.

Institutional homophobic hate speech is most dangerous when it is codified in laws that frame gay people as second-class citizens, not entitled to
the same rights as heterosexuals. Mary, who is white, 61, and from Central
Kentucky, believes that conservative Christians "are out to harm us in substantial, material ways." She said:

The fact of the matter is that the religious Right does us real, true genuine harm. And so it is a danger to us. Those people are dangerous to us. Those people have kept me from being equally compensated with my straight colleagues for twenty years. These people are out to make sure that we fare less well in this society than we would if we were full members of this society, and that's very serious business. So it's not a mere matter of religious belief. These people are trying to manipulate the law to make sure that their biases are captured in coercive law. And it's wrong, and it does us genuine harm. People suffer on account of it, and ultimately people die on account of it, because it contributes to a culture where people think it's just alright to do harm; to sexual and gender minorities, so it contributes to the harmfulness of the culture itself.

Thus, in deconstructing institutional homophobic hate speech, Bible Belt gays typically go through stages of ridicule, logical rebuttal, and concern.

Such hate speech is also "dangerous" and "harmful" because it supports and validates personally directed homophobia and generalized homophobic speech. Generalized homophobic speech is made by someone close to a Bible Belt gay in a personal setting, but is not personally directed. To clarify, consider the difference between someone calling a known or suspected gay man, "you ugly fag!" and the teenager who comments, "that's so gay" to describe someone or something as bad or stupid. The first is a direct attack, the second a frequently repeated homophobic expression that creates a hostile climate for sexual minorities. Illustrations of generalized homophobia are numerous. For the Bible Belt gay, the most painful homophobic speech is made by someone—a teacher, parent, friend, neighbor, relative, preacher—for whom one respects and cares. This hate speech may be personally directed but is more often generalized, and keeps Bible Belt gays, like Ron, in the toxic closet. Ron, who is not out to his parents, shared a time when his mother made a homophobic comment about his college roommate. After a weekend visit, Ron's mother said, "That boy is queer, I can smell him all the way." In addition to being a form of generalized homophobia, this comment also serves as a warning to Ron that he better not be gay and, obviously, that being gay is disgusting and terrible. Every time a gay person hears a homophobic comment, every time a preacher denounces homosexuality, every grunt and sniff of disapproval expressed about homosexuality in the company of a gay person is an example of generalized homophobia. While listening to Ken Ham's DVD recording "The State of the Nation" at the Creation Museum in a half-full auditorium of others during our class field trip, Terry, quoted in chapter 7, felt very disturbed by the reactions of audience members to Ham's framing of gay marriage as part of the "collapse of our Christian nation." After Ham denounced homosexuality, those around us sniffed and muttered their approval of Ham's condemnation. Like Terry, I also felt unsettled and vaguely threatened after this audience response.

In contrast to institutional and generalized homophobic hate speech, personally directed homophobia is targeted at a specific individual. In my case, illustrations of personally directed homophobic hate speech include my neighbor calling homosexuality an abomination after I told him I was a lesbian, a student turning in a homophobic essay to me after I come out in the classroom, a stranger shouting "dyke" at Anna and me while we are walking, and an audience member comparing homosexuality to pedophilia in the Q&A after I give a public talk on being gay in the Bible Belt. These all feel like attacks, usually require me to respond to the perpetrator, arouse strong feelings of fear and anger, and take a heavy toll on my psychological well-being. Sometimes violence accompanies hate speech. In fact, hate speech in the form of epithets (slurs) or literature (pamphlets) is generally part of the evidence that constitutes a "hate crime."[15]

For young people experiencing same-sex attractions, institutional, generalized, and personally directed homophobic hate speech arrest the expression of a gay identity while it is forming. Misty believes that conservative Christian ideology, attitudes, and practices, especially when they are legally enforced, seek to suppress and eradicate gay culture, and dubbed this a form of ethnocide.

"Their Agenda Is One of Prejudice and Greed and War Mongering"

Growing up in the Bible Belt afforded the women and men I interviewed much contact with conservative Christianity. When I asked interview subjects what they thought about people like Pat Robertson and organizations like the 700 Club and the American Family Association, they typically expressed frustration, confusion, hurt, fear, and anger. They critiqued conservative Christian opposition to homosexuality using historical, political, philosophical, practical, economic, moral, and theological arguments. To begin with, unsurprisingly, most interview subjects had extremely negative opinions of conservative Christians, especially the figureheads of such groups. Kimberly, who is white, 32, and from Texas, succinctly said, "I don't like any of those people actually." Misty said:

I think they are bigoted, and I think they are closed minded, I feel like there is no hope for them. I feel like they are so conservative, so right minded, that they have that power of denial, to deny common sense. It is my experience with the religious Right that things that make perfect damn sense can be denied and can be swept away because that does not go with their belief systems.

Cathy, quoted earlier, believes that conservative Christians are hypocrites:

People like that I find tend to be the biggest hypocrites. When I said I think they are all closet homosexuals, I'm kind of joking and I'm kind of not, because I think people, people like that who have such strong and really rigid, rigid, rigid, religious based beliefs about everything else in the world, and they can justify their crazy thoughts about illegal aliens with a Bible verse, those people are hiding something. That's why you see pastors who get caught in relationships with male prostitutes while they are using crystal meth.

Susan, who is white, 41, and from Southern Kentucky, was raised in a Holiness church. Holiness is a charismatic denomination in which parishioners worship with much "hand clapping, shouting, and speaking in tongues." Her grandfather was a Holiness preacher, and Susan was an active participant in church activities throughout her childhood and adolescence. Like Misty, she regularly heard homosexuality condemned from the pulpit and in the pews. Susan still identifies as Christian but does not attend a church because, she said, "I never have really found a church that I felt was affirming and comfortable enough to really consider myself a part of it." She continued:

I have a lot of negative feelings toward them. I totally disagree with what they say and preach. I think that the whole God Christianity thing is supposed to be based on love, and I think that the religious Right in general is just all about hate, and it's all negative. There's nothing positive about it.

Sarah, white, 43, and from Eastern Kentucky, said that she prefers not to think about members of the Christian Right. When she does, she feels sorry for them because "they have a perspective that is so narrow and they are missing out on so much."

Brother Damien expressed a great deal of pent up righteous fury about conservative Christians during our interview. He spoke for 20 minutes on the sins and crimes they commit and argued that by doing so in the name of Jesus, they perform Satan's work. He said:

I believe that the religious Right movement is from the devil, is from Satan. It is being orchestrated by the devil. Because what does the devil do? What does the devil delight in doing? The one thing that Satan delights in more than anything else is to take people who consider themselves to be Christians and to make them, to manipulate them into believing that evil is good, and to embrace hatred and prejudice, which in fact they've done. Basically their agenda is one of prejudice and greed and war mongering, and they justify this by taking Jesus and using him as a figurehead, because their Jesus is not the Jesus of the Gospels.

Damien likened such spokesmen as James Dobson and Pat Robertson to the Pharisees that Jesus condemned in the New Testament. Linda, who is white, 29, and the preacher's kid from Texas, also believes that conservative Christians are poor representatives of Jesus Christ. She said, "I think people like that *like* having someone to hate, to be perfectly honest with you." Linda explained that she has stopped listening to anything conservative Christian leaders have to say:

I don't listen to them at all. I think that they don't have any right to speak for God. I don't think they have any right because if they're half as good at what they do, at being "men of God," then they know damn well, they're fully aware, of what they're putting out there as false. They know damn well it's not true. But they'll still spout it because it's what people are used to hearing. It's what people almost want to hear, because they want to have it confirmed for them that everything they've been told their whole lives isn't based on a lie. I feel like anybody who is so ready to judge another person, so ready to condemn them to the pits of hell, to me, is not a good representative of Jesus Christ, sorry but they're not.

Keith, who is white, 47, and from Northern Kentucky, and his partner, Henry, who is white, 51, and from Illinois, also critiqued conservative Christian attitudes about homosexuality on theological grounds. Keith, a former Catholic priest who was defrocked and excommunicated (following an arrest for having sex in a local park with a man) related:

What we experience in this country are these very fundamentalist, very ridiculous churches that are absolute, and have this power over the media, have money and spend it and try to blackmail people. Try to entice them into fear and all this kind of stuff. Their effect is scary. It's very frightening to me. I do not believe that they are really of God in a sense of . . . they're going to such extremes in trying to separate people and make absolute

186 << "THE OPPOSITE OF FAITH IS FEAR"

statements about who's right, who's wrong, and who's okay and who's not okay and who's legitimate in the church and who's not legitimate, how you do this and how you do that. All they're doing is tearing people apart instead of helping people. I think they're there for power and just trying to influence and confuse people. I think they're foolish. I do not think that technically they should call themselves a church. Not in a strict sense of what the scriptures tell us church is about.

Henry, like Keith, and many Bible Belt gays, observed that leaders of the Christian Right use fear to manipulate people:

It's their way or the highway and they try to put that fear in that only their way is the right way, and their reading of the scriptures. They pick and choose what they want out of the scriptures to justify their hatred, especially [the book of] Leviticus. They always want to quote that when they talk about gay and lesbians. But they don't really want to go into the whole book of it. They quote so much in the Old Testament and not what Jesus says. They manipulate it, and I think it's very political.

Derek, who is white, 39, originally from Ohio but a longtime resident of Kentucky, felt especially frustrated with the ways that conservative Christians have, in his words, "hijacked" Christianity and the identity of Christian in order to exclude gay people. He believes that the media perpetuates this perception by not presenting gay Christian and conservative Christian beliefs with equivalent institutional weight. For example, when publishing perspectives on Christianity and homosexuality, the media will interview the pastor of a local well-known megachurch and balance this with the thoughts of an individual gay Christian. Derek explained:

The media really feeds this by just going to any random person that will talk to them about the issue, but then going to the anti-gay people who are Christian to get their official response. And then you try to say, "well, if you're going to talk to them, why didn't you talk to our official advocacy spokesperson in the Kentucky Fairness Alliance?" They just talked to some random gay person on the street and that's very frustrating.

This kind of media construction stacks the deck against perceiving gay Christians as valid because any single gay Christian stopped on the street is likely not as verbally polished as an institutional leader, nor do such individuals offer a consistent institutional message. The anti-gay Christian perspective, according to Derek, "has the stamp of institutional correctness, whereas talking to the gay person on the street, it's just oh this is my random opinion." Derek observed that members of the Christian Right likely have many more diverse perspectives on homosexuality, as well as many other social issues, than the leaders express. He asked, "How did we come up with the idea of the religious Right anyway? We had significant spokespersons that claimed to voice the opinions of this homogenous group of people that all believe the exact same thing." By sounding a consistent institutional message about sin, hell, and God, conservative Christian leaders model compulsory Christianity for their followers. They preach that there is only one proper way to be a Christian and that any who do not ascribe to this belief system are doomed to hell. This hegemonic message in the Bible Belt panopticon creates a climate of intimidation which discourages those with dissenting opinions from sharing them, and thus produces the impression that everyone is in agreement about what is the best, right, godly way to be.

Mary and Jeff, quoted earlier, and Jordan, white, 51, a lesbian raised in Indiana who lived many years in Kentucky, situated the practices of conservative Christians in a historical context. Mary, a philosophy professor, compared contemporary global expressions of religious fundamentalism to fascism in the 1930s. She explained:

> It's like fascism in the '30s. All of the sudden, it rises. It's in Italy, it's in Spain, it's in Germany. Fundamentalism is in our lifetime the right-wing movement. And I suppose it will pass as other things do, and it's probably going to get more violent and nasty before it passes. As people get more desperate.

Jeff compared the contemporary Christian Right to the Catholic Church in the Middle Ages:

> People were burning witches in the Middle Ages at the same time the nobility and the rich were living high on the hog all in the name of Jesus and God and the church. They were not doing what their teaching said, which was to help the poor. In some ways, the religious Right is the same thing. They are super Christian Yuppies who are making all this money, and they are voting for people who hurt the poor, and hurt the environment, who are doing anti-Christian things, and they can do it because they are doing it under the name of God. It's the same old story with the conquistadors who tortured and killed Indians under the name of God. The church burned witches and oppressed the poor, but they did it in the name of God. If you are benefiting from all this stuff, it's a very convenient rationale.

Jordan, a historian, explored the idea that conservative Christians did not really mean to do harm to gay people, but are rather acting out of ignorance. A commonly held hope is that if homophobic Christians fully understood the reality of gay life and accepted that we are all humans struggling to get by the best we can, homophobic attitudes would dissipate. But, like Mary, Jordan thought conservative Christians understood the arguments in support of gay rights and rejected them as invalid. Jordan related:

> I read somewhere that in the abolition movement, and in civil rights, people have long made the mistake of believing that racists and slave owners were just poorly informed, and that if you just explained it to them enough, they would see the light and change their ways. What they finally had to realize in the abolition movement, what the war was over, is not that pro-slavery people hadn't heard the arguments, they just didn't buy them. They didn't agree with them. I think that's the way it is with people who are homophobic. It's not that they haven't heard the arguments, they just don't agree, they don't buy it.

Mary observed that just as she was certain that no one could produce an argument that would persuade her that gay people were "morally bankrupt, there are people for whom no argument is going to convince them that we are full-fledged human beings and should be treated with full equality." Mary believed that engaging in conversation with people like that is a "real waste of our time." She said that she shared no more moral ground with leaders in the Christian Right than with a "convicted Nazi."

Talking Back

Pray the Gay Away is a story about the toll of homophobia, how individuals resist and negotiate homophobic attitudes, and, most importantly, a narrative of transformation. To this end, I asked each lesbian and gay man I interviewed to, in the words of the scholar bell hooks, "talk back." I asked them to share something about their lives, thoughts, experiences, and realizations that might make a difference in another's negative or uninformed perception of gay people. hooks theorizes that "talking back" is a speech act that liberates the oppressed. She writes, "true speaking is not solely an expression of creative power; it is an act of resistance, a political gesture that challenges politics of domination that would render us nameless and voiceless."[16] The Bible Belt gays I interviewed had much to name and voice.

Annie, who is African American, 23, and from Cincinnati, simply said, "Gay people have feelings, and the only thing that truly separates me from you is me wanting to be with a woman." Jeff said, "Any belief, or sense, you had that gay people are different or 'other' is really a fabrication." Matt, African American, 48, and from Kentucky, explained, "I'm the same as everybody else. We pay bills. I go to church. I have faith. I have religion. I have nieces and nephews. I have animals." Peter wanted to remedy a host of misperceptions about his day to day life:

> I'm a boring person, I go to work, I come home, I go to meetings. I teach my class. I'm not a revolutionary. I'm not out to destroy the family. I've not got any gay agenda. I'm not out to tear down the family. I'm not out to convert your children. I'm not out to steal your husband.

Christina, who is white, 24, and from Central Kentucky, explained that it mystified her when people treated gay people hatefully. Ardent about social justice issues and serving as the adult advisor for a youth gay straight alliance and pride center, Christina was puzzled that some conservative Christians did not perceive how interconnected were all humans. A homophobic heterosexual could still have a gay child, for example. She continued, "I'm going to turn around and laugh one day when your kid comes out. It sounds like a bunch of sappy bull crap, but we're all affected in one way or another" :

> Being really passionate about social justice issues in general and seeing the struggle of all kinds of oppressed people, the thing that always comes to my mind is, why can't people understand that we're all human and we're all connected? That something that affects one person in your community, some way or another, is going to affect you.

This hopeful note—that we are all human, we all suffer, we all pay our bills and mow the yard, and that if you just understand this, everything would be okay—sounded by 90% of the Bible Belt gays I interviewed was tempered by the desire of many that conservative Christians fully comprehend the oppression gay people endure.

"We Have to Do Special Things in Order to Receive the Same Rights"

My interview question on "talking back," a version of "what would you like to say about your life to people who are ignorant about gay people that might create social change?" at first typically confused the Bible Belt gays I interviewed. Most initially responded by stating what, to them, was self-evident: conservative Christians don't listen and are impossible to communicate with.

The assumption that they are always most "right" in their interpretation of God's law prevents them from seriously considering any other point of view.[17] To elicit more reflection after a response like this, I qualified the question with the following sorts of comments: "What would you like to say to those that are in the middle?" " . . . those teetering on the edge?" " . . . those people who would listen and might be affected by what you say?" "What do you want to share that you feel is not heard and not understood?" "What about if one in the parish was open to hearing something different?" "What would you say if it might make a difference in someone else's life?" and "What do you want to say about being gay if you were sure you would be listened to?" The discursive and linguistic efforts I made to explain this concept suggest a finding: Bible Belt gays have had so few opportunities to present their ideas to potentially homophobic heterosexuals, it required extra time and effort to explain the question.

For example, Misty, who had charged conservative Christians with ethnocide, responded, "If they were not combatant to me, I would be willing to express my ideas with them, because I'm really open to expressing my ideas, but if they are the typical conservative person they're going to tell me that I'm wrong. They're going to cut me off, and not listen to me." Misty struggled with being willing to say anything at all to Christians. During a lengthy exchange, we realized that she was so angry that it was not only difficult for her to conceive a situation in which a genuine exchange of ideas might occur, but she was not sure she even wanted to talk with a Christian. After much coaxing, Misty said the following:

> I would make a statement about how it's hypocritical that they preach love and acceptance yet they also preach, "hate the homosexuals," or "we're glad you're dead," or "we wish you were never here." I would like to make them understand how contradictory that is, and I would like, and it would be very impossible, but I would like to let them inside my worldview to understand what the oppression of not having the same rights that they do feels like. I want them to understand oppression.

Partners Susan and Kimberly wanted Christians to take them seriously, not dismiss, abuse and/or ignore them. They explained that the oppression they endured put undue hardship on same-sex relationships in general, and their relationship in particular. Susan said, "I think there is such a misconception of our lifestyle in general. Our relationships are just as real, and intense and committed." Kimberly interjected:

I think we deserve the same opportunities. What makes me mad is that we aren't given the same opportunities. It's hard, as gay couples, to achieve the same things that straight people do sometimes because you really have to struggle to do things together, a lot of things. It's not as easy as just signing your name on the dotted line sometimes. And, I would like to just have equal opportunity.

Tonya, who is white, 30, from Kentucky, echoed Kimberly's comments saying, "We want the same kind of rights as everyone else. We aren't asking for anything special. We are just asking to be who we are. Nobody else is scrutinized like this." I interviewed Tonya with her partner Laura, quoted earlier, and their friend Frank, who is white and 33. All are from Kentucky. After Tonya said this, the four of us segued into a discussion that detailed the complex and tedious intricacies of travel we might take, and the paperwork we could complete, to partially legalize our unions. We shared our collective knowledge on states in which same-sex marriage is legal, and the documents a lawyer might prepare that gave one legal access to a life partner in the hospital, and rights to shared possessions in the case of a partner's death. When Frank commented that he was willing to go through these necessary, if laborious, steps to partly institutionalize his relationship, Tonya made the following observation, "That's not really the point. The point is they talk about us asking for special rights, but we have to do special things in order to receive the same rights, and it's ridiculous."

"A Faithful Person Is Not Fearful"

The theme of fear emerged repeatedly in interviews. Many Bible Belt gays identified fear as the psychological key controlling the imaginations of conservative Christians. Derek, quoted earlier, observed that conservative Christians not only worked to inspire fear in their followers but also acted out of fear:

My view of the religious Right is that they are basically acting out of fear a lot of the time because they don't understand gay people. Rather than directly interacting with gay people, and liberal people, and trying to change hearts and minds one at a time, they would rather act in the political way to make things illegal, to force you to act in what they consider to be a moral way. To perceive things with fear rather than to change hearts. Which, I think if anyone were to look at objectively, just is not the heart of the Christian gospel. It is that God works in your heart to change who you are, and in the actions of your life, you act out what you believe internally. And in law nothing will change that.

Derek especially wanted heterosexual Christians to understand that he was also a Christian who adhered to a similar set of core Christian beliefs. He explained that "people don't make decisions about what they believe based on facts. They believe on a more personal level. So I really believe that having dinner with people like that once a week for six months" would create the most lasting change. Derek shared that he had already tried this with limited success with the students at a local, conservative seminary:

> Last year a couple of times, I sat down with a large group of seminarians, and we talked about what it was like to be gay and Christian. And I spent a good deal of time offering my Christian credentials and talking to them in their language, which I know. I am a Christian, and I am even their kind of Christian in many, many senses, and I can help them really see that I am their neighbor and I am not their enemy. I am one of the us and not one of them. I mean I don't want anybody to be one of them, but maybe we would have fewer of them if they realized I am one of us.

Derek, a self-described "right-wing homophobe," and politically active conservative Christian for much of his life, had well-earned insight into the psychology of conservative Christians. In the early 1990s, after starting, but not finishing a degree in theology—largely because of his struggle over his own same-sex attractions—Derek started work at a Christian publishing company. Through the editor-in-chief, Derek met a notoriously homophobic conservative politician running for the state senate who hired Derek to be "his righthand man." During this time, Derek began dating a man and it became "known more widely in the gay community that 'Candidate Fred' had this gay guy working for him and a few people got upset about that and threatened to out me."

Derek lost friends and was asked not to teach Bible Studies to children at his church when people learned he was gay, even while he was still a self-identified conservative Christian. Under this strain, Derek decided to out himself to "Fred." Derek asked Fred to lunch and, in the privacy of the car, shared that he was gay. Fred responded, "I think it's no worse than somebody that's an alcoholic or has some other personal struggle that they have to deal with, so if you need anything just let me know." Derek explained that he was relieved this had gone so well, but soon found himself shut out of any visible political association with Fred. Although this concerned Derek, he never wanted to consider himself a single-issue voter, and still identified as a conservative, Republican Christian. He explained, "while it bothered me, the things that Fred said about gay people, I was also very much in favor of many of the things that he was pushing, aside from that."

Derek has an "outsider within"[18] and, like many gay people rejected and excluded by once-close friends and family members, an "insider without" perspective on local Republicans and conservative Christians; he believes "that many Christians or conservative Christians or people that are considered to be Christians don't know how to get along in this world with people that are different." One of the defining characteristics of fundamentalism is separation from secular society. Fundamentalists fear that interacting with those who are unsaved may tempt them astray from God's law.[19] Because of this, Derek believes some Christians are afraid to think for themselves and prefer to let a leader think for them. For such people, it is only necessary to wave one's Christian card to be recognized as "one of us." He continued:

They will empower people to take care of this for them because they can't seem to get around their fear of interacting with the world on their own. So, if there are some leaders that do interact with the world in some effective way, and they empower them, this leads to problems because the leaders recognize the fear of their followers and so they try to act on that fear and use it in harmful ways.

Derek explained, "And when they need something, they just look in the Yellow Pages and find anybody that advertises their religious symbol, and then they don't have to be afraid that they are not of their Jesus."

Keith, quoted earlier in this chapter, believes that by focusing on a message of fear and by behaving fearfully, conservative Christians "are slipping away from the true definition of being a church and being a faithful community." While he rose to refill his coffee cup, I could see in his erect posture the years spent officiating Mass and offering succor to the weary and heartbroken as he declared, "I'd like to say that the opposite of faith is fear, that a faithful person is not fearful." Keith's partner, Henry, seemed genuinely puzzled by the fear-driven actions of conservative Christians, and brought up the subject of "fear" several times during our interview. When offered the opportunity to "talk back," what Henry wanted to do was ask a question of homophobic Christians. Henry said:

I want to know why. What are you so afraid of? That marriage has to be between a man and a woman? How is our relationship, the union that we have, different from the union that the persons of the opposite sex have? And you're trying to amend your constitution to say that you want marriage to be defined this way, to alienate us from the same rights that you have as an opposite sex union? I just don't understand.

Peter observed that conservative Christians must be very insecure about the stability of their own relationships to fight so vehemently to prevent same-sex couples from marrying:

> If someone else's marriage is so shallow that gay people being allowed to get married would have the power to undermine their marriage then I feel like they didn't really have a marriage to begin with. I thought people were supposed to get married because they loved each other, because they had a mutual respect for each other, because they share common values and they want to generally to share each other's lives. But if you are so worried about who else can belong to your exclusive group, then your marriage is really a sham as far as I'm concerned.

Clyde Wilcox and Carin Robinson, scholars on the Christian Right, directly address Peter and Henry's confusion about why some conservative Christian seem threatened by gay marriage, and why they put so much effort into anti-gay activism. In their book *Onward Christian Soldiers?* Wilcox and Robinson write that because the Bible promises that children raised in the faith will adhere to it, "this leads many activists to believe that gays and lesbians seduce heterosexuals, and that the gay and lesbian lifestyle is powerfully attractive."[20] Some conservative Christians believe that any public legitimation of homosexuality (i.e., domestic partner benefits, gay/straight alliance clubs, antidiscrimination legislation, same-sex marriage, allowing gay people to serve openly in the military) can tempt children and adolescents into a sinful homosexual lifestyle. In fact, the fear that a gay lifestyle may prove irresistible to suggestive young people does undergird some conservative Christian anti-gay activism.

Brother Damien explained that he was fed up with conservative Christians "up in arms against gay marriage" condemning the "gay lifestyle" and monopolizing the public conversation about morality. He said that he wanted to stand up to them and say:

> Excuse me, I happen to highly disapprove of ultra-conservatives, of nationalists, of nationalism, of people that are war mongers, people that want

to worship the flag, televangelists and the fundamentalists. I have a major problem with these people. I believe I disapprove of their lifestyle. Many progressives would say we disapprove of their lifestyle. There are tens of millions of us, does this mean, therefore, that if we disapprove of their lifestyle, which we do, do we choose if they marry or not? Should we then? That's a part of our philosophy, that's a very deep part of us. We very much disapprove of their lifestyle, and that's part of our religious beliefs in many cases, or our deeply felt beliefs. There are tens of millions of us, shouldn't we have the right to decide if these people that we disapprove of get to marry or not? Why hasn't that argument been brought up more often?

This is both a good question and a unique perspective on conservative Christian practices, and I appreciated that Brother Damien accomplished the challenging task of centering progressives from a gay perspective. Ultimately, I believe his argument has not been raised more often because gay people are still very peripheral to heterosexuals, and legislating social attitudes is in opposition with a progressive vision of social life.

What Would Jesus Do?

Many of the people I interviewed discussed their own Christian identity and deliberated over how Jesus would likely minister to gay people. Jeff said:

> Science doesn't know for sure why people are gay. Jesus said, "treat each other as you would want to be treated." A lot of things in the Bible people don't follow, like eating pork or cutting their hair. You have to use your mind as well. You don't win anything by being mean to people.

Katie, Black and 26, whom I interviewed in Texas, wanted Christians to care for her like they believe Jesus would:

> I want to say that I'm human. I don't feel as though I am committing a crime. I don't feel as though I am hurting anyone. As someone who has also been raised in the church, when you listen to Jesus and the things that He has done, He has always told us to love everyone and He never showed hate towards anyone. So anyone who is listening to this who is religious and thinks that I'm going to hell, I think they are entitled to their opinion but I would like it if they would treat me the same way Jesus would have treated me, which would be with love and understanding.

Caroline, who is white, 52, and from Kentucky, queried, "Is it better for me to love, or them to hate?" To which her partner, Jennifer, who is white, 39, and also from Kentucky, responded, "You can sort of turn that statement around from us to them: love the sinner but just hate their sin. It's just hate." Jennifer perceived conservative Christians as "sinful" in their attitudes and behaviors toward homosexuals.

Celia, who is white, 40, and from Eastern Kentucky, sounded frustrated when she said, "Being different is not a threat. It's important for people to be able to live their lives with integrity. I mean, if you can't do that, what's the freaking point?" She continued:

> The Bible says a lot of stuff about a lot of things, and contradicts itself on many occasions. It doesn't have to be the tool that people use to scapegoat people. Jesus also said, "do unto others as you would have them do unto you." Let's just treat people with some compassion and move on. That's what I wish people would adopt, and that's how I wish people would behave.

Keith thought that sitting down and talking with leaders in the Christian Right would not change anything, and he did not want to engage in any such arguments. Keith, in fact, was concerned that others I interviewed might speak out of "anger or rebellion" and that might drown out a "much more profound message." He continued:

> If the person would really sit there and listen, I would say "I just want you to meet me. I want you to realize that I'm 47 years old, and I was an ordained priest 27 years ago, and that I have a church, that I have a congregation, that I've preached the gospel every Sunday, that I very much believe in God and believe in Jesus Christ and the Holy Spirit. And I believe that it has had a hand in my life and it has changed me. It has not changed me to be straight, nor will it. Nor do I feel in any way I need to. I don't have any bad feelings about being gay. You're telling me I should is not going to change that dynamic. Nor would I ever try to tell you that you should be gay, because that's the way God created you and if you would take time and think about it, then maybe you'll be in a better place." I think that's what I would try to do. I wouldn't try to argue, because it's not going to do any good.

Like Keith, many Bible Belt gays wanted others to understand that they did not choose to be gay.

Conclusion: "It can't be wrong to be something that you are."

In the beginning stages of this study, in December 2006, John, a white, 18-year-old, first-year student from Eastern Kentucky, sought me out to talk about being gay when he learned of this project from a story in our university newspaper. As I wrote in chapter 2, John had heard only negative messages about homosexuality and, when he came out to his mother, she told him that she'd have preferred that he lie to her about being gay and hide it. Yet, in spite of this, John was confident enough in his own self-worth and self-knowledge to find and talk with me about his ideas on homosexuality. He explained:

> I was made this way. I didn't choose to be this way. The only choice you have is whether you want to be happy or not, and I don't think that God, or whatever you believe, I don't think that people will be this way if they weren't meant to act upon it because it's really just hurting yourself if you do something like that. Because you're not only hurting yourself if you get married and you're gay, you're hurting your wife and your kids and everything like that. So it can't be wrong to be something that you are. It's as simple as that.

His youthful clarity rings with internal consistency: this is obviously how I am supposed to be because this is the way I am. John is certain there is nothing wrong with him in spite of all the negative messages he has heard about homosexuality. Jenna, who is African American, 22, from Kentucky, and also a student, expressed a similar youthful certainty about her sexual identity. She explained, "I would say that being gay is part of who I am. It's something I can't change. Just like my skin color. I can't change it. I'm very proud of who I am, and I'm proud of the people who are like me."

The idea that sexual identity is essential, that we are "born that way," is a contentious claim among some activists and researchers. Some sexuality scholars maintain that the "born that way" argument perpetuates heterosexist ideology because underlying it is the assumption that no one would "choose" to be in a same-sex relationship if they could "choose" to be in a heterosexual one.[21] As Janet R. Jacobsen and Ann Pellegrini write in *Love the Sin: Sexual Regulation and the Limits of Religious Tolerance*:

> We want to recast the debate, shifting from arguments over origins (is homosexuality "inborn" or "chosen"?) and analogies of race to robust public discussions of sexual ethics. In our view, it does not matter how one becomes homosexual, *because there is nothing wrong with homosexuality*.[22]

Even worse, the "born that way" argument allows conservative Christians to set the terms of the debate over homosexuality: it is an argument about choice rather than the importance of sexual freedom to a society. Regardless of activist and scholarly problematizing of this argument, almost all of the gay men and lesbians I interviewed used a born-this-way framework to describe how they experienced themselves. To illustrate, Chris, (see the introduction), whose parents tried to pray the demon of homosexuality out of her, used the argument with her mother:

> My mom, for the longest time, seemed to think that it was a choice, my sexuality was a choice, that I could choose whom to fall in love with, who to love. I said to her on the phone not too long ago, "Mom, who would choose to live the lifestyle if all your public demonstrations of affection are closeted? You have to watch the verbiage of your language. Who would choose that? Who would choose to live a life of seclusion and secrecy? Who would choose that? I don't think it's a choice. I think you're born that way."

Several interviewees wanted Christians to understand that they believed sexual orientation is not a choice for gay people or heterosexuals. Cathy observed:

> People get so caught up in the sex part of it that they don't understand that you've got two people who love each other, period. And if you want to start quoting the Bible and basing it on religious kinds of things, the God that I know is all about love in whatever form it comes in. I didn't choose this. This is just the way that he made me. People don't choose to be gay, you don't make that choice. People don't choose to be heterosexual. It just is what you are. It's just whether or not you choose to accept it. We want the same mediocre things that straight people get, and why is it bad? Why is it bad that I love a woman? I mean, why is that a bad thing? That's not evil, that's not wrong, that's what God is. God is love.

Elena, who is Hispanic, 20, and from Texas, echoed Cathy on her thoughts about God and love, saying simply that since God is love, loving is not a sin. Further, she wondered, as did many other Bible Belt gays, "why would you condemn me for being happy?" Jose, who is Hispanic, 19, and also from Texas, reiterated John and Elena's thoughts. He said, "What makes us happy is what we are supposed to be."

Like oppressed groups throughout history, gay people struggle to articulate our lives so that we appear as human in the eyes of our oppressors. The political strategist Suzanne Pharr theorizes in her book *In the Time of the Right: Reflections on Liberation* that "domination politics" renders violence done to those constructed as inferior as either invisible or "deserved." To counter this, bell hooks argues, speech—the sharing of stories and insights—can transform members of marginalized groups from objects to subjects in the eyes of the larger culture, and make visible what was invisible.[23] Among my goals with this study is to help make religious-based abuse visible and provide a place for Bible Belt gays to share their stories. We do not really know what gay culture is, or might be, were it allowed to thrive free of religious-based homophobia in the Bible Belt. The next chapter explores how Bible Belt gays choose happiness and will illustrate that everyone benefits from the expansion of gay cultural expression, not its destruction.

8

"God Can Love All of Me"

Living the Life

No one can tell you how to live your life. No one can tell you when
to be happy or when to be sad. No one owns your happiness.
—Eric Alva, Hispanic, 37, from Texas

Imagine life is a river endlessly moving, and you, a single person in a small,
sturdy boat are navigating the currents. At any point in your life you can
choose to go with or against the flow of the river. If you paddle against the
current, upstream, you expend an enormous amount of physical and emotional energy fighting the impersonal flow, and you do not go very far. The
river is stronger than you are. You need to rest and eat and play while the
river never stops moving. If you are determined to go upstream, you have
to be vigilant, guarded, and careful because any brief respite may sweep you
back in another direction. There is little time and energy to explore enticing
tributaries when you are locked in a battle against the flow of your life. For
Bible Belt gays, being in tension with homosexuality is a constant state of
trying to paddle upstream.

At some point, each of the gay men and lesbians I interviewed decided
that fighting the current was futile, unnecessary, and a waste of time. Each
lifted up the paddle and let the current sweep them somewhere new, somewhere unexplored and unpredictable. They *allowed* homosexuality, in spite

of all its accompanying barriers of discrimination, oppression, and rejection, and in doing so freed up a vast reservoir of energy and joy. This is not to say that any claimed their lives were suddenly perfect after coming out, but to the degree that they could simply let their homosexuality *be*, they had more time and energy to invest in their own happiness. As Eric Alva, the first soldier wounded in the Iraq War succinctly stated, "No one owns your happiness." In rejecting conservative Christian theology about homosexuality and heterosexual expectations about partnerships, my interview subjects learned how to choose happiness. This was something, they explained, that they deeply appreciated.

The final interview question I asked of my participants was simply, "What do you value about being gay?" After one to two hours spent analyzing and critiquing their observations and experiences of homophobia in a variety of forms, this last question usually shifted the tone of the interview. After a moment or two of confusion (many remarked that it was an unusual question, one they had never before been invited to contemplate), the air grew lighter, we breathed more deeply, we smiled, laughed, and enjoyed paying attention to this new topic: what was special and wonderful, what we loved about being "gender outlaws" as the gender theorist Kate Bornstein posits. Jeff, who is white, 42, and from North Carolina, explained, "straight people's lives are laid out for them. We have another path, our own special destiny." Although this path may contain a great deal of discrimination and oppression, almost everyone I interviewed found much to appreciate about their queer lives and gay culture.[1] For example, Jason Johnson, who is white, 20, from Kentucky, and expelled from the University of the Cumberlands for being gay, believes that we are still trying to figure out what it means to be gay. This is a journey that Jason enjoys:

> I don't want to follow the tried and true path. I don't want to follow the path that is easy. I want to make my own path, and not let anybody else say you have to be this, or you have to be that. I want to be who I want to be. And I think being gay gives me the freedom to do that.

Jason values thinking for himself, deciding his own life, and the emotional and psychological expansion such internal freedom provides. Most of the Bible Belt gays I interviewed, like Jason and Jeff, worked for their mental freedom by engaging in lengthy self-reflection on what it means to be different around people who are scared of difference. In doing so, they earned the unique gaze they have on the social world. Like a musician or dancer or chef or scholar who has logged hundreds (even thousands) of hours practicing their profession and thus can perform complicated tasks with an effortless grace mystifying to others, interview subjects demonstrated a facility to both detect hypocrisy and follow their own truths.[2] They demonstrated what Martin E. P. Seligman, a psychologist and former president of the American Psychological Association, classified as *Character, Strengths, and Virtues*: "kindness, fairness, authenticity, gratitude, and open-mindedness."[3] Several candidly shared that they believed being gay had made them *better people*: more interesting, more honest, more loving, and less judgmental.

"It Has Been Good for Me to Be an Oppressed Minority"

Colin, who is white, 30, and from Western Kentucky, explained that "the best thing about being gay has been that it has changed my worldview." He continued:

> It has been good for me to be an oppressed minority. I feel like it has shaped my world view for the positive. Had I not been, I worry that I could have been one of these people who feel very entitled to his privilege. I think I have enough self-awareness to know that I very easily could have been that. I think that the biggest blessing of being gay is having walked a mile with no shoes, being unreasonably and irrationally denied full citizenship or full acceptance, gives a really positive insight into how you should treat people.

Colin's partner, Jeff, agreed, "For me the same thing. I think that if I had been born a straight, white male southerner, I don't think I would have as much of an understanding of women, or other people, as I do." Derek (see chap. 7), had a similar insight into his character. Derek said bluntly, "I'll just say that had I not ended up being gay, I would have been an asshole." Derek identified as a conservative Christian before he came out and maintained his Republican political identity for some time afterward. In terms of their gender presentations, Colin, Jeff, and Derek easily "pass" as heterosexual. They are tall, reasonably handsome, and reasonably butch, white men. Each recognized that, had they not been gay, this set of personal qualities, coupled with class and educational privilege, would likely have made them more selfish, less caring people. Derek elaborated:

> Now there may be some people who think I'm an asshole anyway, but significantly fewer. Because the experience of being gay and being a nonmainstream person has opened me up to understanding and relating to

the whole world of people that are different in other ways that I can't even relate to. I just don't think I could understand what people are talking about when they're saying there are people that don't get along with the current structure of marriage, and there are people that are of different races that have been downtrodden and experience systemic institutional discrimination each day and things like that. I just wouldn't have any clue about that stuff had I not experienced othering myself.

Derek, Colin, and Jeff experience the benefits of being a majority member in every area of their lives except sexual identity. Were they heterosexual men, without a gay window into what it feels like to be discriminated against for no good reason, each believes he might never have perceived oppression at all, in anyone's experience, either by race, gender, class, age, or level of ability.

William, who is white, 24, from Southern Kentucky, and Derek's partner, expanded upon Derek's comment on "othering":

Once people have judged you based on some otherable characteristic about yourself it forever changes you, and I think for the better. It opens up your eyes. You see people do things that are racist or sexist, or some serious discrimination based on religious identity—how you can't get off work for Ramadan. You just start to notice it all the time because you know what it looks like. So I think that has made me a more interesting person. I like the fact that I know that about myself.

"Othering," as the French feminist Simone de Beauvoir described in her book *The Second Sex,* is to perceive those who are different as inferior, not belonging, not "one of us," and therefore not fully human.[4] Although only a few specifically used the language of "othering," most of the Bible Belt gays I interviewed explained that they believed experiencing oppression had made them more empathetic and compassionate. Laura, who is Native American, Melungeon, and white, 37, from Kentucky, and a Special Education teacher related:

I think that it has helped me to see through other people's eyes, through oppressed people's eyes. Especially when I'm dealing with my kids, because I think that they are really oppressed. They have to depend on someone for almost everything. I have some high kids, but I have some low kids too. I think it helps me to be able to see through their eyes and to understand better. We can make a judgment, but you hold off on judgment. You just see the situation for what it is and then you get up and go from there.

Katie, who is Black, 26, interviewed in Texas, felt that being a lesbian had taught her much about other people, especially to notice when someone is left out, ignored, and/or dismissed:

> Having to go through the experience, even as horrible as the experiences were, I think I have learned a lot about people being a lesbian. I've learned a lot about what it feels like to not be considered a part of a group. So, even reading newspaper articles about any situation, I always tried to look at the small man, or try to listen to the voice that's not heard because I feel like my voice wasn't heard and I would have loved it if someone would have listened to me, or maybe looked out for me. So, I think living as a lesbian makes me a little bit more sensitive to certain issues.

Ernesto Scorsone, who is white, 54, a former state senator, attorney, and currently a judge in Central Kentucky, felt that being gay provided him a greater "sensitivity to things that are outside the norm." Ernesto, whose family immigrated to Kentucky from Italy when he was eight, said:

> That whole experience, which parallels my experience of being an immigrant in this country and being different, I think it's made me a little more reluctant to prejudge people, and issues, and subjects. That doesn't mean that I can't have knee-jerk reactions, 'cause I can, but I think it makes me a little more open to people. It's really good in the criminal justice system. I do criminal defense work where my job is to defend people that have been charged with some type of horrible crime. People have knee-jerk reactions to people that commit horrible crimes understandably, but, my job is to find some good in folks, and to articulate that to the court.

Ernesto believed that his lived experience as a gay man increased his efficacy in his work and, like many of my interview subjects, made him a better person. He continued:

> I do the best that I can for my clients. Being a member of a minority that's been discriminated against in horrible ways makes me a little more sensitive to groups and individuals that suffer that same kind of discrimination. I think that, in some ways, it has made me a little more sensitive to people that get discriminated against, and that makes me a better person.

Like Ernesto, Jeff recognized that being gay had made him more aware of differences among people, more appreciative of those differences, and more interested in treating those who are different with respect. He drew on a scriptural metaphor to illustrate: "It has given me a deeper understanding of the commandment, or the rule, that says treat others as you would want to be treated." In interview after interview, my research participants explained, like Jeff, that for all the bad that comes with being gay, "the good that comes from it is pretty awesome if you can harness it."

View from the Margins

Many of the Bible Belt gays I interviewed valued what Mary, who is white, 61, and from Central Kentucky, described as "the view from the margins." Being an oppressed minority—in the case of my interview subjects, being gay— enables a person to see aspects of social life often invisible to those who are privileged.[5] The sociologist Patricia Hill Collins theorized that when members of oppressed groups interact in intimate settings with majority members, they have a "distinct view of the contradictions between the dominant group's actions and ideologies."[6] To illustrate, Collins described the "peculiar marginality" of Black female domestic workers in white families. Closely involved in the day-to-day functioning of a family, a Black domestic worker may form relationships with family members, especially the children, and see "white power demystified." At the same time, Black domestic workers are not family members, usually economically exploited, and remain outsiders. Collins defined this insider gaze coupled with an outsider status as the location of "outsider-within." Like Black domestic workers and, as Collins theorized, Black women in general, so too do many Bible Belt gays occupy the status of "outsider-within" in their families, churches, workplaces, and neighborhoods.

Although he expressed that he was concerned it might be a cliché, Ron, who is white, 36, and from Eastern Kentucky, believed that this view from the margins meant that "gay people have more open hearts." He continued:

> They appreciate differences, maybe not all of us, but certainly I think we're a little bit more empathetic because of the troubles we've endured. One thing I tell people about being friends with a gay person is that you are not going to be judged as harshly as you would by a straight guy.

Because gay people, as Mary explained, "see things that people who are privileged don't see," they may better understand how power and dominance operate, and consequently, develop strategies to resist, circumvent, and/or transform stressful situations. Mary elaborated:

When you're in an oppressed position, you learn a lot about power that you don't learn when you're in the powerful position. You learn all sorts of alternatives to raw power. The people who are reflective have a whole different kind of knowledge that just isn't accessible to people who have it easier in the world.

With the phrase "people who are reflective," Mary means those minority members who question inequality, those who do not accept the dominators' perception of them. Linda, who is white, 29, and the preacher's kid from Texas, can be counted among those "who are reflective." Linda believes she better understands social injustice because she is a lesbian, and she appreciates this insight:

> I call it a realization process. The last couple of years when I realized, "oh by the way, I'm gay," has made me much more aware of the social injustices in this country that I wasn't really aware of beforehand. Because it didn't affect me, so I didn't really notice. I wish I could say otherwise, but that wouldn't be honest. It's really made me aware that this country has come so far and has done so much, but we have still got a long way to go to be who we proclaim ourselves to be. So I value the insight that I've gained.

Under conditions of social inequality, people are irrationally divided based on subjectively selected characteristics such as sex, race, class, and/or sexual orientation; and power is defined in terms of control, force, and scarcity. Suzanne Pharr argues that domination politics relies on ideologies of scarcity, exclusivity, and meritocracy to perpetuate inequality (see chap. 7).[7] An ideology of exclusivity divides people into an "us" and a "them"; in other words, "you are either with us or against us," while the myth of meritocracy defines people as "deserving" or "undeserving" based on their level of material and social success. Finally, a society that draws on a model of scarcity to imagine social life sees power as a zero-sum game. Only one person or one group can win. This means if someone, or some group, gets more power— more resources, more rights, more attention, a "bigger piece of the pie"— people believe there is less for everyone else. Conservative Christians who argue that "gay marriage threatens the sanctity of marriage" operate from a paradigm of scarcity. To make certain that they are the "winners," members of dominant groups protect their piece of the pie with physical force, political legislation, and ideological manipulation. Because the ways in which institutional power, authority, and privilege advantage members of majority groups is confusing to most Americans, often deliberately so, people learn to blame individuals for social problems. In my gender classes, I describe this kind of power as "power-over." The power-over paradigm establishes a hierarchy in which inequality is inevitable and unchangeable.

What the view from the margins allows is a different, more egalitarian, feminist paradigm of power: power-with. When a group of people adopt the "power-with" framework, fear of scarcity evaporates. One can see that there is plenty to go around when people are willing to share, and that our real wealth—our ideas, creativity, love, caring, our connections to one another—do not diminish the more another of us receives and expresses. In a power-with paradigm, the more we share the less we fear and try to control, and the more we all benefit. Why fight over one pie when we can each make a pie and share it with others? Being an outsider-within allows a minority member to see beyond a power-over paradigm and sometimes transform it.

Speaking a Common Language

Judy Dlugacz, who is Jewish, 54, founder of Olivia Records and Olivia Travel, and not a Bible Belt gay, shared a story that well illustrated a transformative engagement with a power-over dynamic. In 2008 Anna and I celebrated our 10th-year anniversary with an "Olivia" vacation. Olivia Travel caters to women only and especially to lesbians. Worries about being out or negotiating homophobic heterosexuals are an additional burden same-sex couples face with vacation travel. After once vacationing at a South Carolina beach where we felt inhibited from even holding hands during a sunset stroll, Anna and I decided to splurge on an Olivia trip. I asked Judy if she would be willing to be interviewed for this project, and she graciously agreed. For close to twenty years at that time, Judy had observed lesbians from all over the United States sign up for Olivia vacations and relax. I expected she might have insights about closeting and being out, and she did. However, her most moving story was about interrupting a power-over, exclusive dynamic between lesbian travelers and native protestors in the Bahamas.

Many Olivia cruises go to the Caribbean. Certain Caribbean islands are more homophobic than others, including the Bahamas. On one visit, Judy explained, an evangelical group planned a demonstration against an Olivia ship docking in Nassau. Judy explained:

> We had been there ten times. We had no problems and we went a day after Easter. The bishops of the Caribbean had gotten together and they had condemned homosexuality. The day after Easter everyone had the day off, so now these groups, these really evangelical Christian groups were

planning to have a demonstration because Olivia was coming. So I get a call from the cruise line that says, "'Judy, we think there's going to be a demonstration when we arrive in Nassau." They said, "there is a very good likelihood that there will be a demonstration, but usually demonstrations are small."

There was a planned excursion to a private island, so the Olivia travelers had to go from the pier to waiting boats. Judy explained that she tried to minimize any anxiety the travelers might be experiencing by saying that the "government of the Bahamas has promised to protect the pier." She continued:

> So, when we woke up that morning I went out to see, was there a demonstration happening? It's a long way from where we dock to the end of the pier. There was a demonstration. There were people standing. There were speeches being made. Maybe 150 people were there. I said I wanted to talk to the leader. I don't know if he was a bishop or if he was one of the clergy, and I said to him, "we just want you to know we're here on vacation, and we're here to enjoy the town and to spend our money and, you don't even know us. We are wonderful people, and if you knew us you wouldn't be saying all these terrible things about us. We're mothers, we're daughters." He finally said, "well, you're going to burn in hell, and Jesus said . . . " And he went on and on. Then a group was starting to surround us. They said, "go back, go back [to the ship]. We want you to go back." So I said, "okay."

On her way back to the ship, Judy realized that there was no government protection on the pier, and that the demonstrators were following her back to the ship. She radioed the Olivia staff that the protestors were coming and told them to close up the ship. The staff sealed the ship, leaving Judy on the pier with the protestors. She explained what happened next:

> They are screaming at the ship, and the women were watching. They are not in any danger, and they are watching them scream at them down below. Then the demonstrators started singing a hymn. It's a beautiful four-part harmony hymn. They just start singing this hymn because they are trying to show Jesus will save you if you just stop. But, what they didn't realize was the women on board, most of whom were Christian at some point in their lives, knew the same hymn.

The Olivia vacationers then joined in the hymn with the protestors:

So the women on board are singing back to them, and waving their hands and it completely took the anger and the fierceness out of the demonstrators. Like, you could watch the power go whoop, out of them. And they finished the song and they quietly left the pier.

This is not just a story of homophobia but potentially of colonialism, neo-colonialism, racism, and class inequality. From a Bahamian perspective, any visiting cruise ship may represent greedy American tourists who feed like locusts on the resources of native people and places. And arguably, anyone who can afford a vacation abroad is materially advantaged next to those living on very little and who do not have the money to travel for pleasure and refreshment. Alternatively, while Olivia vacations are, to me, a little pricey, it is not only wealthy women who take them. Olivia offers a payment plan, and many of the guests are middle and lower-middle class. Some save for months to take an Olivia vacation, like we did, to celebrate a special event. So, while this encounter could just as easily be explored in terms of neocolonialist narcissism as belligerent homophobia, what is most interesting to me is how a divisive situation became defused through speaking a common language, that of music. I prefer to read this story in terms of transformation rather than of oppression and exploitation, because it is this reading that models how we might better connect with instead of fear one another. Because the lesbians aboard the Olivia ship spoke the same language of Christianity as did those opposing homosexuality, joining in the singing of the hymn potentially opened up common ground between the different groups and, according to Judy, drained some of the anger out of the demonstrators. And likely, what enabled the participants, both those on the pier and those on the ship, to see one another as people, and not "others," was a view from the margins—a different conception of power—that members of *each* group could access.

Community, Culture, and Connection

The majority of the people I interviewed, in some way or other, discussed that it was important and meaningful to them that they "belonged to something" and felt "a sense of membership in a club," "like we're all in this together." Julie, who is white, 51, from Central Kentucky, and Mary's partner, especially appreciated the tangible sense of female solidarity she experienced at women's music festivals. The annual Michigan Womyn's Music Festival that Julie regularly attends is a 5-day, all-female event featuring musicians, workshops, and vegetarian food in a rural part of Michigan. Women travel from all over the world to attend the festival, camping on the grounds in tents and RVs.

> The women's music is fabulous, and straight people don't even know about it, they don't even know what they're missing. And the culture is great. There is this underdog feeling, and being at the Womyn's Music Festival is powerful. Knowing that we're all fighting the good fight together basically, because living in the real world is hard no matter how good you are. So you know all those other people who are here for a little rest because out there it's so hard and here they can rest and be themselves. So I guess that's part of being the underdog. It's who I am. I mean I value it a lot more than the lie I was living before.

Peter, who is white, 29, and from Western Kentucky, talked at length about his perception of gay culture and how much he enjoyed being a part of a group that had its own language:

> I think no matter how well you fit into a heterosexual group there's something really comforting about sitting in a group of people who are just like you. Wear the same things, and know the lingo, and can talk to that. I've found comfort in being in a group of people where I can say, "oh do you think he's family?" And have everybody understand that, because by and large terms that we take for granted, like "so and so is a leather queen," or I might say, "she's a lipstick lesbian." The terms we throw about with great ease and everyone in our culture understands these terms. By and large, the straight population is still really ignorant of those things, so there's a great comfort in being able to throw these terms out and know that they are understood.

With this comment, Peter is referencing something more than a shared language among gay people. He also values not having to hide who he is with other gay people and sees gay culture as an arena in which he can stake a claim, participate, and openly interact. Peter enjoys relating with people who are like him. He continued, "no matter how supportive your straight friends are, I don't think they're ever really going to understand what it is to be gay, just like I'm never going to understand what it is to be a Black person or a Hispanic person." This shared experience of being gay is the foundation for many meaningful relationships, what Matt, who is African American, 48, and from Kentucky, identified as "that special friendship we have because of the things we went through." Like Matt, Frank, who is white, 33, and from

Southern Kentucky, described what the anthropologist Kath Weston called "families we choose."[8] Frank said:

> We actually formed another family. I think the biggest benefit is the connection that we all have with each other is emotional, and we can carry that on for years and years just because of that. We find ourselves being so reclusive back home, but once we do find the special bond, it makes it even stronger. It's like when you've gone a long time without eating and that cracker tastes so good. We've found friendships that will last forever.

Many interview subjects attributed that "special friendship" with gay people to a shared experience of oppression, like Peter, Matt, and Frank. Robert, who is African American, 24, and from Texas, also felt that by overcoming hardship, he was better equipped to help others. After describing his rocky journey coming out in his conservative Christian home, Robert said, "The one thing that journey has allowed me to do is to help other people on a similar journey. To show that you can go through the roughest of the rough, and still come out being who you are."

Caroline, who is white and 52, and Jennifer, white and 39, live largely closeted lives in a rural Kentucky county and socialize mostly within a regular group of 10–15 local lesbians and friendly heterosexual women. They explained that they appreciated the connection they had with other lesbians as well as the intensity of the bond they shared with one another. Although they explained that their small social circle sometimes felt insular, enmeshed, and incestuous (with such a narrow dating pool, members of their social circle inevitably ended up dating and partnering with someone else's ex-girlfriend), Jennifer said "I like the camaraderie with other lesbians. It seems like we all have a common bond. Not only that I have so many of the same interests with my friends, it's kind of like we're all in this together, you know." Jennifer, who tried for years to pray the gay away, even participating in ex-gay ministries, explained, "I'm a very sensitive person and I find that being able to open up my emotions to other women is so much easier with women than it is with men."

Several of the people I interviewed explained that being with the same sex offered them a "head start" on better understanding their partners, and that they experienced much greater intimacy with a member of the same sex than they felt was possible in a heterosexual coupling. For example, Sarah, who is white, 43, and from Eastern Kentucky, had been married to a man for many years; she said that had been a good relationship for much of it. Nonetheless, she felt she experienced much deeper intimacy in lesbian relationships, "The intimacy that you have with a woman you can't compare it to being with a man, and I was in a good male/female relationship for a long time, but the intimacy is so different. The connection and the community of other women that are together is different." Linda echoed Sarah:

> I value the immense intimacy and closeness that my girlfriend and I are able to share together unlike any other relationship I've ever had before. Being this way has enabled me to be more feminine than I was in any other aspect of my life beforehand, even when I was married to my husband. It's just allowed me to really relax and to be who I am. And I really value that. Darlene makes me value my femininity. She makes me feel comfortable with it and enjoy it, and see it reflected in her. Some of the things I find beautiful about her, she makes me see some of those things about myself, which I hadn't seen before her.

Among my interview subjects, both women and men (though more women than men) talked about the special connection they felt with a person of the same sex. Intimacy, intensity, and greater understanding came up over and over in descriptions of lesbian pairings. The following exchange between partners Erin, who is white, 22, and Jenna, African American and 22, both in college in Eastern Kentucky, was typical:

> ERIN: I like being with a girl because you can relate. Being with a guy, they can read magazines all they want to about what we like, what we want, but they're not really, truly going to understand anything. They're not going to understand your pains, you know, during your times. When you're with a girl, she can understand emotional stuff.
>
> JENNA: And we understand each other's boundaries. When I want to be left alone, she knows to leave me alone and just the idea of being close. The idea that I have a friend, she's my best friend, and she's my lover and she's my soul mate. That's how I feel. The best thing about being a lesbian is that she's always there. I may not have to say anything, and she knows what's on my mind. That's what I really love.

Annie, who is African American, 23, and from Cincinnati, explained that her favorite part of being gay was simply being with women. Annie shared that she felt "completed" by her partnership with a woman in a way that she was incapable of feeling with a male partner. She said:

> What I like about being gay is that I'm a very dominant person, I'm outspoken and I like to do what I like to do. I can identify with women so

much more. I used to be bi for a certain period of time, and guys could never get along with me because I wanted something and so did they and then we wanted to fight about it. What I find, a lot of women that I go out with, they're a little more docile and they kind of complete that half of me that I need. I guess, to be quite damn honest, I need somebody else who wants to depend on me to help complete me.

Some of the Bible Belt gays I interviewed believed that the quality of the connection they experienced with their partners was *only* possible between members of the same sex. Partners Susan, who is white, 41, and from Kentucky, and Kimberly, who is white, 32, and from Texas, explored this. Susan said, "I don't think there's any way that a man and a woman can connect in the same way that two women can." She continued:

They understand each other, the way we think and the way we feel. There's more intensity, really quickly if you make that connection with somebody. The relationship in general, I think it's a lot greater than what it could be with men because I don't think that men can understand women.

Kimberly immediately concurred:

I agree. I've always felt that. I have dated men. I used to date men in high school and when I first went to college and I think that there's definitely more of an emotional connection that you can have with a woman than you could ever have with a man. It's a more intuitive relationship.

Gender role socialization is likely at least partially responsible for the great intimacy lesbian interview subjects described. Our culture encourages women to be emotionally expressive.[9] Thus, a lesbian couple arguably has double the skill set of a heterosexual couple for relating, expressing, and creating intimacy with one another. I explain this to my students by asking the young women to imagine their most intense female friendship; one in which they spent every day for a year or longer talking daily or weekly, and sharing every single thought and experience with another girl. Most girls have had at least one such relationship with another girl, one that was so intense, each knew the inside of the other best friend's mind and heart like it was her own, the connection was so strong and the empathy so great, each suffered her friend's pain and expanded joyously with her happiness. I have had more than 20 such relationships with other women so far, not including my lesbian partnerships. I ask my students to re-imagine this connection and then weave in passionate romance and sexual exclusivity to understand what a lesbian pairing might be.[10] After Jennifer had explained that she found it much easier to open up emotionally with a woman than a man, her partner Caroline chimed in:

> You know what we hear a lot, from our heterosexual friends, is that they have lesbian envy because we're so close. My sister, she's been married to her husband for oh gosh, a million years, but she says she wishes she could have a bond with him that two women can have. She says that seems to be missing and she is completely heterosexual. I've had many of my straight friends say that they wish that they could have that connection with their husband.

Although woman after woman I interviewed discussed the powerful connections they felt with their female partners, they did not romanticize them. No one claimed that these intense connections were problem free. The girl who is your best friend is also the girl who can hurt you the most. My female students are sometimes loathe to pluck that special female friendship out of their memory banks to inspect and ponder because it has usually ended, a casualty of some irreparable hurt that was itself a consequence of the greater intimacy the girls had achieved.

Keith, who is white, 47, from Northern Kentucky and a former Catholic priest, believed, like Susan and Kimberly, that being the same sex as one's partner gave one a "head start" on understanding one another. Keith drew on his experience of premarital counseling with heterosexual couples when he was in the priesthood to explore this:

> As a minister who has counseled them, heterosexual relationships are extremely complicated, very difficult because they really never get to know the other one. They try and try, but they never really get to know the other one. I'm not saying in gay relationships that the two men know each other terribly well either, but they have a head start on it, and two women in their relationship have a head start on it. At least they know the other person's body as their own, and know what's going to work to a certain extent. So if there's anything that I really like about being gay, it's easy, it's really not terribly complicated to sit with a group of guys and chat and have fun and relate and have sex, it's a relatively simple thing to do. I don't have to second-guess the dynamic.

The people interviewed for this study identified as gay, so it is hardly surprising that many appreciated the quality of the emotional, physical, and spiritual connections they experienced with a member of the same sex. As Annie explained, being with a woman "completed" her. Keith ventured that members of the same sex have an easier time relating to one another. Misty, who is white, 24, and from Eastern Kentucky, said, "I like the fact that I know my lover's body because she's not a man, so I don't have to figure that out." Lesbian after lesbian referenced the "intensity" of the connection possible between women. Whether gay couples achieve *greater* intimacy than heterosexual couples is outside the scope of this study. Such a claim would be difficult to empirically support, and is not necessary to the primary story I perceive Bible Belt gays to be telling about their lives. The more important finding here is that the women and men I interviewed highly valued the intimacy they shared with their same-sex partners.

"It Is My Life, This Is not TV"

Sarah, whose youthful connection to Grace was summarily squelched by her mother and who had the misfortune to get pregnant the first time she had sex with a man and subsequently spent sixteen years in a heterosexual marriage, felt that she was finally choosing her own life when she came out. She explained that she had felt dissociated while married to a man, as if she were an actor reading a script someone else had written. Sarah elaborated:

> It is my life, this is not TV. This is me. Before, I think it wasn't me, it was TV. I was doing what TV said you should do. Even though I was the main character in it, I still felt like it was being directed by someone else. Someone else was writing it, someone else was producing it. Now I produce, I direct, I create, and I am the main character in my show, and that makes life so much fuller.

Robert echoed Sarah:

> The thing I value about being gay is that being gay is a part of me. Within the black gay community, I still see a lot of people who haven't gotten to that point to where they feel even comfortable in their own skin. They have to act a certain way at one point, and a completely different way at another way at another point. I have gotten to the point where I am who I am all the time. I used to remember when I was younger. I used to say, "man, I have given some academy award winning performances because I would be acting my behind off. I wouldn't be authentic to who I am. Now, I feel I am authentic to who Robert is.

Sarah and Robert observed, like many Bible Belt gays, that this process of self-discovery, of deliberately choosing the path not taken, directing one's own life story, and becoming authentically themselves overall made them freer, happier, more open, and more courageous people.

Elena, who is Hispanic, 20, and from Texas, described coming out as a progressive journey during which she had the great good fortune to learn new things about herself. She explained that being a lesbian allowed her to examine and reflect upon elements of her inner self, to *realize* herself. Elena related:

> So many straight people never get to experience what it is like to discover something about yourself that is different. That is going to make you happy. You don't have to grow up and realize that something about yourself, and how you are, and have to come to terms with it, and accept it, and be happy about it, then have pride in it. So I just really think it's an awesome thing to be able to fight for what we get, and be proud of who we are. I realize a lot of people coming out aren't proud right away, and I didn't come out being full of gay pride, but I've gained a sense of self and that's pretty cool, because a heterosexual might never get that. They might never get to be able to say, "I am so proud of the fact that I am straight. I had to figure out that I was straight and like, wow man, straight is . . . Yeah!" But, I get to say that, and I've never thought about that, and it makes me feel happy.

Elena rejoiced in the fact that being a lesbian allowed her to *earn* her sexuality. Darlene, who is white, 37, and from Eastern Kentucky, expressed something similar: "I've learned a lot more about myself and I've learned that I learn different. Developing my sexuality and realizing the positive side to myself that I was different but there wasn't anything wrong with me."

The majority of Bible Belt gays referenced their own happiness when reflecting upon what they valued about being gay. Christina, who is white, 24, and from Central Kentucky, succinctly illustrated this: "I like being gay. I'm happy. It's who I am." John, who is white, 18, and from Eastern Kentucky, also simply stated, "I like who I am." Eric Alva said, "What I value about being gay is just getting to be who I am—loving who I am and the person I am. It is my life." Coming to terms with homosexuality—recognizing, accepting, and making life choices that affirm it—illustrates an individual capacity for self-actualization. The psychologist Abraham Maslow described the human need for self-actualization in his book *Motivation and Personality* as "the desire to become more and more what one idiosyncratically is, to become everything that one is capable of becoming."[11]

Gender Freedom

Several interview subjects also expressed that they highly valued the gender freedom that accompanied homosexuality. Although gay people are often represented in two-dimensional, stereotyped ways in the media, the real-lived experience of being gay can be a refreshing alternative to stultifying traditional heterosexual gender role expectations. Gender freedom allows self-actualization. John explained:

> I like that I am not held to any particular stereotype. Most straight guys, if they were to listen to Kelly Clarkson [country and pop singer], people would look down upon you for that. But you really can't be looked down upon if you're gay. I'm not held to any standards. I don't have to be anything because I'm not a particular category. I can be whoever I am, and not have to care what anyone else thinks about it basically.

Jason Johnson shared that he enjoyed the "atmosphere of freedom" he experienced being a gay man:

> I think society is very rule oriented. There are gender rules, males do these things, females do these things, boys play sports, girls dance—these gender roles that people and society is very defined by. What I really enjoy about being gay is that I can be as effeminate or as masculine as I want, and I can pick the parts that I like the best. I can be in theater and I can do dance, but at the same time I can enjoy playing video games and working on computers and I can enjoy cooking. I like to be able to be a mix of all the different roles of life together, and nobody's like, "well that's weird." They aren't like, "you are a strange person because you like that," they are just like, "okay."

The women and men I interviewed, in this case more men than women, loved the gender flexibility they had as gay people. Given how narrow and constraining are the rules of masculinity for men in the United States, it is not surprising more men than women reveled in their gender freedom.[12] Gay men are subject to much harassment, insults, and the threat of physical violence. The slurs "fag," "queer," "homo," and "pussy" serve interchangeably to devalue everything that is not 100% butch, macho masculinity, and to the degree that they do not or cannot play the "tough guy" game, gay men face a daunting amount of social sanctioning.[13]

The gay men I interviewed also observed that they were not held to the same butch standard of preferences and behaviors as their heterosexual peers, and they *liked* that. Henry, who is white, 51, and originally from Illinois, summed this up saying, "We don't have to pretend to be something that we are not." The appreciation a gay person has for their gender freedom, I speculate, is not limited to those living in the Bible Belt. Recognizing that one is gay can be paradigm breaking and can open up previously unimagined possibilities not only about compulsory participation in rigid gender roles but a whole host of other life choices for gay people across the United States. To offer one small example, among the gay men and lesbians I interviewed, six separate people wryly offered some version of Peter's comment: "What I like about it is that I never have to worry about having any children."

"The Beauty of Difference Instead of Conformity"

Full conformity to mainstream relationship standards was not really possible for the Bible Belt gays I interviewed. In most cases, they lacked their family's support, the church's blessing, and their friends' full participation in their lives. Homophobia also inhibits commonplace daily chatting about what happened last weekend, and co-worker bonding over complaints about a spouse's dishwashing aversion. In short, Bible Belt gays cannot count upon external validation for being gay or their current partnership. Lacking external validation encourages, one might say even *forces* (boot-camp style), some Bible Belt gays to validate themselves. Celia, who is white, 40, and from Eastern Kentucky, explored this:

> I think, as humans, we like conformity to a certain extent. I think that it makes us comfortable with everybody and everything. I was very much like that. I had very black-and-white thinking that, frankly, was encouraged by the culture at large. You go to schools, you drive this kind of car, wear these kind of clothes, and then you're okay. It's easy to buy into. I think life is so much more interesting and beautiful if you don't buy into that. Maybe those shoes that are kind of ugly are really comfortable and I like them so I'm going to wear them even though they might not be the right brand. I think that's been a personal evolution on my part.

Cathy, who is African American, 35, and from Lexington, Kentucky, explained that she learned self-validation as a teenager watching her parents try to keep up appearances while struggling with her brother's drug addiction. She said, "We were just as crazy and as dysfunctional as everybody else. It was a good show." Cathy said that "growing up that way was real frustrating, because it was like here we go . . . trying to hide the fact that my brother is a crack head. Everybody's got a crack head in their family." She believed this family situation taught her to identify and reject hypocrisy early in life, and her youthful insight facilitated her coming out as a lesbian. Cathy prefers to experience oppression than feel like a hypocrite, and she values being with other gay people because:

> There's not that rush to keep up goals, like the pressure in my family to keep up appearances. There's not that much pressure to keep up appearances in the gay community because everybody looks different, everybody acts different, and everybody likes different things. I think gay people accept more.

This capacity to think for and validate oneself, to accept more in oneself and others, coupled with the mental freedom to reject conformity and choose difference, illustrates character strengths and virtues that positive psychologists argue "enable human thriving."[14] Celia continued:

> I feel more of a sense of validation about who I am and what I can bring to the table, what I can do, and I appreciate those things in other people, and know that they are not always the same thing and that's what's good. I've found a certain amount of camaraderie with other lesbians who weren't always okay with being who they were and having to go through some of the same struggles, with religion and with family. I feel that makes them appreciate differences, and the beauty of difference instead of conformity.

Tonya (see chap 7) felt that being a lesbian forced her out of a narrow mold and freed her up to embrace other kinds of differences:

> Where we were brought up, we weren't around a lot of diversity. Being gay opens up the doors for that. It opens you up to different cultures and different ways of life. You feel comfortable going into any situation. We go into Indian restaurants, we don't feel weird, whereas you take the regular Jo Schmo from Hazard, KY and you put him in an Indian restaurant, he'd probably be like, "what in the Sam hell is this?" I think in a way it opens your eyes up to different possibilities and I think it's helped me.

For all the discrimination she's experienced, including a homophobic mother, Tonya still feels that being a lesbian has opened more doors for her than it closed. Similarly, Ron felt that being gay had given him a greater appreciation of difference. Ron said, "I love diversity. I love having persons of color in class, I love having lots of women in class."

"God Can Love All of Me, and All of Me Can Love God"

The theme of spirituality often emerged in interviews. Jeff, for example, is hungry for more conversations about queer spirituality. He believes that "there is a mystical purpose to everything" and that gay people have our own path to travel. Jeff longs to find the queer God during this journey. He said:

> We are a small group of people compared to the population, but I think we each individually have to discover something that is much more powerful and apparent to us than it would be for a straight person. There is something that is unique to all of us, but it's not been written down or talked about and discussed that we openly know. Sometimes I long for a movement among gay people about our spirituality. We are gay, but let's look into ourselves, let's go into ourselves. Where does it lead us? What is our own path? Where is our own religion? What is God? Where is our queer God?

Frank compared coming out to spiritual enlightenment. Frank was glowing when he said the following, "I absolutely love being gay! It's the best thing that has ever happened to me. It's almost like having a spiritual enlightenment. Like a light shined on me and all of a sudden I knew, 'it's not bad being gay.'" For everything that interview subjects suffered in the name of conservative Christianity, religious-based condemnation of homosexuality also inspired them to wrestle with scripture and engage in much internal reflection upon their own relationship with the Divine. This deep engagement with religious thought and experience laid the foundation for a rich spiritual life for some *after* they accepted their same-sex attractions. Others, like Joshua (see chap. 3), Celia, and Misty, felt wounded by religion and wary of it any form. But some, like Jason Johnson, discovered that adversity had strengthened their understanding of faith, God, and spirituality. Jason confided that being kicked out of the Christian college, the University of the Cumberlands, for admitting he was homosexual was "a blessing in disguise." He explained:

> It's a blessing in disguise because it has not only empowered me, not to just give me a topic to talk about, but it said to me that this is also a way God speaks to me. God spoke to me during this, and He said, "You are going to

stay strong. You are going to have hardships where people are not going to like who you are, but you will live through it because you are being real. You are being who you were supposed to be. You were being the child that I made you to be."

Whether Jason had an actual conversation with God is beyond the scope of this book to verify. What is evident in this interview excerpt is that severe social sanctioning for homosexuality encouraged Jason to draw on *internal* (God, as Jason interprets God) rather than *external* (religious dogma, others' approval) validation. In this way, Jason not only experienced self-actualization but he demonstrated *spiritual* actualization. Specifically, Jason found his faith strengthened because he believed he received evidence that God values all forms of love:

That's how I've been able to affirm and bring faith back into my life. Now my faith feels like a piece of the puzzle that fits. God heard me, he says to me, "you are my kid, you are my child, and I love you no matter what. Because I am a God of love, anything born out of love is never wrong." I always believed this, and now I finally can back that up by saying, "this is what I believe God is telling me." This is what's right for my life and God would never give me anything that wasn't right for my life.

Like Jason, Derek believed that his journey coming to terms with being a gay man permitted him to arrive at a new understanding of God. Derek explained that he is more spiritually integrated since he accepted his homosexuality:

I feel like I'm much more integrated as a person in general, but also spiritually because, as I related earlier, growing up as a spiritual person, I felt like there was a good part of me and a bad part of me, the part of me that God loved and the part of me that God hated. So there was this civil war inside myself, but as I accepted myself as gay, I can be spiritual. God can love all of me, and all of me can love God.

Sarah also expressed that coming out—taking the path less traveled— opened her up for a richer relationship with God. When she was in heterosexual relationships, Sarah felt there was a void in her life. She clarified that the void was not a consequence of the people she was around, but that in a heterosexual relationship she was not in full alignment with herself. Because she was not well connected with herself, she could not be fully connected with God, the manifestation of one's transcendent self that Sarah now simply calls "Source." Sarah recalled:

> I was giving, giving, giving, and there was still this void of something. I don't think it really had to do with those people. I think I was still not connected the way that I needed to be connected to God, or to Source, or whatever word you want to put on it.

In the process of coming out, Sarah realized that focusing on her own happiness not only gave her personal peace and spiritual fulfillment but also allowed her to have more empathy for others. She continued:

> So it's not trying to make them happy, it's knowing that they can make their own self happy, I can make my own self happy. Source is okay with what makes me happy because I am just supposed to seek joy on this planet. I'm not supposed to save anybody. I'm not supposed to change anybody's mind about anything. I'm just to seek joy, and everything else is just going to fall into place. It's very fulfilling for me to do that, and I feel if somebody would say, "Sarah, do you try to live like Jesus lived?" I would say, "yeah, I do." I treat everybody with kindness. I try to uplift them. I try not to make problems with anybody. I try to be empathetic, not just sympathetic. I try to see them as a 3-year-old, because we were all 3-year-olds at one time and we all had the same needs and wants, and that is to be joyful, and to be loved.

Helen, who is white, 55, from Central Kentucky, and had been involved with ex-gay ministries, similarly found that the elements of her life fell into place when she accepted her same-sex attractions. Helen had struggled with the fear that she was offending God in the first on-again, off-again year of her relationship with her partner, Leslie. After grappling with scripture and consulting with almost everyone who crossed her path, she said, "you talk to this person and you agree, 'yeah I think this sounds right.' You talk to this person and you agree, 'well I think that sounds right.' Well, they both can't be right." Helen finally decided to give the matter over to God. She continued, "if it's wrong, if You really believe this is wrong, if this is really, really wrong God, then stop me." As soon as Helen and Leslie decided to leave it up to God to stop them if it was "really, really wrong," she exclaimed, "the very opposite happened. Once we came together it was like heaven opened up and we felt assured that what we were doing was okay." After making the decision to try trusting her inner guidance, Helen turned downstream in the current of her life, and was swiftly rewarded with psychological, relational, and spiritual actualization.

From the outside looking in, being gay in the Bible Belt, is full of institutional, social, and familial constraints that sideline the full participation of gay people in social life. *Pray the Gay Away* has systematically chronicled the destructive consequences of such social ostracism. At the same time, from the inside looking out, from the Bible Belt gay perspective, life as a gender outlaw includes much that is personally rewarding, even joyous. My interview subjects learned that they were more fulfilled by a homosexual union than a heterosexual one through trial and error: trying and failing to fully connect with the opposite sex, suppressing their same-sex yearnings, then exploring their feelings at gay bars, online, and in intimate friendships that evolved into romantic relationships. Since American cultural narratives about romance, dating, marriage, and family are so heterocentric, and the messages about homosexuality in the Bible Belt so negative, each person I interviewed had to engage in much personal reflection to acknowledge his same sex attractions, and then take explicit, sometimes scary actions, to find romance, sex, and a partner. Same-sex attractions were a difference that burdened most interview subjects at times but also allowed them to choose their own happiness. Although living in such close contact with intimate others who are ignorant about and fearful of homosexuality created great distress for the Bible Belt gays I interviewed, it also taught them the psychological practice of self-validation and encouraged many to engage in deep spiritual reflection.

Keith, the former Catholic priest from Northern Kentucky, gives talks on lesbian and gay spirituality. He believes that one of the gifts gay people offer the world is that we challenge others to grow. Keith said:

When I do my talks about gay and lesbian spirituality, I usually try to talk of the gifts that gays and lesbians themselves bring to the world. Another thing that I would say is positive and wonderful about being gay is that I believe that right now, in our time, gays and lesbians are challenging our world to grow, and that's a good thing. It's hard to struggle, but it's very exciting when it finally gets there. It won't be as prejudiced. It will be a different kind of dynamic because of gays and lesbians. Look at how we've changed in the last ten years: the news coverage, the commercials, the TV stuff, with comics and stuff, it's much better and wholesome. Many changes have occurred. And if that level of change can happen in the next four years, we will be in an entirely different space than we are now.

This is among the elements of being gay that I also value highly. As rough as the little traveled path can be, walking on it means that one is doing one's small bit in a larger social transformation toward equality, justice, and freedom. Any Bible Belt gay who is out to anyone else in this religiously and politically conservative region is a de facto part of this social change. I concur with Keith who concluded, "It's fun to be part of this social dynamic that challenges this world to grow."

9

What the Future Holds

In May 2011, ABC aired a "What Would You Do" news feature of a waitress harassing a lesbian couple who were ordering breakfast with their children at Norma's Cafe in Farmers Branch, Texas.[1] The waitress, the lesbian couple, and the children were all actors ABC hired to engage in controversial public behavior with the goal of assessing spectator's responses. In this episode, the waitress questioned the couple about their relationship status, and then loudly made a number of openly homophobic comments such as, "I mean it's bad enough you're lesbians but you're also parents and they don't have a father. I think that's kind of bad . . . . I think this is terrible. I think they need a dad!" She also calls them "disgusting," and finally refuses to serve them. Texas, incidentally, is one of 29 states in which a gay person can be refused service in public accommodations for being a homosexual.

During this role-play, most of the other diners looked acutely uncomfortable, and 24 out of 53—almost half—confronted the server on how rude and inappropriate she was behaving. One man pulled her aside and said, "It's completely inappropriate that when someone comes into a restaurant to have breakfast with their family that you question them about their life choices." Other customers made comments like the following: "I've never felt so uncomfortable and so beside myself with anger. You are a horrible person and a horrible waitress, and you need to leave," "You're the hate monster," "This is not the place for a political debate. This is a place for you to do your job," and "You are not king. You are not God. You have no choice. You have no place to put anybody in their place." One man told the server that Jesus did not judge. The producers of the story shared that they repeated this experiment in the more liberal state of New York. In New York, out of 100 customers, fewer than 12 spoke up for the harassed gay couple. When questioned about their lack of interest, New Yorkers responded, "It's none of my business" and "we're here to eat." Watching the episode, I felt inspired by the responses of the patrons of Norma's Café and hopeful about the future for Bible Belt gays.

For me, *Pray the Gay Away* has always been a social justice project that uses the individual experience to unpack the mechanics of domination. Among the original goals of this study was to sociologically examine and articulate what, to many, is a largely unseen world: that of the lives of Bible Belt gays. As the stories featured here illustrate, conservative Christian beliefs and practices affect people in an especially concentrated form in the Bible Belt. However, as the ABC news feature suggests, and survey data supports, Bible Belt residents also adhere to a strong culture of manners, and attitudes about homosexuality are shifting. The question remains: What are the broader implications of the stories and analysis featured here?

After six years of ethnographic observation, interviewing and study, I now understand that a certain percentage of conservative Christians are unlikely to change their belief systems to accommodate homosexuality no matter what argument or evidence is offered. The existence of the Creation Museum, and the accompanying enthusiasm of most of its guests to creationist arguments, is proof alone of this. Those conservative Christians interpret their beliefs within a total system that allows no shades of gray. For them, homosexuality is unsanctified and those engaging in same-sex behavior are sinners. Cracking open their belief system a tiny bit to accommodate gay people means the dissolution of their religious structure and the prospect of facing a great, cavernous unknowing about deep moral questions of good and evil, as well as what happens when we die. Further, many conservative Christians are taught that thinking for oneself is dangerous and sinful, and they thus have few skills to put to practice in considering alternative views. They may also cling to homophobic mind-sets to avoid being targeted and ostracized should they appear to question a literal interpretation of the

Bible. Many do not want to shake up the system that benefits them. Some, in particular political and religious leaders, appear to enjoy the power they wield over large numbers of followers. Others really believe that God hates homosexuals.

Yet, while some individuals and institutions are unlikely to ever embrace homosexuality as part of God's design, some Christian denominations do welcome gay people, and others are beginning to do so. For example, the Episcopal Church declared in 1976 that gay people are children of God and in 2003 ordained Gene Robinson as bishop of New Hampshire. Robinson is the first openly gay, noncelibate bishop in a major Christian denomination. Additionally, the United Church of Christ ordains openly gay people to the pastorate. Regions of the Christian Church (Disciples of Christ), a denomination born in Kentucky, are either now ordaining gays and lesbians or are having conversations about it. In May 2011, the Presbyterian Church voted to change its constitution to allow openly gay people to be ordained.

Ernesto Scorsone (see chap. 8) believes that social attitudes about homosexuality are changing, even in the Bible Belt. He has lived in Kentucky since 1965 and is still the first and only openly gay member of the Kentucky General Assembly. When I interviewed him in 2007, he was serving in the state legislature. He left the General Assembly to become a judge with the Fayette County Circuit Court in 2008. He explained that he was happy to be publicly out because it provided him personal relief and furthered gay rights. Ernesto believes that the 2004 election period was a high-water mark for Christian conservatives, and since then, they have begun to lose credibility and support.[2] He explained that he was hopeful about the future:

> I have this concept of homophobia as one of those giant ice sculptures that you see at functions, just slowly melting away. Sometimes we turn up the heat in the room, and it melts faster. Sometimes it gets cold and it doesn't melt as fast, but essentially, the ice sculpture is not going to be there. It's going away and I feel that it's going to keep going fast.

Ernesto thinks that the conservative Christian influence on politics is waning and, consequently, their position is going to get "lonelier and lonelier." He said, "I don't think we'll relive such a hateful time again."

National attitudes toward homosexuals, and growing institutional and political support of gay people, support Ernesto's prediction. Since 2008, the Obama administration has made considerable progress in advancing gay rights. Perhaps the biggest and potentially most important change for Bible Belt gays is the repeal of the military policy "Don't Ask, Don't Tell."

Soon gay people will be able to serve openly in the military. I expect that such institutional support of gay people, especially given the large number of military bases located in the Bible Belt, will have a trickle-down effect into individual communities and families. It may not sway those who are most certain homosexuality is wrong, bad, and unsanctified, but it will likely help more moderate Christians support the gay people in their midst. Additionally, in 2009, Congress passed the Matthew Shepard and James Byrd Jr. Hate Crimes Prevention Act that recognized sexual orientation and gender identity as protected statuses in federal hate crimes legislation. It is also the first federal law that protects transgender people. And, in May of 2012, President Barack Obama historically declared that he believed same sex couples should have the right to legally marry.

Also on the gay marriage front, in July 2011, New York State legalized gay marriage, and the mayor of New York City, Michael Bloomberg (R), officiated at the union of two staffers on the first day that gay people could legally marry. New York is the largest state to allow gay marriage since California voters repealed same-sex marriage during the 2008 political election. I predict that Kentucky will legalize same-sex marriage within the next two decades. Pew Research data demonstrates that in just two years—between April 2009 and May 2011—support for gay marriage increased by ten percentage points.[3] I believe we have reached and passed a cultural "tipping point," as the author Malcolm Gladwell defined, "the moment of critical mass, the threshold, the boiling point" about acceptance of homosexuality.[4] While we may never be fully rid of homophobia, it is already becoming less culturally acceptable to be openly homophobic, even in the Bible Belt. Like Ernesto Scorsone, I think the 2004 political election season marks this tipping point. Although 2004 was not the first time Americans heard a virulent political discussion about gay rights, the fact that so many states featured an anti-gay marriage amendment for voters to decide during a period when gay people were increasingly coming out, and various media outlets represented gay life more favorably, made homophobic prejudice particularly visible and distasteful to many.

At the same time, the groups that are most resistant to same-sex marriage and acceptance of homosexuality in general, continue to be Republicans, especially conservative Republicans, those from the South, and those identifying as evangelical.[5] This is the intersection of groups found in most concentrated form in the Bible Belt. Yet, even here, research data shows an increasing—although slower than the rest of country—arc of acceptance for gay people and same-sex relationships. When asked the survey question about whether the "impact of more gay and lesbian couples raising children is bad for society," Republican opposition to gay parenting dropped 17 points from 70% in 2007 to 53% in 2011, and white evangelical opposition dropped 15 points from 78% in 2007 to 63% in 2011.[6] National survey data illustrate that we are in a period of rapidly changing social attitudes about homosexuality.

For Bible Belt gays, quickly changing social norms about "being out" can result in misunderstandings in many people's daily lives as expectations and assumptions about sexual orientation vary. Confusing social interactions about sexual orientation are not confined to the Bible Belt. However, because of a widespread absence of institutional support for homosexuality, individuals in the Bible Belt have fewer resources to draw on when managing sexual orientation issues and thus handle them on their own. Negotiating such issues on an individual level is not necessarily detrimental, but it does make an out Bible Belt gay more vulnerable to homophobic retaliation in school, in the workplace, and/or in church than a gay person in states with legislative protections. Further, a Bible Belt gay over the age of 40 grew up and developed strategies of expression and concealment about her sexual orientation with fewer media role models than currently exist (i.e., the television show *Glee*), and before the widespread use of the Internet. To illustrate, a 15-year-old in 1985 could not go online to search for resources on sexual identity formation. Thus, it is possible that a Bible Belt gay over 40 may be especially wary about being out in his workplace, as the following story illustrates, even when working for a company that has a nondiscrimination policy directly addressing sexual orientation.

Change Is Messy

Patty is white, 40, and from Eastern Kentucky. She works for a technology office in Central Kentucky. She is gender nonconforming, that is to say, she is butch, and she is "out" at work. By out, she means that all her co-workers and supervisor know that she is a lesbian, and she assumes her customers know she is one, but she rarely talks about anything personal with them. If directly queried by a customer, Patty is willing to share that she is a lesbian, especially by indicating that she is partnered with a woman. Patty's job as a fieldworker entails repairing technology at a variety of businesses. She shared a story of helping a co-worker, "Bob," who is also gay, and also gender nonconforming (Patty called him "very queeny"), to fix a computer at a hospital. Bob is not officially out to anyone except the other gay people at his office, which include Patty and their supervisor. Bob is white, 41, and from Central Kentucky. Patty shared that she overheard the following exchange between Bob and a young, white, heterosexual woman, "Sandy," a customer at the hospital, when they were repairing the machine. Bob and Sandy had been bantering about dating when Bob said to Sandy, "you're not my type." Sandy teased back, "Of course not, everybody knows you're gay." Patty explained that Sandy was not hostile when she said this, but playful and matter of fact. But still, Bob got very red in the face after this comment, looked angry, said nothing, and the atmosphere grew strained. He never discussed the incident with Patty, though she believes he probably did so with their supervisor.

This small incident is one illustration of how changing social norms about homosexuality can be confusing and create miscommunications. From Patty's account, Sandy did not appear to be homophobic and simply assumed Bob was out. I've watched students make similar assumptions about other students who are gender nonconforming but not explicitly out. Sometimes gay people come out when another assumes she or he is gay. They might reference a partner if they have one, like Patty does, for example. Sometimes the assumed gay person neither comes out nor claims heterosexuality by skillfully diverting the conversation to other matters. These individuals appear most comfortable with the condition of inarticulation. Sometimes the assumed gay person explains that she is heterosexual, even if she is not, and sometimes the assumed gay person is just gender nonconforming but heterosexual. Sometimes, like Bob, they get angry and don't say anything at all. After the conflict with Bob, Patty said that Sandy approached her and explained that she "knew Bob was gay because he slept with a friend of mine" and that she hadn't meant to offend him.

Among the possible factors responsible for Bob and Sandy's miscommunication are age, sex, gender presentation, heterosexual privilege, and contradictory messages about being out. Sandy is almost 20 years younger than Bob and thus a member of a generation that is, overall, more accepting of homosexuality. One of the biggest changes that we have seen, and that my research supports, is that young people are most accepting of homosexuality. A May 2011 Pew study found that 69% of young people aged 18–29 believe homosexuality should be accepted by society, compared to 59% of those aged 30–49, 55% of those aged 50–64, and 47% of those over 65.[7] These generational differences can create some complicated tensions in workplaces, as Patty's story demonstrates. Because they are already more likely to perceive being gay as nothing remarkable, young people sometimes don't understand why anyone bothers with the rickety relic of the closet. Bob, on the other hand, is from a not-so-accepting generation in a Bible Belt state. He is also a gender nonconforming man who probably experienced some ridicule and harassment for presenting as effeminate. Sandy is heterosexual and never had to hide her sexual orientation. As a majority member, she might assume other people don't either. Finally, in the same workplace, with the same company, Patty is out and Bob and their supervisor are not. Customers, like Sandy, as well as co-workers, no matter what their sexual orientation, receive mixed messages because of this. A customer or co-worker might assume because Patty is out, Bob is too. Logically, someone who knows that Patty is a lesbian but who does not know whether Bob is or is not gay might wonder, "Why is Patty out and Bob isn't? Is Bob really gay? He seems gay. How come she is out and okay, but he's not?" This may be especially confounding when considering that Bob and Patty both work for a company with a nondiscrimination policy for sexual minorities.

All this speculation and confusion can lead to messy and/or strained social interactions. In such cases, I believe it is best not to confuse gender presentation with sexual orientation, not to assume anyone's sexual orientation, to interact normally, demonstrate support for gay rights, and provide opportunities for another to claim a sexual identity, or not. This unfortunately complicated and laborious linguistic process is one of the costs heterosexuals, as well as gay people, pay for living in a homophobic culture. The upside to these accumulated interactions about homosexuality, no matter how uncomfortable they sometimes are, is that over time they add up to more contact between minority and majority group members, and thus, under the appropriate circumstances, reduce prejudice.

Transformation and the Contact Hypothesis

The psychologist Gordon Allport theorized about the role of contact in reducing prejudice in his book *The Nature of Prejudice*.[8] Allport argues that contact between minority and majority members can reduce prejudice if the contact is sustained, and the participants are of equal status and have shared goals and similar values. Gregory M. Herek (see chap. 5) tested Allport's contact hypothesis in a number of studies, finding in all cases that certain kinds of contact between heterosexuals and gay people are highly effective in diminishing prejudice against homosexuals.[9] In other words, coming out, as gay rights groups have advocated for years, reduces prejudice.

One of the central questions I have grappled with throughout researching and writing *Pray the Gay Away* is what causes personal transformation. What makes someone reject a fundamentalist mind-frame while another embraces it? What set of variables or experiences allow one to value sexual and gender diversity rather than fearing it? What moment(s) can an individual point to that marks the change from shame to self-acceptance? Interview subjects, friends, family members, colleagues, even acquaintances at barbeques have all willingly engaged in dialogue about the nature of change, and gracefully endured relentless probing into their personal biographies to find some answers to these difficult questions. These conversations suggest that there is no one specific path or formula, and what works for one person will not necessarily work for another. Further, change often happens gradually so there may be no moment of epiphany one can identify. Chris's story of reconciliation with her parents is such an illustration of gradual change occurring through sustained contact.

During our interview, Chris, who is white, 42, and from Eastern Kentucky, not only shared the frightening tale of facing down her parents during an attempted exorcism (see introduction), she also explained how her parents slowly, over many years, have come to terms with the fact of her homosexuality and her 16-year partnership with Deanna. She explained that, since she first came out to them, her parents have changed "180 degrees" in their interactions with her. In the early days, they "stalked" Deanna:

> They stalked Deanna for quite some time. They would show up in Lexington unannounced. They knew where she lived. And they knew where I was living at the time. They tried to tell her things, just tried to sway her from not staying with me.

This continued for five to seven years and changed only when they realized they were going to lose Chris completely if they did not stop treating Chris and Deanna with hostility. Chris was prepared to let them go. She said, "I was not okay with it, but if that's the way that I had to live my life and be true to myself then that was going to be the way it was going to be." Chris chose herself. Now, after 16 years, they welcome Deanna into their home and treat her lovingly although Chris's mother prefers to read Chris and Deanna's relationship as best friends and not life partners. Chris said, "She has to think of it that way." She continued:

> One time my mother said to me, "Christina Lynn, do you think that you're married to Deanna? Do you look at your all's relationship as you being married?" And I said, "yeah, sure. After seven, eight, nine, ten years with somebody? Yeah, we're married. If we can't legally get married it's as close to a marriage as we can get." So they love Deanna. They've accepted Deanna as a part of my life. As the partner part of my life—I don't know.

Chris thinks that her family does not perceive her relationship with Deanna as equal to a heterosexual relationship, but Chris has come to terms with this. She related:

> My brother acknowledges Deanna as my life partner and I think again my parents do too, it's just not the definition of partner that I would use to describe our relationship. They use a different definition. They have to think of it in a different context than I do. And you know what, quite frankly, that's okay. That's okay, because I've come from being totally terrified by them, and not wanting to be any part of their lives, to okay, if they have to think of it this way, then I'm alright with that. Because, like Deanna quoted to you before, they fought for me. Hers didn't. Hers didn't fight for her. Hers just let her fall by the wayside. And I think that our commitment to each other after all these years and our behavior, it might not be the old man and woman thing, but it's working. Deanna and I have been together in our family longer than anybody. My brother's divorced. My cousins have divorced. Deanna and I are the long-term relationship.

Chris's parents have even offered support when the couple has gone through some rough times, encouraging Chris and Deanna to work out their differences and stay together. I asked Chris if there was any one moment, or revelation, or event that she could identify that caused this change in their attitude. Chris explained that there was no one moment. Their fears about homosexuality diminished because of daily contact over time. Chris said:

> Being a part of our lives, being an active part of our lives and seeing what our relationship was about. We were just like a heterosexual relationship, the daily routine, the daily living of life. It's not different. You might love a person that's of your same sex, but all the trials, tribulations, good times, moments of joy, they're all the same whether you're with someone of the same sex or the opposite sex. The support, the recognition, the acknowledgement, all that's the same. Regardless. And I think they're finally seeing that.

Chris's story is a single account of slow change over time in one family committed to maintaining ties and loving one another, even when it was challenging to do so. Significantly, not only do Chris and Deanna benefit from their continued involvement with Chris's extended family, so does the whole family unit. In other words, support for gay people and for same-sex couples has tangible material, emotional, psychological, and spiritual advantages for *both* gay people and heterosexuals.

Two-Spirited

Many of the women and men I interviewed were gender nonconforming: they did not fit neatly into mainstream expectations of gender expression. Some indigenous North American native cultures use the term "two-spirited" to describe people whose gender presentation does not match their biological sex according to the contemporary social construction of gender. The term suggests that such individuals are a little closer to the Divine because they embody two spirits intertwined. Someone who is two-spirited, or gender nonconforming, such as a butch woman or femme man, typically strikes others as visibly, identifiably gay, whether they actually are or not. Because of this, they are likely to be treated differently than someone who "passes" as heterosexual. In this way, the daily experience of a gender nonconforming individual, like my partner, Anna, more closely resembles that of a racial minority than someone like me because she is visibly "different" and I am not. Feminists have written extensively about how patriarchal social systems police gender expression, and I concur with these analyses.[10] At the same time, the two-spirited life is not only one of social sanctioning as the following two examples demonstrate.

I recently became friends with "Gabriel," who is white, 45, and from Eastern Kentucky. Gabriel is a Wiccan hippie. He has long gray hair, which he usually wears in a pony tail. Gabriel dresses in androgynous shoes and clothes, and paints his toenails blue. He has a huge flower garden. Gabriel and his partner host large pagan gatherings on their country farm. Recently Gabriel shared with me that he has never had any negative encounters because of his gender presentation or sexual orientation in the rural communities within which he is a lifelong member. Rather, he said, he noticed that his "obvious gayness" allowed heterosexual women, in particular, to treat him better than they did their female friends. He said, "You know, women can be competitive with one another, and mean sometimes, but they don't do that to me. They can be very loving with me." Because Gabriel is a gay man, his female friends and acquaintances do not seek his sexual attention. Further, they do not appear to compete with him for a higher status in beauty and sexual attractiveness, as Gabriel observed them doing with other women. Gabriel and I speculated that his femme gender presentation freed women of the dual sexist paradigms of sexualization by men and competition with women. We wondered if this allowed them to express pent-up affection and appreciation for the feminine, "the Goddess" Gabriel said, in a nonthreatening other. Gabriel believes that his femme gender presentation benefits himself and others, and he would not change it if he could.

Similarly, my partner, Anna, who is butch, has unique relationships with some heterosexual men. First, in general, men do not sexualize her. She is not an object of the "male gaze."[11] Men instinctively treat her as "one of the guys." She talks football, basketball, fishing, technology, and yard work with them. Not only does she have easier interactions with heterosexual men because she shares a common set of socially constructed butch interests, some men are just more relaxed around Anna. Like Gabriel, she does not require sexual attention so there is no lurking sexually objectified script that might uncomfortably emerge. Finally, and perhaps most significantly, because she is a woman, men do not need to compete with her for a higher macho status nor do they need to worry that any gender slippage of their own will result in a homophobic response. To clarify, men can easily talk about sports and relationships and feelings with Anna, unfettered by the fear that something they do or say might make them seem "gay." I speculate that two-spirited people like Anna and Gabriel allow heterosexual men and women to honor rather than fear the butch and the femme. I think that this improves the quality of the interactions Anna and Gabriel have with others, and this can be psychologically, emotionally, and spiritually healing for heterosexuals. These two examples suggest that further research on the advantages of non-normative gender expression might reveal important findings.

The Power of Stories

Gay rights organizations, such as the Human Rights Campaign, the Equality Federation, and the "It Gets Better" Campaign, sponsor the telling of stories as a political strategy, and *Pray the Gay Away* is in full alignment with this tactic. In the second decade of the twenty-first century people from red and blue states, rural and urban areas, coasts, plains, and mountains need a map out of the polarized "culture wars," not more ammunition. The stories of Bible Belt gays offer us just such a guide: they have lived with and love, and are loved by, conservative Christians. They grew up worshipping God side-by-side with one another. Bible Belt gays understand the religious doctrine that makes their family members, friends, and neighbors fear and condemn homosexuality. Several of the women and men I interviewed, like Chris, also evinced much compassion for the pain their family members suffered for having a gay relative. When I look at the Bible Belt through my interview subjects' eyes, I see a place defined by homophobia but also a place complicated by family and community ties with a uniquely caring culture. "Those" people, the conservative Christians voting against gay civil rights, are the grandparents and sisters and uncles and cousins and neighbors of gay people. Many of these Bible Belt heterosexuals have cared for their gay relatives and friends all their lives, even if they don't know it, and they deserve better than to be lumped into a fundamentalist soup, ridiculed and disregarded. As the author Alice Walker observed in an open letter to president-elect Barack Obama in 2008, "Most damage that others do to us is out of fear, humiliation and pain . . . . We must learn actually not to have enemies, but only confused adversaries who are ourselves in disguise."[12]

The science fiction writer Elizabeth Scarborough explored this thesis—the idea that the "enemy" is a socially constructed category—in her speculative novel *Nothing Sacred*. The novel is set in the mountains of Tibet. A Bodhisattva, a spiritual leader, gathers a number of people in a remote area to survive a coming apocalypse.[13] The world is at war at the opening of the book, and the people assembled in Tibet are prisoners and guards of a camp. After a nuclear event devastates the globe, the characters in the novel slowly begin to learn that the roles they were playing of "guard" and "prisoner," and the emotions they ascribed to those roles, "righteous sentinel" and "abused victim who must escape," were meaningless. Each experienced a consciousness shift in which that person realized that the Bodhisattva had assembled this specific group to this sacred place to survive, and she had only made use of the form of "camp" to gather people and supplies. In the novel, transformation occurs when the jailers recognize that the social construction of "rehabilitation camp" is a hollow shell that traps them as much as it does the prisoners. In turn, the captives stop seeing the guards as the "enemy." The social and physical bars that separate prisoners from guards dissolve with the dawning awareness that the game of "prison camp" no longer needs to be played.

Once guards and prisoners began to see one another as human, the remote mountain hollow transforms from a penal colony into a community. This transformation was possible when the characters let go of their constraining social roles, and the accompanying desire to be "right" and one of "the good guys," and perceived the "other," "them," and the "enemy" as fully human. Although no Bible Belt gay specifically referenced this sort of speculative science fiction in our interviews, person after person made comments that echoed Scarborough's hopeful thesis: artificial social barriers that separate groups can evaporate when "the enemy" understands, 'I'm just like you.'" The single idea most expressed by Bible Belt gays in interviews is the desire that others understand that we are all human and all connected, for we are all, as Alice Walker wisely noted, one another "in disguise." For those readers who have little personal acquaintance with gay people, this book serves as a contact and introduction to Bible Belt gays, perhaps making the foreign lives of sexual minorities a little less strange and scary, and, hopefully, a little more familiar and welcoming.

Being gay in the Bible Belt encouraged my interview subjects to live the "examined life."[14] In doing so, they not only earned their sexuality and partners but many also earned enduring friendships, increased happiness, and a richer spiritual life. I do not see a group of people either destroyed by homosexuality or homophobia. I perceive much to admire and appreciate about Bible Belt gays. I see funny people who are more likely to shoot an over-the-shoulder eye-roll than engage in pointless confrontation, who can tune out other people's ill will and listen to the song in their own head, who tend to be conscious of and care about being kind to others, who appreciate difference and value diversity. If I were setting out to prove that these qualities allowed one a richer, more meaningful, more expansive, and altogether more fun life, the stories of Bible Belt gays make me hopeful. It's not only that the lives of Bible Belt gays illustrate the maxim: "having endured much, they are stronger for it," although their stories do suggest this, but that the personal work each engaged in to come to terms with being different gave them a greater capacity to think for themselves, and thus made them more powerful and independent.

INTRODUCTION

1. Thomasville is a pseudonym as are most of the names of the people featured in *Pray the Gay Away*. I use a person's real name only if that person is a public figure or if the individual requested I use her real name.

2. Conservative Christians draw on the following six biblical passages to condemn homosexuality as sin: Gen. 19:5, Lev. 18:22 and 20:13, Rom. 1:26—27, 1 Cor. 6:9, and 1 Tim. 1:9–10. The passage Jim quotes to me is from Lev. 18:22, "You shall not lie with a male as those who lie with a female; it is an abomination."

3. Ammerman 1987.

4. Barton 2011b.

5. Barton 2010, 480.

6. Joshua requested that I use his real name.

7. Ray 2006.

8. Another difference between racism and homophobia is that oppression and widespread economic exploitation are often linked for people of color. White, and particularly white and middle-class gay men and lesbians, will experience great oppression but not suffer economic exploitation. And, of course, a gay person of color experiences a triple jeopardy. See Pharr 1996 for further discussion on this.

9. http://www.statemaster.com/graph/peo_rom_cat_per_of_cat-people-roman-catholicism-percentage-catholics.

10. http://www.jewishvirtuallibrary.org/jsource/US-Israel/usjewpop.html.

11. Typically, the southern tip of Florida and the states of Delaware and Maryland are not considered part of the Bible Belt.

12. Although 57.9% is a large percentage, and this GSS data clearly indicates a larger percentage of respondents who identify as fundamentalist in Bible Belt than non–Bible Belt regions, secondary data sets, such as General Social Survey data, rarely perfectly measure any individual researcher's query, and this is the case for me as well. Among the options of "fundamentalist, moderate, and liberal" in this politically conservative area of the United States, it is not surprising that such a

large percentage of respondents consequently chose "fundamentalist." It is important, thus, to note that 57.9% may be inflated.

13. Lakoff 2004, xv. In his book *Don't Think of an Elephant*, Lakoff analyzes the results of the 2004 election season and argues that one reason why conservative policies receive support is because conservatives develop better frames for their policies than do progressives.

14. Marsden 1991.

15. Stephens and Giberson 2011; and Balmer 2006. Randall Balmer, an Episcopal priest, author, and well-known professor of religious history, is currently a visiting professor at Dartmouth College in Hanover, New Hampshire.

16. Balmer, 2006, ix. For example, *Sojourners Magazine*, with editor in chief Jim Wallis, is an example of leftist evangelical politics.

17. White 2006, 11.

18. Woodberry and Smith 1998.

19. Ammerman 1987, 55.

20. Ibid.; Woodberry and Smith 1998.

21. H. L. Mencken, *Heathen Days, 1890–1936* (New York: Alfred A. Knopf, 1943), 231–34; Michael Williams, "Sunday in Dayton," *Commonweal* 2 (July 29, 1925): 285–88.

22. Balmer 2006, xvi.

23. Personal correspondence with Lynne Gerber.

24. Hankins 2008, 145.

25. See Pharr 1996 for her discussion of "domination politics."

26. Herman 1997; White 2006.

27. Like the 2004 and 2006 anti-gay marriage amendments on ballots, the 1990s ballot initiatives mobilized both conservative Christians and gay activists. Bull and Gallagher 1996.

28. For further detail on the history of American fundamentalism, see Balmer 2006; Bull and Gallagher 1996; Fetner 2008; Hankins 2008; Marsden 1991; White 2006.

29. Howard 1997, 108.

30. Books that critique conservative Christian attitudes (Dawkins 2006; Herman 1997; Hitchens 2007; Joyce 2009; White 2006) as well as those that describe, explore, and critique recent manifestations of evangelical Christianity (Aguilar 2008; Goldberg 2006; Sheler 2006; Stephens and Giberson 2011), and works reflecting on individual's personal experiences with religious-based bigotry (Campbell 2009; Gold 2008; Perez 2007; White 1995, 2006) have informed the ideas explored in this manuscript. None of the works cited here examines Christianity from the perspective of Bible Belt gays.

31. Denzin and Lincoln 2003, 5.

32. I explore methodological issues that emerged researching *Pray the Gay Away* in greater detail in the article "My Auto/Ethnographic Dilemma: Who Owns the Story?" Barton 2011b.

33. Geertz 1973.

34. The Second Vatican Council, lasting from 1962 to 1965, reviewed church doctrine on both social and theological matters with the goal of making the Roman Catholic Church more modern. Among the changes instituted after Vatican II was that the Catholic Mass would be held in the language of the country of origin, not Latin. There was also a move away from a literal to inspired interpretation of scripture.

35. http://www.boston.com/news/local/massachusetts/articles/2009/03/09/number_of_ne_catholics_tumbles/

36. I use the word "femme" here and the word "butch" later to describe gender expression. Briefly, femme lesbians typically present to others in gender-conforming feminine ways of dress, talk, and mannerisms. Although the word "butch" has a negative association for many in homophobic societies, some lesbians choose to self-identify as butch, and some lesbians use "butch" to describe the type of woman they are attracted to. Butch women usually appear to others as more androgynous or masculine than feminine. For a fuller description and analysis of butch and femme, see the following anthologies: *Femme: Feminists, Lesbians and Bad Girls* (1997), edited by Laura Harris and Elizabeth Crocker; *The Feminine Mystique* (1995), edited by Leslea Newman; *The Persistent Desire: A Butch Femme Reader* (1992), edited by Joan Nestle. See also Leslie Feinberg, *Stone Butch Blues* (1993) and Elizabeth Lapovsky Kennedy and Madeline D. Davis, *Boots of Leather, Slippers of Gold: The History of a Lesbian Community*.

37. Peggy McIntosh's (2007) widely cited essay "White Privilege, Male Privilege" describes privilege as a set of unearned advantages that an individual has because they belong to a dominant group. One key element of privilege is that is invisible to those who have it. Privilege feels normal and earned when it is neither. For another excellent discussion of privilege, see Allan G. Johnson, *Privilege, Power and Difference* (2006).

38. Snowball sampling is a qualitative method of finding research participants in which individuals who participate in the study identify, recommend, and sometimes recruit future subjects for the researcher. Snowball sampling is not random or generalizable.

39. Cooley 1902.

40. Pharr 1996; Frye 1983.

41. Collins 2000.

42. hooks 1989, 9.

43. Weston 1995.
44. Collins 2000.
45. Currier 2007, 190.

CHAPTER 1

1. All the names of churches are pseudonyms.
2. Foucault 1979, 201.
3. Barton 2011a.
4. Foucault 1979, 202.
5. Campbell 2009; Gray 2009; Offut 2002.
6. Ammerman 1987.
7. Jake, a pseudonym, a 25-year-old white man, wrote this story in a course paper. He gave me permission to share it here. All identifying information has been altered to protect the confidentiality of those discussed.
8. Jones 1997, 81.
9. We perceive the affects of personalism in conventional attitudes about southerners and northerners. Southerners often perceive northerners as rude, while northerners are mystified by southerners who are cordial to them to their face while holding negative, unspoken attitudes about them.
10. Gray 2009, 5–6.
11. Ammerman 1987.
12. Pharr 1996.
13. Flory and Miller 2008.
14. Jeff also agreed to be interviewed, and excerpts from his interview can be found throughout *Pray the Gay Away*.
15. When observing and interacting in conservative Christian environments, I made the methodological choice to allow those present to perceive me as heterosexual. I did not claim a heterosexual identity, nor did I come out. Because of my conventional gender presentation, most people assume I am heterosexual unless I explicitly say otherwise. I made this decision because I felt coming out in conservative Christian environments to conservative Christians would be simultaneously laborious, confusing for those present, potentially disruptive, and affect the data I gathered. In this, I follow the lead of other gay sociologists who researched conservative Christians, including Thomas Linneman, Arlene Stein, and Dawne Moon. For more discussion on the ethics of coming out, see Barton 2011b.
16. The University of Kentucky basketball team is often ranked among the final four teams competing for the NCAA title. Kentuckians are

enthusiastic basketball fans said to "bleed blue," a reference to the University of Kentucky school colors of blue and white.

17. Altemeyer and Hunsberger 1992; Bendroth 1993; Finlay and Walther 2003; Joyce 2009; Kirkpatrick 1993; Pharr 1996; Robinson and Spivey 2007; Shaw 2008; Stein 2001.

18. Ammerman 1987

19. Ibid. 7.

20. Ibid. 72.

21. Herman 1997, 19.

22. Ammerman 1987.

23. Ibid.

24. This documentary explores the story of a teenage girl from Lubbock, Texas, who worked to get sex education taught in the public schools. Her activist journey eventually caused her to question homophobia.

25. Stein 2006, 111.

26. Parts of this chapter have appeared in Barton 2011a, 2011b.

CHAPTER 2

1. Center for Disease Control Massachusetts Department of Education Youth and Risk Behavior Survey. For a discussion of suicide rates for gay youth also see Silenzio et al. 2007 and Ryan et al. 2009.

2. Ryan et al. 2009.

3. Griffin 2006, 10.

4. Janet Parshall is a conservative Christian talk show host. She also anchored the 2004 documentary *George W. Bush: Faith in the White House*. She was selected by George W. Bush to represent the White House in the capacity of public delegate to the United Nations Commission on the Status of Women.

5. Stephens and Giberson 2011, 7.

6. In researching churches in the Bible Belt, I found a wide range of attitudes about women's participation in church. Many are patriarchal in that only men are allowed positions of authority. Some are so extreme that women are not allowed to speak in the church at all, must sit in the back, wear long dresses, and cannot cut their hair.

7. Melungeon is controversial ethnic identity in which members typically have Caucasian features and dark skin. Melungeon people originate in Appalachia from mixed-race origins, usually a combination of Caucasian, African American, and Native-American.

8. One difference between the older interview subjects like Mary, 61, compared to John, 18, is that John did come out to his mother, though she responded poorly, while Mary never did. This difference may be a

consequence of more gay-themed media. In her book *Out in the Country*, Mary L. Gray (2009) noted the importance of gay-affirming media representations on television, and on-line resources for rural gay youth.

9. http://www.insidehighered.com/news/2011/04/25/texas_house_votes_ to_require_colleges_with_sexuality_centers_to_promote_traditional_ values_too.

10. http://www.insidehighered.com/news/2011/04/25/texas_house_votes_ to_require_colleges_with_sexuality_centers_to_promote_traditional_ values_too.

11. http://www.insidehighered.com/news/2011/04/25/texas_house_votes_ to_require_colleges_with_sexuality_centers_to_promote_traditional_ values_too.

CHAPTER 3

1. Joshua Taylor is planning to elaborate upon the ideas he expresses in his interview with me in his future graduate work.

2. Ammerman 1987,106.

3. Ibid. 100.

4. O'Brien 2004, 185.

5. Ferraro and Johnson 1983; Nash and Hesterberg 2009.

6. This "stuckness," this struggle to reconcile one's gay identity with homophobic Christian dogma is well-illuminated in the film, *Prayers for Bobby* that first aired on the Lifetime channel in January 2009.

7. Boykin 1996; Cohen 1999; Collins 2004; Griffin 2006.

8. Griffin 2006; Cohen 1999.

9. Cohen 1999, 284.

10. Founded by Troy Perry in 1968 to serve gay Christians, MCC has 250 affiliated churches in 23 countries.

11. Collins 2004, 111–12.

12. Ibid. 112.

13. Cathy J. Cohen (1999) noted that AIDS activists felt the following four concerns about how the Black church responded to the AIDS crisis in Black communities: (1) is the Black church following the teachings of Christ; (2), the Black church need to address homosexuality openly to effectively help those with AIDS; (3) claims that the Black church only wishes to service certain segments of the black community; and (4) that too much attention is paid to the church as a service provider (280).

14. Boykin 1996, 155.

15. Ibid. 126.

16. Founded by Rev. Mel White, former ghost writer for a number of famous Christian fundamentalist leaders, the nonprofit activist organization Soulforce, whose mission is to free LGBT people from

religious-based oppression, estimates between 200 and 300 colleges and universities have official policies *against* LGBT students. The exact number of schools with discriminatory policies is difficult to track down, likely because it is not information educational institutions are eager to publicize.

17. An April 2011 *New York Times* article explores the rising phenomenon of students attempting to form gay clubs on Christian campuses. These groups are experiencing mixed results. Most schools do not expel students for experiencing same-sex attractions, but only for same-sex behavior. Heterosexual sexual activity is also grounds for expulsion. Even in the more liberal of the Christian schools, there is still an attitude that homosexuality is sinful, and thus gay students, faculty, and staff are not encouraged to be out. Privately struggling with same-sex attraction is tolerated. Coming out in social media sites is not received well. Please see http://www.nytimes.com/2011/04/19/us/19gays.html for further discussion on this.

18. The philosopher Marilyn Frye explores oppression as a cumulative series of barriers that constrain people using the analogy of a birdcage in her 1983 book *The Politics of Reality: Essays in Feminist Theory.*

19. O'Brien 2004; Walton 2006; Wilcox 2003; Wolkomir 2006.

20. O'Brien 2004, 181.

21. Parts of this chapter appeared in Barton 2010.

22. Jerry Falwell and D. James Kennedy have died since Mel White published *Religion Gone Bad* in 2006. However, this argument continues to apply to megachurch pastors like Rick Warren of the Saddleback church who use their considerable influence to condemn homosexuality. Saddleback, with a weekly attendance of 23,000 people, is the largest church in California and the fourth largest church in the United States. During the 2008 election, Warren endorsed Proposition 8, urging people to "preserve the biblical definition of marriage" while comparing homosexuality to pedophilia and bestiality. http://www.onenewsnow.com/Church/Default.aspx?id=298544.

23. In addition to providing the ideological rhetoric fueling anti-gay legislation, Mormon, Roman Catholic, and Evangelical groups made large financial contributions to the Prop. 8 campaign in California in 2008.

CHAPTER 4

1. Adams 2010; DiPlacido 1998; Feinberg 1993; Gold 2008; Griffin 2006; Jay and Young 1972; Sears 1991; Sedgwick 1993; Seidman 2004; Signorile 1993; White 1995.

2. Adams 2010; Lorber 1994.

3. Adams 2010, 234.

4. Kaufman and Raphael 1996.
5. A bisexual identity is extremely difficult to express in our culture so defined are we by the sex of our most current partner.
6. Barton 2006.
7. Cass 1979; Davies 1992.
8. Davies 1992, 76.
9. Peter Davies distinguishes between individuation and disclosure in the coming out process. As noted in the text, individuation is the process of self-acceptance. Disclosure is the process of sharing one's gay identity with others. Davies explains that, theoretically the safest strategy of disclosure entails either telling no one or telling everyone. His central point is that "partial disclosure creates some strain." (82) In the lives of Bible Belt gays, partial strain is inevitable because, no matter how out one is, there are always new people to tell.
10. Seidman 2004, 181.
11. Cain 1991; Davies 1992; Peacock 2000; Riggle and Rostosky 2012.
12. Adams 2010; Davies 1992; Halley 1989; Savin-Williams 1998; Troiden 1987; Urbach 1996.
13. Sedgwick 1993, 46.
14. Adams 2010, 239.
15. Bawer 1993.
16. The following six states have laws banning discrimination based on sexual orientation: Wisconsin (1982), Massachusetts (1989), New Hampshire (1997), Maryland (2001), New York (2002), Delaware (2009). This information was compiled by the National Gay and Lesbian Task Force, updated on June 14, 2011. The following fifteen states and the District of Columbia ban discrimination based on sexual orientation and gender identity/expression. The year indicates when the antidiscrimination legislation was passed. If there are two years listed, the first indicates a law based on sexual orientation and the second on gender identity: Minnesota (1993); Rhode Island (1995, 2001); New Mexico (2003); California (1992, 2003); District of Columbia (1977, 2005); Illinois (2005); Maine (2005); Hawaii (1991, 2011); New Jersey (1992, 2006); Washington (2006); Iowa (2007); Oregon (2007); Vermont (1992, 2007); Colorado (2007); Connecticut (1991, 2011); Nevada (1999, 2011). This information is available at http://www.thetaskforce.org/reports_and_research/nondiscrimination_laws.
17. Even well-meaning and supportive heterosexuals may lack language to respond appropriately to gay people. For example, in their article, "Mistakes that Heterosexual People Make When Trying to Appear Non-Prejudiced: The View from LGB People," Conley et al. (2001) collected

data on 97 LGB individuals' impressions of "interactions between homosexuals and heterosexuals." (24) Only 7% of respondents felt they had experienced non-prejudicial interactions. The most common mistakes heterosexuals made were relying on stereotypes, ignoring gay issues, and not owning up to their discomfort (34).

18. Frye 1983.
19. Adams 2010.
20. Stereotypically, heterosexual privilege is linked with children and being gay, or in a same-sex relationship linked with childlessness. This conflation of heterosexuality with procreation and homosexuality with childlessness is problematic. Gay couples with children interrupt this assumption (Garfinkel 1967), and manage interactional disorientation with surprised others. Again, the burden will rest upon the gay person to make comfortable those whose assumptions have been challenged.
21. Pharr 1996.
22. Kimmel and Mahler 2003.
23. Levy 2005.
24. In this speculation, I draw on an "ideal type" (Weber 1978) of parenting that many children and youth may not receive, including heterosexual ones, i.e., Mom may not respond appropriately to the suffering heterosexual child either. My point is that the closeted gay youth develops from a disadvantaged place.

CHAPTER 5

1. Albert Mohler has made national headlines for, among other public statements, advocating a genetic solution to homosexuality. In a 2007 blog post, Mohler wrote, "If a biological basis is found, and if a prenatal test is then developed, and if a successful treatment to reverse the sexual orientation to heterosexual is ever developed, we would support its use as we should unapologetically support the use of any appropriate means to avoid sexual temptation and the inevitable effects of sin." http://www.jewsonfirst.org/07b/mohler_womb.html.
2. In 1998 Mohler facilitated the renaming of Boyce Bible School to Boyce College.
3. Erzen 2006.
4. Ammerman 1987.
5. I have found no data that estimates the percentage of Christian counselors who have a credential that would also be recognized by a secular authority (i.e., a state licensing board). Because conservative Christian groups value the authority of the Bible over secular licensing, and indeed may purposely avoid secular institutions for fear of their contaminating influence, I believe it is likely that a large number of

individuals seeking support from Christian institutions to eliminate their same-sex attractions are open to receiving spiritual guidance from those without a state-sanctioned credential (based on data gathered in this study).

6. http://www.gaytoday.com/viewpoint/081803vp.asp.
7. Erzen 2006, 14.
8. For additional information on Exodus International see Erzen 2006 and Wolkomir 2006.
9. Erzen 2006.
10. Ibid.
11. DVDs of all the proceedings at the Exodus conference were available for purchase. I was present at this opening ceremony, and purchased a DVD copy. I fully transcribed it for this chapter.
12. Bennett 2003; Erzen 2006; Gerber 2008.
13. Halperin 1997, 63.
14. Green 2002,522.
15. Jagose 1996, 1.
16. Erzen 2006, 14. In his article "Love Me Gender: Normative Homosexuality and 'Ex-gay' Performativity in Reparative Therapy Narratives," Jeffrey A. Bennett (2003) explored how John and Anne Paulk's use of the language of ex-gay resists the homosexual/heterosexual binary and is thus an illustration of queer theory.
17. Gerber 2008, 8.
18. See Burack and Josephson 2004, 9.
19. Wolkomir 2006.
20. Ibid., 102.
21. Burack and Josephson (2004) note in their report on a "Love Won Out" conference that a "number of speakers emphasized the importance of gender-normative roles, behaviors, and modes of dress and grooming as crucial to the healing of homosexuality. They also presented gender non-normative forms of dress, behavior, and roles, as both signs and reinforcers of homosexuality." (5) I observed this in Christine Sneeringer's gender presentation. Exodus literature also instructed participants to conform to gender norms. At the same time though, I was surprised by the number of men in gender non-normative clothing, as well as the leader of the "Roots and Causes of Lesbianism" workshop distinguishing gender presentations from sexual orientation. It is possible that there has been a slight shift in attitudes about gender presentation since 2004 among the Exodus leadership, but my time spent with ex-gay groups is too short to make a claim either way.

22. In her article, "The Opposite of Gay: Nature, Creation, and Queerish Ex-Gay Experiments" Lynne Gerber (2008) explores the idea that ex-gay ministries suspend the closet, allowing "gender-variant Christians a quasi-legitimate location within the evangelical world." She writes, "The ex-gay category provides a gender/sex position that does not require the complete repression and social isolation of the closet for those who experience same-sex attractions and that counters their complete abjection with the possibility of engagement and compassion, a possibility that is valuable as well to straight evangelicals with gay friends and family members" (25).

23. Brown 2006.

24. Tanya Erzen (2006) notes, "the movement as a whole . . . tends to be male dominated and focused on male homosexuality" (30).

25. This description is reconstructed from intensive notes taken at the time.

26. Erzen 2006; Gerber 2008. Exodus leaders use the work of Irving Bieber (1962), *Homosexuality: A Psychoanalytic Study of Male Homosexuals*, Charles W. Socarides (1978), *Homosexuality*, Joseph Nicolosi (1991), *Reparative Therapy of Male Homosexuality*, and Elizabeth Moberly (1983), *Homosexuality: A New Christian Ethic*, among others. The therapies these authors advocate conceptualize homosexual attractions as a response to an early childhood trauma and/or consequence of parental deficiencies in childhood.

27. Attachment theory is an interdisciplinary theory that explores the importance of the primary caregiver's response to a child during infancy and the early toddler stage. If the primary caregiver does not respond appropriately, that is, meets the child's basic needs for food, comfort, and love in a timely manner, a child may later lack the tools to develop secure adult attachments and instead have attachment styles that are insecure, avoidant, ambivalent, disorganized, and/or anxious. For an overview of attachment theory, see John Bowlby, *Attachment*, 2nd ed., 1983.

28. D'Ann did not clarify whether bisexuality was itself innate. Likely, those involved in ex-gay ministries might argue (if queried) that only heterosexuality is godly and any other sexual expression a consequence of our sin nature. In other words, whether any sexual orientation is innate is irrelevant because we all should be more concerned with following God's plan. Gerber (2008) notes that ex-gay advocates argue that "Christian" is a more natural orientation than homosexuality. Gerber illustrates, "Joe Dallas writes that the Christian life needs to be lived as scripturally dictated and evangelically understood, regardless of whether it comes naturally, and Exodus president Alan Chambers says that the discovery of a gene for homosexuality would not shake his faith

in God but would only explain why the process of change he has under-taken has been so very difficult" (18).

29. This description is also reconstructed from notes.

30. Like many ethnographers (Linneman 2003; Moone 2004; Stein 2001), I introduced myself with "partial truths" (Thorne 1980, 287). In her article "You Still Takin' Notes?: Fieldwork and Problems of Informed Consent," Barrie Thorne (1980) wrote, "Reviewing ethnographies to examine modes of self-introduction (when they are mentioned at all), I have been struck by the widespread use of partial truths" (287).

31. Blee 1991, 6.

32. In *God, Sex and Politics: Homosexuality and Everyday Theologies,* a study of two Methodist congregations—one gay-affirming and one not—Dawne Moon asked a similar question of conservative Christians. Her interviews subjects responded with a "love the sin, hate the sinner" argument. They felt it was ultimately more loving to point out the sin and help the sinner than accept the homosexual and condemn him or her to eternal damnation.

33. Goffman 1963.

34. Burack and Josephson 2004, 11.

35. Wendell 2000.

36. See Barton 2011b for more discussion on this.

37. Harding 1991.

38. A portion of this chapter appeared in Barton 2011b.

39. http://www.exodusinternational.org/content/view/43/87/.

40. http://www.miaminewtimes.com/2010-05-13/news/how-george-alan-rekers-and-his-rent-boy-got-busted-by-new-times/.

41. Herek 1998. For an additional critique of problems in Cameron's research see Bull and Gallagher 1996, 26–28.

42. George Rekers served as an "expert witness" to support a ban on same-sex couples adopting children in Arkansas in 2004 and Florida in 2008. Paul Cameron is an unlicensed psychologist and sex researcher. In 1983 the American Psychological Association expelled him for failing to cooperate with an ethics investigation.

43. Wolkomir 2006, 149.

44. Ibid.

45. http://www.beyondexgay.com/who.

46. http://www.beyondexgay.com/conference/why.

47. Michael Bussee and Gary Cooper, co-founders of Exodus, helped orga-nize the first Exodus conference in Anaheim, California, in 1976. At that time both were married and had children. Three years later Bussee and Cooper fell in love, publicly denounced Exodus, divorced their wives, and became partners. They were together until Cooper died in 1991. For

further details on Bussee and Cooper's journey, see Wolkomir 2006, 28–30.

48. The statements of Bussee, Bogle, and Marks have been fully transcribed from the following video-recording: http://www.youtube.com/watch?v=aDiYeJ_bsQo&feature=related.

49. Darlene Bogle shares her autobiography in her book *A Christian Lesbian Journey: A Continuation of Long Road to Love* (2007), BookSurge Publishing.

50. See Hughes 1945.

51. Blumer 1969.

52. Schwalbe 2008, 100.

53. Burack and Josephson 2004, 6.

54. Ibid. 13..

55. http://www.citizenlink.org/content/A000010719.cfm.

CHAPTER 6

1. http://creationmuseum.org/about/.

2. http://creationmuseum.org/about/give/volunteer/faq/.

3. http://www.answersingenesis.org/about/faith.

4. I also asked my students to share their impressions over email with me and with one another; I included an essay question on their final exam about the Creation Museum and have their permission to share their written comments publicly. All the students' names are pseudonyms.

5. Special thanks to Dawne Moon for feedback on my Creation Museum analysis.

6. Jesus receives little attention in the Creation Museum. The story of Jesus' birth, crucifixion, and resurrection is confined to the very end of the exhibits in one 20-minute video presentation titled "The Last Adam."

7. For additional description and analysis of creationism and the Creation Museum in particular, see Rosenhouse 2012; and Stephens and Giberson 2011.

8. Ammerman 1987, 99.

9. Ibid. 4.

10. Toumey 1994.

11. Ammerman 1987, 15.

12. Ibid.; Wilcox and Robinson 2010.

13. New International Version.

14. Ammerman 1987, 165.

15. Foucault 1979.

16. Unlike the other two times I visited the Creation Museum, during our class field trip, a uniformed officer with a leashed dog patrolled the

facility. He was not friendly to me, refusing to return a smile, nor was he friendly with any of the students. On this particular day, Ken Ham himself was scheduled to appear, sign autographs, and do a general meet-and-greet with museumgoers. I speculate that perhaps there was extra security present because of this.

17. Glen Branch shared with me, "One of NCSE's members, a former police officer, told me (in abundant detail) that the security apparatus at the museum is much more elaborate than he considered necessary for a building of its nature, which suggests that the panoptic effect is real."

18. Creation Museum brochure.

19. On each of my three visits to the Creation Museum, I observed large contingents of people in Amish-style dress.

20. Duncan 2009, 18.

21. Scott and Branch 2003, 284.

22. Ibid., 283.

23. Museum Souvenir Guide.

24. Stein 2006.

25. Ibid. 126–27.

26. These publications are only a sample of the news outlets that have run stories about the Creation Museum.

27. http://www.nytimes.com/2010/12/06/us/06ark.html?_r=1.

28. http://www.livescience.com/culture/creation-museum-fundamentalists-christians-discrimination-100818.html.

29. In February 2011, a gay male couple tried to attend a dinner sponsored by AiG. "The event included dinner, musical performances and a talk from museum founder Ken Ham about love and the biblical view of marriage." http://www.sfgate.com/cgi-bin/article.cgi?f=/n/a/2011/02/20/national/a153110S37.DTL. At first, the two men were admitted but then expelled. AiG refused to return their $71 admittance fee.

30. See Ken Ham personal response to the article http://blogs.answersingenesis.org/blogs/ken-ham/2010/08/23/crowds-keep-pouring-in/.

31. http://www.answersingenesis.org/articles/2010/08/20/feedback-please-stop-the-hate.

32. The political scientists Clyde Wilcox, Carin Robinson (2011), and Matthew C. Moen (1994) observed that leaders of the Christian Right deliberately adopted the language of liberalism, "rights" and victimization in the early 1990s. In their book *Onward Christian Soldiers? The Religious Right in American Politics* Wilcox and Robinson write, "Candidates and groups that attack the Christian Right are now routinely accused of religious bigotry, and Christian Right leaders charge that opposition to their policies comes from those who discriminate against people of faith" (51).

33. Ammerman 1987, 201.
34. Bull and Gallagher 1996; Fetner 2008.
35. Ammerman 1987, 197.
36. Pharr 1996.
37. Hankins 2008; Wilcox and Robinson 2011; White 2006.
38. Pharr 1996, 44.

CHAPTER 7
1. http://www.afa.net/FAQ.aspx?id=2147483680.
2. http://www.afa.net/FAQ.aspx?id=2147483680.
3. De Beauvoir 1952.
4. Article 7 of the *1994 Draft United Nations Declaration on the Rights of Indigenous Peoples* states: Indigenous peoples have the collective and individual right not to be subjected to ethnocide and cultural genocide, including prevention of and redress for: (a) any action which has the aim or effect of depriving them of their integrity as distinct peoples, or of their cultural values or ethnic identities; (b) any action which has the aim or effect of dispossessing them of their lands, territories or resources; (c) any form of population transfer which has the aim or effect of violating or undermining any of their rights; (d) any form of assimilation or integration by other cultures or ways of life imposed on them by legislative, administrative or other measures; (e) any form of propaganda directed against them. http://www.wce.wwu.edu/Resources/NWCHE/Mission.shtml#ethnocide.
5. http://www.enotes.com/genocide-encyclopedia/ethnocide.
6. See Fetner 2008 for findings and analysis on how the religious Right shaped lesbian and gay activism.
7. http://www.ct.gov/shp/lib/shp/pdf/same-sex_marriage_stress.pdf. See also Feigenbaum 2007 for further discussion on heterosexual privilege and the passage of an anti-gay marriage amendment in Ohio.
8. http://static.texastribune.org/media/documents/FINAL_2010_STATE_REPUBLICAN_PARTY_PLATFORM.pdf.
9. Blee 2004,100–101.
10. Schwalbe 2008.
11. Blee 2004, 101.
12. Frye 1983.
13. Jerry Falwell died in May 2007.
14. In February 1999, Falwell's media outlet, the National Liberty Journal, published an unsigned article claiming that a children's television character, the Teletubby Tinky Winky, was intended to be a gay role model, and that this was damaging for children. This assertion was supported by the evidence that Tinky Winky was

the color purple—a gay pride color, had an antenna shaped like a triangle—a gay pride symbol, and carried a magic purse.

15. Blee 2004.
16. hooks 1989, 8.
17. Wilcox and Robinson 2011.
18. Collins 2000.
19. Ammerman 1987; Wilcox and Robinson 2011.
20. Wilcox and Robinson 2011, 162.
21. Jacobsen and Pellegrini 2004; Whisman 1996; Wolkomir 2006.
22. Jacobsen and Pellegrini 2004,16.
23. hooks 1989.

CHAPTER 8

1. The one exception was Kelly, Hispanic, 21, from Texas, and whose family had disowned her not two weeks before our interview. This last question left her literally speechless. After some reflection, Kelly said, "I honestly have never thought about it. I don't know how to answer that. I wouldn't know where to start. I'm still learning to accept that it's okay, it's normal, it's natural."
2. In their book *A Positive View of LGBTQ: Embracing Identity and Cultivating Well-Being*, researchers Riggle and Rostosky (2012) compiled the responses of a national sample of LGBTQ individuals about the strengths and benefits of their identities. Among the positive elements their participants reported included the value of authenticity, self-awareness, personal growth, the freedom to create new rules, stronger emotional connections with others, greater compassion and empathy, creating social change, and belonging to a community. In his online article "The Gay Factor: What Are Our Special Gifts?" life coach Clint Griess writes that gay people have a built in "bullshit detector." Griess explains, "In the end, the result of living a dual life gives gay people a well-developed ability to discern between reality and illusion."
3. Seligman et al. 2005, 4114. 1952.
4. De Beauvoir expanded upon philosophical theories exploring the "other" in contrast to the "same" through an examination of gender roles. Within a patriarchal social system, she argued, woman is "other."
5. McIntosh 2007; Johnson 2006.
6. Collins 2000, 11.
7. Pharr 1996.
8. Weston 1991.
9. Lorber 1995.
10. I share this to describe, not romanticize, lesbian partnerships. The double socialization to connect has its downside as well. Lesbian couples

can be too interdependent and enmeshed. For more discussion and analysis of lesbian relationships, see Weinstock and Rothblum 2004.

11. Maslow 1970, 22.
12. Jensen 2008; Kimmel 2009.
13. *Tough Guise* (1999), a Media Education Foundation documentary featuring Jackson Katz, an anti-sexist activist.
14. Seligman et al. 2005, 411.

CHAPTER 9

1. To read about the episode and watch it in its entirety go to: http://abcnews.go.com/WhatWouldYouDo/hidden-cameras-roll-cafe-patrons-defend-gay-parents/story?id=13631544.
2. Wilcox and Robinson (2011) support this claim as well writing, "When Bush won reelection in 2004, it seemed a high-water mark for the Christian Right" (53).
3. http://pewresearch.org/pubs/1994/poll-support-for-acceptance-of-homosexuality-gay-parenting-marriage.
4. Gladwell 2000, 12.
5. http://pewresearch.org/pubs/1994/poll-support-for-acceptance-of-homosexuality-gay-parenting-marriage.
6. http://pewresearch.org/pubs/1994/poll-support-for-acceptance-of-homosexuality-gay-parenting-marriage.
7. Wilcox and Robinson (2011) concur: "Fundamentalists and evangelicals are far more liberal about gay rights than they were just eight years ago. More important, younger fundamentalists and evangelicals are far more liberal than their parents and grandparents" (61).
8. Allport 1954.
9. Herek 1987b; Herek and Glunt 1993; Herek and Capitanio 1996.
10. See for example Pharr 1997; and Kimmel 2009.
11. Mulvey 1999.
12. www://theroot.com/id/48726;
13. Scarborough 1991. In Tibetan Buddhism, a bodhisattva is an enlightened individual who reincarnates in a physical form to help others achieve enlightenment.
14. Nozick 1990.

Aguilar, Rose. 2008. *Red Highways: A Liberal's Journey into the Heartland.* Sausalito, CA: PoliPointPress.

Adams, Tony E. 2010. "Paradoxes of Sexuality, Gay Identity and the Closet." *Symbolic Interaction* 33 (2): 234–256.

Allport, Gordon W. 1954. The Nature of Prejudice. Reading, MA: Addison-Wesley Publishing.

Altemeyer, Bob, and Bruce Hunsberger. 1992. "Authoritarianism, Religious Fundamentalism, Quest, and Prejudice." *International Journal for the Psychology of Religion* 2 (2): 113–133.

Ammerman, Nancy Tatom. 1987. *Bible Believers: Fundamentalists in the Modern World.* New Brunswick, NJ: Rutgers University Press.

Balmer, Randall. 2006. *Thy Kingdom Come, an Evangelical's Lament: How the Religious Right Distorts the Faith and Threatens America.* New York: Basic Books.

Barton, Bernadette. 2006. *Stripped: Inside the Lives of Exotic Dancers.* New York: NYU Press.

———. 2010. "'Abomination'—Life as a Bible Belt Gay." *Journal of Homosexuality* 57 (4): 465–484.

———. 2011a. "1CROSS + 3NAILS = 4GVN: Compulsory Christianity and Homosexuality in the Bible Belt Panopticon." *Feminist Formations* 23 (1): 70–93.

———. 2011b. "My Auto/Ethnographic Dilemma—Who Owns the Story?" *Qualitative Sociology* 34 (3).

Bawer, Bruce. 1993. *A Place at the Table: The Gay Individual in American Society.* New York: Simon and Schuster.

———. 1997. *Stealing Jesus: How Fundamentalism Betrays Christianity.* New York: Three Rivers Press.

Bendroth, Margaret Lamberts. 1993. *Fundamentalism and Gender: 1875 to the Present.* New Haven, CT: Yale University Press.

Bennett, Jeffrey A. 2003. "Love Me Gender: Normative Homosexuality and 'Ex-gay' Performativity in Reparative Therapy Narratives." *Text and Performance Quarterly* 23 (4): 331–352.

Berzon, Betty. 2004. *Permanent Partners: Building Gay and Lesbian Relationships That Last*. New York: Plume.

Bieber, Irving. 1962. *Homosexuality: A Psychoanalytic Study of Male Homosexuals*. New York: Basic Books.

Blee, Kathleen M. 1991. *Women of the Klan: Racism and Gender in the 1920s*. Berkeley, CA: University of California Press.

———. 2004. "Positioning Hate." *Journal of Hate Studies* 3 (95): 95–105.

Blumer, Herbert. 1969. *Symbolic Interactionism*. Englewood Cliffs, NJ: Prentice-Hall.

Bornstein, Kate. 1995. *Gender Outlaw: On Men, Women and the Rest of Us*. New York: Vintage.

Bowlby, John. 1983. *Attachment*. 2nd ed. New York: Basic Books.

Boykin, Keith. 1996. *One More River to Cross: Black and Gay in America*. New York: Anchor Books.

Brown, Karen McCarthy. 2006. "Fundamentalism and the Control of Women." In S. M. Shaw and J. Lee, eds., *Women's Voices, Feminist Visions*, 681–685. New York: McGraw Hill.

Bull, Chris, and John Gallagher. 1996. *Perfect Enemies: the Religious Right, the Gay Movement and the Politics of the 1990s*. New York: Crown.

Burack, Cynthia, and Jyl J. Josephson. 2004. *A Report from "Love Won Out: Addressing, Understanding, and Preventing Homosexuality."* National Gay and Lesbian Task Force Policy Institute.

Cain, Roy. 1991. "Stigma Management and Gay Identity Development." *Social Work* 36 (1): 67–73.

Campbell, Susan. 2009. *Dating Jesus: A Story of Fundamentalism, Feminism and the American Girl*. Boston: Beacon Press.

Cass, Vivienne C. 1979. "Homosexual Identity Formation: A Theoretical Model." *Journal of Homosexuality* 4 (3): 219–235.

Cohen, Cathy J. 1999. *The Boundaries of Blackness: AIDS and the Breakdown of Black Politics*. Chicago: University of Chicago Press.

Collins, Patricia Hill. (1991) 2000. *Black Feminist Thought: Knowledge, Consciousness and the Politics of Empowerment*. New York: Routledge.

———. 2004. *Black Sexual Politics: African Americans, Gender, and the New Racism*. New York: Routledge.

Conley, Terri D., Christopher Calhoun, Sophia R. Evett and Patricia G. Devine. 2001. "Mistakes that Heterosexual People Make When Trying to Appear Non-Prejudiced: The View from LGB People." *Journal of Homosexuality* 42 (2): 21–43.

Cooley, Charles. 1902. *Human Nature and Social Order*. New York: Scribners.

Currier, Ashley. 2007. *The Visibility of Sexual Minority Movement Organizations in Namibia and South Africa*. PhD diss., University of Pittsburgh, Department of Sociology.

Davies, Peter. 1992. "The Role of Disclosure in Coming Out among Gay Men." In K. Plummer, ed., *Modern Homosexualities*, 75–83. New York: Routledge.

Dawkins, Richard. 2006. *The God Delusion*. New York: Houghton Mifflin Company.

deBeauvoir, Simone. 1952. *The Second Sex*. New York: Vintage.

Denzin, Norman K., and Yvonna S. Lincoln. 2003. Collecting and Interpreting Qualitative Materials. Thousand Oaks, CA: Sage Publications.

DiPlacido, Joanne. 1998. "Minority Stress Among Lesbians, Gay Men, and Bisexuals: A Consequence of Heterosexism, Homophobia and Stigmatization." In G. Herek, ed., Stigma and Sexual Orientation: Understanding Prejudice against Lesbians, Gay Men, and Bisexuals, 138–159. Thousand Oaks, CA: Sage Publications.

Duncan, Julie. 2009. "Credibility, Profitability, and Irrefutability: Why Creationists Are Building Museums." NCSE Reports 29 (5): 17–20.

Erzen, Tanya. 2006. Straight to Jesus: Sexual and Christian Conversions in the Ex-Gay Movement. Berkeley: University of California Press.

Feigenbaum, Erika Faith. 2007. "Heterosexual Privilege: The Political and the Personal." Hypatia 22 (1): 1–9.

Feinberg, Leslie. 1993. Stone Butch Blues. Ithaca, NY: Firebrand Books.

Ferraro, Kathleen J., and John M. Johnson. 1983. "How Women Experience Battering: The Process of Victimization." Social Problems 30 (3): 325–339.

Fetner, Tina. 2008. How the Religious Right Shaped Lesbian and Gay Activism. Minneapolis: University of Minnesota Press.

Finlay, Barbara, and Carol S. Walther. 2003. "The Relation of Religious Affiliation, Service Attendance, and Other Factors to Homophobic Attitudes among University Students." *Review of Religious Research* 44 (4): 370–393.

Fisher, Randy, Donna Derison, Chester F. Polley III, Jennifer Cadman, and Dana Johnston. 1994. "Religiousness, Religious Orientation, and Attitudes towards Gays and Lesbians." *Journal of Applied Social Psychology* 24 (7): 614–630.

Flory, Richard, and Donald E. Miller. 2008. *Finding Faith: The Spiritual Quest of the Post-Boomer Generation*. New Brunswick, NJ: Rutgers University Press.

Foucault, Michel. 1979. *Discipline and Punish: The Birth of the Prison*. New York: Vintage Books.

Frye, Marilyn. 1983. *The Politics of Reality: Essays in Feminist Theory*. Freedom, CA: Crossing Press.

Garfinkel, Harold. 1967. *Studies in Ethnomethodology*. Englewood Cliffs, NJ: Prentice-Hall.

Geertz, Clifford. 1973. "Thick Description: Toward an Interpretive Theory of Culture." In C. Geertz, ed., *The Interpretation of Culture*. New York: Basic Books.

Gerber, Lynne. 2008. "The Opposite of Gay: Nature, Creation, and Queerish Ex-Gay Experiments." *Nova Religio: The Journal of Alternative and Emergent Religions* 11 (4): 8–30.

Goffman, Erving. 1963. *Stigma: Notes of the Management of Spoiled Identity.* New York: Simon and Schuster.

Gold, Mitchell. 2008. *Crisis: 40 Stories Revealing the Personal, Social, and Religious Pain and Trauma of Growing up Gay in America.* Austin, TX: Greenleaf Book Group Press.

Goldberg, Michelle. 2006. *Kingdom Coming: The Rise of Christian Nationalism.* New York: W. W. Norton.

Gray, Mary L. 2009. *Out in the Country: Youth, Media and the Politics of Visibility in Rural America.* New York: NYU Press.

Green, Adam Isaiah. 2002. "Gay but Not Queer: Toward a Post-Queer Study of Sexuality." *Theory and Society* 31: 521–545.

Griffin, Horace L. 2006. *Their Own Receive Them Not: African-American Lesbians and Gays in Black Churches.* Cleveland, OH: Pilgrim Press.

Haddock, Geoffrey, and Mark P. Zanna, M. 1998. "Authoritarianism, Values, and the Favorability and Structure of Antigay Attitudes." In Herek, *Stigma and Sexual Orientation,.* 82–107. Thousand Oaks, CA: Sage Publications.

Halley, Janet E. 1989. "The Politics of the Closet: Towards Equal Protection for Gay, Lesbian and Bisexual Identity." *UCLA Law Review* 36:915–976.

Halperin, David. 1997. *Saint Foucault: Towards a Gay Hagiography.* New York: Oxford University Press.

Hankins, Barry. 2008. *Evangelicalism and Fundamentalism: A Documentary Reader.* New York: NYU Press.

Harding, Sandra, ed. 2004. *The Feminist Standpoint Reader: Intellectual and Political Controversies.* New York: Routledge.

Harding, Susan. 1991. "Representing Fundamentalism: The Problem of the Repugnant Cultural Other." *Social Research* 58 (2): 373–393.

Harris, Laura, and Elizabeth Crocker, eds. 1997. *Femme: Feminists, Lesbians, and Bad Girls.* New York: Routledge.

Henley, Nancy, and Fred Pincus. 1978. "Interrelationship of Sexist, Racist, and Antihomosexual Attitudes." *Psychological Reports* 42:83–90.

Herek, Gregory M. 1987a. "Religious Orientation and Prejudice: A Comparison of Racial and Sexual Attitudes." *Personality and Social Psychology Bulletin* 13 (1): 34–44.

———. 1987b. "The Instrumentality of Attitudes: Toward a Neofunctional Theory." *Journal of Social Issues* 42: 99–114.

——— 1998. "Bad Science in the Service of Stigma: A Critique of the Cameron Group's Survey Studies." In Herek, *Stigma and Sexual Orientation,* 223–255.

Herek, Gregory M., and Eric K. Glunt. 1993. "Interpersonal Contact and Heterosexuals' Attitudes toward Gay Men: Results from a National Survey." *Journal of Sex Research* 30 (3): 239–244.

Herek, Gregory M., and John P. Capitanio. 1996. "'Some of My Best Friends': Intergroup Contact, Concealable Stigma, and Heterosexuals' Attitudes toward Gay men and Lesbians." *Personality and Social Psychology Bulletin*, 22 (4): 412–424.

Herman, Didi. 1997. *The Antigay Agenda: Orthodox Vision and the Christian Right*. Chicago: University of Chicago Press.

Hitchens, Christopher. 2007. *God Is Not Great: How Religion Poisons Everything*, New York: Twelve.

hooks, bell. 1989 *Talking Back: Thinking Feminist, Thinking Black*. Boston: South End Press.

Howard, John. 1997. "The Library, the Park and the Pervert: Public Space and Homosexual Encounter in Post World War II Atlanta." In J. Howard, ed., *Carryin' on in the Gay and Lesbian South*, 107–131. New York: NYU Press.

Hughes, Everett C. 1945. "Dilemmas and Contradictions of Status." *American Journal of Sociology* 50:353–354.

Jacobsen, Janet R., and Ann Pellegrini. 2004. *Love the Sin: Sexual Regulation and the Limits of Religious Tolerance*. Boston: Beacon Press.

Jagose, Annamarie. 1996. *Queer Theory: An Introduction*. New York: NYU Press.

Jay, Karla, and Allen Young, eds. 1972. *Out of the Closets: Voices of Gay Liberation*. New York: NYU Press.

Jensen, Robert. 2008. *Getting Off: Pornography and the End of Masculinity*. Boston: South End Press.

Johnson, Allan G. 2006. *Privilege, Power, and Difference*. New York: McGraw Hill.

Jones, Loyal. 1997. *Appalachian Values*. Ashland, KY: The Jesse Stuart Foundation.

Joyce, Kathryn. 2009. *Quiverfull: Inside the Christian Patriarchy Movement*. Boston: Beacon Press.

Kaufman, Gershen, and Lev Raphael. 1996. *Coming Out of Shame: Transforming Gay and Lesbian Lives*. New York: Doubleday.

Kennedy, Elizabeth Lapovsky, and Madeline D. Davis. 1993. *Boots of Leather, Slippers of Gold: The History of a Lesbian Community*. New York: Penguin Books.

Kimmel, Michael S., and Matthew Mahler. 2003. "Adolescent Masculinity, Homophobia and Violence." *American Behavioral Scientist* 46:1439–1458.

Kimmel, Michael. 2009. *Guyland: The Perilous World Where Boys Become Men*. New York: Harper.

Kirkpatrick, Lee. 1993. "Fundamentalism, Christian Orthodoxy, and Intrinsic Religious Orientation as Predictors of Discriminatory Attitudes." *Journal for the Scientific Study of Religion* 32 (3): 256–268.

Lakoff, George. 2004. *Don't Think of an Elephant!: Know Your Values and Frame the Debate.* White River Junction, VT: Chelsea Green Publishing.

Laythe, Brian, Deborah Finkel, and Lee A. Kirkpatrick. 2001. "Predicting Prejudice from Religious Fundamentalism and Right-Wing Authoritarianism: A Multiple-Regression Approach." *Journal for the Scientific Study of Religion* 40 (1): 1–10.

Levy, Ariel. 2005. *Female Chauvinist Pigs: Women and the Rise of Raunch Culture.* New York: Free Press.

Linneman, Thomas J. 2003. *Weathering Change: Gays and Lesbians, Christian Conservatives and Everyday Hostilities.* New York: NYU Press.

Lorber, Judith. 1995. *Paradoxes of Gender.* New Haven, CT: Yale University Press.

Lorde, Audre. 1984. *Sister Outsider.* Freedom, CA: The Crossing Press.

Marsden, George M. 1991. *Understanding Fundamentalism and Evangelicalism.* Grand Rapids, MI: William B. Eerdmans.

Maslow, Abraham H. 1970. *Motivation and Personality.* 3rd ed. New York: Harper and Row.

Moon, Dawne. 2004. *God, Sex and Politics: Homosexuality and Everyday Theologies.* Chicago: University of Chicago Press.

McIntosh, Peggy. 2007. "White Privilege and Male Privilege." In S. Shaw and J. Lee, eds., *Women's Voices, Feminist Visions: Classic and Contemporary Readings,* 91–98. New York: McGraw Hill.

Moberly, Elizabeth R. 1983. *Homosexuality: A New Christian Ethic.* Cambridge, UK: James Clarke and Co.

Moen, Matthew C. 1994. "From Revolution to Evolution: The Changing Nature of the Christian Right." *Sociology of Religion* 55 (3): 345–357.

Nash, Shondrah Tarrezz, and Latonya Hesterberg. 2009. "Biblical Framings of and Responses to Spousal Violence in the Narratives of Abused, Christian Women." *Violence against Women* 15 (3): 340–361. doi:10.1177/1077801208330437.

Nestle, Joan, ed. 1992. *The Persistent Desire: A Butch Femme Reader.* Boston: Alyson Publications.

Newman. Leslea, ed. 1995. *The Femme Mystique.* Boston: Alyson Publications.

Nicolosi, Joseph. 1991. *Reparative Therapy of Male Homosexuality: A New Clinical Approach.* Northvale, NJ: Jason Aronson.

Nozick, Robert. 1990. *The Examined Life.* New York: Simon and Schuster.

O'Brien, Jodi. 2004. "Wrestling the Angel of Contradiction: Queer Christian Identities." *Culture and Religion* 5 (2): 179–202.

Offutt, Chris. *No Heroes: A Memoir of Coming Home*. New York: Simon and Schuster.

Peacock, James R. 2000. "Gay Male Adult Development: Some Stage Issues of an Older Cohort." *Journal of Homosexuality* 40 (2): 13–28.

Pelosi, Alexandra C., producer and director. 2009. *Right America: Feeling Wronged—Some Voices from the Campaign Trail*. Documentary.

Perez, Joe. 2007. *Soulfully Gay: How Harvard, Sex, Drugs, and Integral Philosophy Drove Me Crazy and Brought Me Back to God*. Boston: Integral Books.

Pharr, Suzanne. 1996. *In the Time of the Right: Reflections on Liberation*. Berkeley, CA: Chardon Press.

———. 1997. *Homophobia: A Weapon of Sexism*. Berkeley, CA: Chardon Press.

Ray, Nicholas. 2006. *Lesbian, Gay, Bisexual and Transgender Youth: An Epidemic of Homelessness*. New York: National Gay and Lesbian Task Force Policy Institute and the National Coalition for the Homeless.

Riggle, Ellen, and Sharon S. Rostosky. 2012. *A Positive View of LGBTQ: Embracing Identity and Cultivating Well-Being*. Lanham, MD: Rowman and Littlefield Publishers.

Robinson, Christine, and Sue E. Spivey. 2007. "The Politics of Masculinity and the Ex-Gay Movement." *Gender & Society* 21 (5): 650–675.

Rosenhouse, Jason. 2012. *Among the Creationists: Dispatches from the Anti-Evolutionist Front Line*. New York: Oxford University Press.

Rostosky, Sharon, Ellen Riggle, Sharon Horne, and Angela Miller. 2009. "Marriage Amendments and Psychological Distress in Lesbian, Gay and Bisexual (LGB) Adults. *Journal of Counseling Psychology* 56 (1): 56–66.

Ryan, Caitlin, David Hubener, Rafael M. Diaz, and Jorge Sanchez. 2009. "Family Rejection as a Predictor of Negative Health Outcomes in White and Latino Lesbian, Gay and Bisexual Young Adults." *Pediatrics* 123 (1): 346–352.

Savin-Williams, Ritch C. 1998. "The Disclosure to Families of Same-Sex Attraction by Lesbian, Gay and Bisexual Youths." *Journal of Adolescence* 8 (1): 49–68.

Scarborough, Elizabeth. 1991. *Nothing Sacred*. New York: Bantam Books.

Schwalbe, Michael. 2008. *Rigging the Game: How Inequality Is Reproduced in Everyday Life*. New York: Oxford University Press.

Scott, Eugenie C., and Glen Branch. 2003. "Antievolutionism: Changes and Continuities." *BioScience* 53 (3): 282–285.

Sears, James T. 1991. *Growing Up Gay in the South: Race, Gender and Journeys of the Spirit*. New York: Harrington Park Press.

Sedgwick, Eve Kosofsky. 1993. "The Epistemology of the Closet." In H. Abelove, M. Barale, and D. Halperin. eds. *The Lesbian and Gay Studies Reader* New York: Routledge.

Seidman, Steven. 2004. *Beyond the Closet: The Transformation of Gay and Lesbian Life*. New York: Routledge.

Seligman, Martin E. P., Tracy A. Steen, Nansook Park, and Christopher Peterson. 2005. "Positive Psychology Progress: Empirical Validation of Interventions." *American Psychologist* 60 (5): 410–421.

Shaw, Susan M. 2008. "Gracious Submission: Southern Baptist Fundamentalists and Women." *NWSA Journal* 20 (1): 51–77.

Shelcr, Jeffrey L. 2006. *Believers: A Journey into Evangelical America*. New York: Viking.

Signorile, Michelangelo. 2003. *Queer in America: Sex, the Media and the Closets of Power*. Madison: University of Wisconsin Press.

Silenzio, Vincent, MD, MPH, Juan B. Pena, PhD, Paul D. Duberstein, PhD, Julie Cerel, PhD, and Kerry L. Knox, PhD. November 2007. "Sexual Orientation and Risk Factors for Suicidal Ideation and Suicide Attempts among Adolescents and Young Adults." *American Journal of Public Health* 97:2017–2019.

Socarides, Charles W. 1968. *Homosexuality*. New York: J. Aronson.

Speechless: Silencing the Christians. February 2009. American Family Association one-hour television special.

Stein, Arlene. 2001. *The Stranger Next Door: The Story of a Small Community's Battle over Sex, Faith, and Civil Rights*. Boston: Beacon Press.

———. 2006. *Shameless: Sexual Dissidence in American Culture*. New York: NYU Press.

Stephens, Randall J., and Karl W. Giberson. 2011. *The Anointed: Evangelical Truth in a Secular Age*. Cambridge, MA: The Belknap Press of Harvard University Press.

Swank, Eric, Vicky Eldridge, and Lisa Mack. 2006. "Comfort with Homosexuality in Rural America." *Journal of Homosexuality* 51 (2): 39–56.

Thorne, Barrie. 1980. "'You Still Takin' Notes?'": Fieldwork and Problems of Informed Consent. *Social Problems* 27 (3): 284–297.

Tough Guise: Violence, Media and the Crisis in Masculinity, featuring Jackson Katz. 1999. Media Education Foundation Film.

Toumey, Christopher P. 1994. *God's Own Scientists: Creationists in a Secular World*. New Brunswick, NJ: Rutgers University Press.

Troiden, Richard R. 1988. "Homosexual Identity Development." *Journal of Adolescent Health Care* 9 (2): 105–113.

Truluck, Rembert. 2000. *Steps to Recovery from Bible Abuse*. Gaithersburg, MD: Chi Rho Press.

Urbach, Henry. 1996. "Closets, Clothes, DisClosure." *Assemblage* 30:62–73.

Walton, G. 2006. "'Fag Church': Men Who Integrate Gay and Christian Identities." *Journal of Homosexuality* 51 (2): 1–17.

Weber, Max. 1978. *Economy and Society.* 2 vols. Berkeley: University of California Press.

Weinstein, Jacqueline S., and Esther D. Rothblum, eds. 2004. *Lesbian Ex-Lovers: The Really Long-Term Relationships.* New York: Harrington Park Press.

Wendell, Susan. 2000. "The Flight from the Rejected Body." In A. Minas, ed., *Gender Basics: Feminist Perspectives on Women and Men,* 54–64. Belmont, CA: Wadsworth.

Weston, Kath. 1991. *Families We Choose: Lesbians, Gays, Kinship.* New York: Columbia University Press.

———. 1995. "Get Thee to a Big City: Sexual Imaginary and the Great Gay Migration." *GLQ* 2:253–277.

Whisman, Vera. 1996. *Queer by Choice: Lesbians, Gay Men and the Politics of Identity.* New York: Routledge.

White, Mel. 1995. *Stranger at the Gate: To Be Gay and Christian in America.* New York: Plume Books.

———. 2006. *Religion Gone Bad: The Hidden Dangers of the Christian Right.* New York: Penguin Group.

Whitley, Bernard. 1999. "Right-wing Authoritarianism, Social Dominance Orientation, and Prejudice." *Journal of Personality and Social Psychology* 77 (1): 126–134.

Whitley, Bernard, and Stefania Egisdottir. 2000. "The Gender Belief System, Authoritarianism, Social Dominance Orientation, and Heterosexuals' Attitudes toward Lesbians and Gay Men." *Sex Roles* 42 (11/12): 947–967.

Whitley, Bernard, and Sarah E. Lee. 2000. "The Relationship of Authoritarianism and Related Constructs to Attitudes toward Homosexuality." *Journal of Applied Social Psychology* 30 (1): 144–170.

Wilcox, Clyde, and Carin Robinson. 2011. *Onward Christian Soldiers? The Religious Right in American Politics.* Boulder, CO: Westview Press.

Wilcox, Melissa. 2003. *Coming Out in Christianity: Religion, Identity and Community.* Bloomington: Indiana University Press.

———. 2006. "Outlaws or In-laws? Queer Theory, LGBT Studies, and Religious Studies." *Journal of Homosexuality* 52 (1/2): 73–100.

Wolkomir, Michelle. 2006. *Be Not Deceived: The Sacred and Sexual Struggles of Gay and Ex-gay Christian Men.* New Brunswick, NJ: Rutgers University Press.

Woodberry, Robert D., and Christian S. Smith. 1998. "Fundamentalism et al.: Conservative Protestants in America." *Annual Reviews Sociology* 24:25–56.

ABOUT THE AUTHOR

Bernadette Barton is Professor of Sociology and Women's Studies at Morehead State University and author of *Stripped: Inside the Lives of Exotic Dancers*, also published by NYU Press